Prologue

TO THE ENDS OF THE EARTH: THE QUEST FOR THE TEN LOST TRIBES OF ISRAEL

Rivka Gonen

This book was set in 11 pt. Souvenir by Alpha Graphics of Pittsfield, New Hampshire and printed and bound by Book-Mart Press, Inc. of North Bergen, NJ.

Copyright © 2002 by Rivka Gonen

10 9 8 7 6 5 4 3 2 1

All rights reserved. No part of this book may be used or reproduced in any manner whatsoever without written permission from Jason Aronson Inc. except in the case of brief quotations in reviews for inclusion in a magazine, newspaper, or broadcast.

Library of Congress Cataloging-in-Publication Data

Gonen, Rivka.
    To the ends of the earth : the quest for the ten lost tribes of Israel / Rivka Gonen.
      p. cm.
    Includes bibliographical references (p.) and index.
    ISBN: 978-0-7657-6146-0
    1. Lost tribes of Israel. 2. Jews—Origin. I. Title.
Ds131 .G65 2000
909'.04924—dc 21   00-035540

Printed in the United States of America on acid-free paper. For information and catalog, write to Jason Aronson Inc., 230 Livingston Street, Northvale, NJ 07647-1726, or visit our website: www.aronson.com

"The Ten Tribes shall not return again, for it is written: And he cast them into another land like this day (Deuteronomy 29:28). Like as this day goes and returns not, so do they go and return not. So Rabbi Akiva. But Rabbi Eliezer says: Like as the day grows dark and then grows light, so also after darkness is fallen upon the Ten Tribes shall light hereafter shine upon them."

Mishnah Sanhedrin 10:3

Acknowledgments

This book was born out of a small advertisement in the *Daily Mail* of 1985, which I saw while staying in London, offering an explanation to the mystery of the alleged disappearance of the Ten Lost Tribes of Israel. I wrote to the address noted in the advertisement, discovered the British Israelites, and learned of their belief that the British people were the lost tribes. This novel idea kindled my excitement, and caused me to spend long days in the British Library scanning books, popular and learned magazines, and pamphlets, expanding my knowledge of the strange ways in which the disappearance of the Ten Lost Tribes has been extended both geographically and ethnically. I could not possibly exhaust all the vast literature on the subject, and consequently did not attempt to sketch in this book an all-inclusive picture of the past and present quest for the Ten Lost Tribes of Israel. This would have been a monumental but repetitive task. I chose some outstanding case studies, which I feel adequately illustrate the means and ways used by tribe seekers over the centuries.

Over the years in which I worked on and off on the subject, many people were subjected to my enthusiastic ramblings about the devious ways the search has been taking. My close family, and especially my husband Amiram, had to bear this burden for many years. Several people read the manuscript or parts of it in its various stages, edited some, and made many useful comments. I wish to note especially Ilana Korenbluth, who encouraged me to keep on with the work, Yvonne Fleitman, who introduced me to important manuscripts relating to central and south America, and Amazia Porat, who brought to my attention the story of the Englishmen Cadmeon. Rabbi Eliyahu Avihail of Amishav—The Dispersed of Israel Organization, Jerusalem—shared with me information on the tribes of Mizoram, India, and introduced me to a member of the "Tribe of Menasseh." The National and University Library, Jerusalem, and its deputy director Dr. Jonathan Yoel, were kind enough to permit me to photograph books in their holding. Photographer Peter Lanyi, Jerusalem made photographs from books, and photographer Aran Patinkin, Jerusalem, kindly let me use photographs he made in India and China. Beit Hatefutzot, The Nahum Goldman Museum of the Jewish Diaspora, Tel Aviv, its Visual Documentation Section, and Zipi Rosen, kindly helped me locate relevant photographs in their collection, and duplicated them for me.

However, all this effort would have come to nothing were it not for the perseverance of Ronald Goldfarb of Goldfarb & Silverman Law Office of Washington, D.C., and especially of Robbie Ann Hare of that office. Without their efforts, this book would never have seen the light of day. I wish to thank them all.

Table of Contents

List of Illustrations		ix
Prologue:	The Ten Lost Tribes of Israel in the World Today	xv
Chapter 1:	The Man from Cush—Firsthand Account of the Ten Tribes	1
Chapter 2:	Enigma—Where Are the Ten Lost Tribes?	11
Chapter 3:	Jews in Search of Their Lost Brethren	31
Chapter 4:	Mountain Tribes and Plain Tribes—Israel in the Caucasian Mountains and Beyond	53
Chapter 5:	Lost in the Land of Assyria—The Patans of Afghanistan	81
Chapter 6:	The Tribes in the Land of the Rising Sun—Israel in Japan	103
Chapter 7:	The Thrust to the West—How the Israelites Got to Britain	125
Chapter 8:	The Red and the White—Israel in America	145
Chapter 9:	Israel in the Far Reaches of the World	169
Conclusion:	Why the Search?	183
Bibliography		191

List of Illustrations

Figure 1: A venerable elder of the Ethiopian Jewish community, Israel, 1983.
Government Press Office, The State of Israel.
Photographer: Harnik Nati.   xvi

Figure 2: Operation Solomon 1991: Ethiopian immigrants aboard an Israeli air force plane.
Government Press Office, The State of Israel.
Photographer: Alpert Nathan.   xvii

Figure 3: Official declaration by Israel Sephardi Chief Rabbi Ovadia Yoseph that the Ethiopian Jews are from the Tribe of Dan. Jerusalem, 1973.
Chief Rabbinate, Hechal Shlomo, Jerusalem.
Photo courtesy of Beth Hatefutsoth, Tel Aviv.   xx

Figure 4: Ethiopian immigrant demonstrating. Jerusalem, 1983. Government Press Office, The State of Israel. Photographer: Harnik Nati.   xxi

Figure 5: Title page of *The Book of Eldad ha-Dani*. Constantinople, 1766.
Jewish National and University Library, Jerusalem. Photo courtesy of Beth Hatefutsoth, Tel Aviv.   5

Figure 6: Jaillot, Alexis-Hubert, 1632–1712.
Map of the Holy Land divided into the Twelve Tribes of Israel.
Hand-engraving, ca. 1690.
Norman Bier Section for Maps of the Holy Land, The Israel Museum, Jerusalem. Photographer: Peter Lanyi.   13

Figure 7: Assyrian siege on the town of Ekron. Palace of Sargon at Khorsabad.
Botta, P.E. & Flandin, E. *Monuments de Ninive II*. Paris, 1849, pl. 145.
Photographer: Peter Lanyi. 16

Figure 8: A city taken by assault, and the inhabitants led away captive.
Layard, A. H. *The Monuments of Nineve II*. London, 1853.
The Israel Museum, Jerusalem. Photographer: Peter Lanyi. 18

Figure 9: Jewish captives from the town of Lachish. Palace of Sennacherib at Nineveh.
Layard, A. H., *Nineveh and Babylon*. London, 1853.
The Israel Museum, Jerusalem. Photographer: Peter Lanyi. 19

Figure 10: Detail of an Assyrian letter from Tel-Halaf (biblical Gozan), mentioning Neriah and Paltiyahu. Seventh century B.C.
Harper, R. F. *Assyrian and Babylonian Letters*. Chicago, 1895. Photo courtesy of Beth Hatefutsoth, Tel Aviv. 22

Figure 11: The legendary king Prester John.
Alvares, F. *The Prester John of the Indies*. Lisbon, 1640. Photo courtesy of Beth Hatefutsoth, Tel Aviv. 35

Figure 12: A family of Yemenite Jews walking through the desert, 1949.
Government Press Office, The State of Israel. Photographer: Kluger Zoltan. 40

Figure 13: A Jewish man from Haban, 1946.
Government Press Office, The State of Israel. Photographer: Kluger Zoltan. 42

Figure 14: A Jewish woman from Haban, 1946.
Government Press Office, The State of Israel. Photographer: Kluger Zoltan. 44

List of Illustrations xi

Figure 15: "A true portrait of Shabbetai Zvi, by an
 eyewitness in Smyrna, 1666."
 From Thomas Coenen's chronicle of
 Shabbetai Zvi's life and exploits, Amsterdam,
 1669.
 Jewish National and University Library,
 Jerusalem. Photo courtesy of
 Beth Hatefutsoth, Tel Aviv. 48

Figure 16: Armies of the Lost Tribes from the Caucasus
 who, according to rumor, are coming
 to fight the Turks and to redeem the
 "Promised Land."
 News from Rome. London, 1606. Photo
 courtesy of Beth Hatefutsoth, Tel Aviv. 55

Figure 17: Derbent Pass.
 Department of Jewish Ethnography photo
 archive, The Israel Museum, Jerusalem. 68

Figure 18: Caucasus Jews in traditional costume. Engraving,
 Caucasus, 1905.
 The Jewish Encyclopedia. New York,
 1901–1906.
 Jewish National and University Library,
 Jerusalem. Photo courtesy of
 Beth Hatefutsoth, Tel Aviv. 74

Figure 19: Caucasus Jews in traditional costume, ca. 1920.
 Department of Jewish Ethnography photo archive,
 The Israel Museum, Jerusalem, courtesy
 of Rivka Avshalomov, Tel Aviv. 79

Figure 20: The Agronov family, Derbent, 1920.
 Department of Jewish Ethnography photo archive,
 The Israel Museum, Jerusalem, courtesy of
 Agronov family, Hadera. 80

Figure 21: Members of the Durani tribe, of the Pathan tribe
 group of Afghanistan who call themselves
 "Bani Israel." Drawing.
 Recluse, E. *Nouvelle Geographie Universelle.*
 Paris, 1876–1894.
 Jewish National and University Library,
 Jerusalem. Photo courtesy of
 Beth Hatefutsoth, Tel Aviv. 83

Figure 22: An Afghan of Damaun: or Man of the "Beni Israel."
Forster, Charles. *The One Primeval Language.*
London, 1851.
Jewish National and University Library, Jerusalem.
Photographer: Peter Lanyi. 85

Figure 23: A Eusof-Zye or Afghan of "The Tribe of Joseph."
Forster, Charles. *The One Primeval Language.*
London, 1851.
Jewish National and University Library, Jerusalem.
Photographer: Peter Lanyi. 94

Figure 24: Afridis.
Forster, Charles. *The One Primeval Language.*
London, 1851.
Jewish National and University Library, Jerusalem.
Photographer: Peter Lanyi. 97

Figure 25: Gion Festival in Kyoto, with portable shrines
carried along the streets.
McLeod, N. *Illustrations to the Epitome of the
Ancient History of Japan.* Nagasaki, 1879.
Jewish National and University Library,
Jerusalem. Photographer: Peter Lanyi. 104

Figure 26: Alleged march of the Israelites to Japan.
McLeod, N. *Illustrations to the Epitome of the
Ancient History of Japan.* Nagasaki, 1879.
Jewish National and University Library,
Jerusalem. Photographer: Peter Lanyi. 111

Figure 27: Jewish Temple musical instruments envisioned
as Japanese instruments.
McLeod, N. *Illustrations to the Epitome
of the Ancient History of Japan.*
Nagasaki, 1879.
Jewish National and University Library,
Jerusalem. Photographer: Peter Lanyi. 116

Figure 28: The Japanese emperor.
McLeod, N. *Illustrations to the Epitome of the
Ancient History of Japan.* Nagasaki, 1879.
Jewish National and University Library,
Jerusalem. Photographer: Peter Lanyi. 117

List of Illustrations

Figure 29: Professor Avraham Tashima, head of the Makoya sect, 1973.
Government Press Office, The State of Israel.
Photographer: Milner Moshe. 121

Figure 30: Japanese pilgrims of the Makoya sect in Jerusalem, 1986.
Government Press Office, The State of Israel.
Photographer: Sa'ar Ya'acov. 122

Figure 31: "The Four Past Great World Empires and the Fifth (indestructible) Stone Kingdom." The British Israelites believe that all white inhabitants of the Fifth Empire are descended from the Tribes of Israel.
Ferris, A. J. *Great Britain and the U.S.A. Revealed as the New Order*. London, 1941.
Jewish National and University Library, Jerusalem.
Courtesy of Beth Hatefutsoth, Tel Aviv. 136

Figure 32: Genealogy of the House of Israel, Great Britain, and the United States.
Ferris, A. J. *Great Britain and the U.S.A. Revealed as the New Order*. London, 1941.
Jewish National and University Library, Jerusalem. 142

Figure 33: Bishop Bartolomeo de las Casas. Engraving: Tomas Lopez Enguidanos, 1550s. 146

Figure 34: Persecuting idolaters.
Descrepcion de Tlaxcala. 1582–1583.
The Israel Museum, Jerusalem. Photographer: Peter Lanyi. 147

Figure 35: Manasseh Ben Israel. Etching by Rembrandt, 1636. Photo courtesy of Beth Hatefutsoth, Tel Aviv. 150

Figure 36: First Page of the report of Antonio de Montezinis.
Ben Israel, Manasseh. *Spes Israelis*. Amsterdam, 1650.
Jewish National and University Library, Jerusalem. Photo courtesy of Beth Hatefutsoth, Tel Aviv. 152

Figure 37: Domestic Rituals of the Indians.
Bishop Bernardino de Sahagun, *Florentine Codex II*.
The Israel Museum, Jerusalem. Photographer: Peter Lanyi. 153

Figure 38: Musicians and dancers.
Bishop Bernardino de Sahagun. *Florentine Codex I*.
The Israel Museum, Jerusalem. Photographer: Peter Lanyi. 155

Figure 39: Prayer at a "Tribe of Menasseh" synagogue, Mizoram, India, 1995.
Photographer: Aran Patinkin, Jerusalem. 172

Figure 40: Members of the "Tribe of Menasseh." Mizoram, India, 1995.
Photographer: Aran Patinkin, Jerusalem. 172

Figure 41: Madai family in festive attire, Cochin, ca. 1900.
Courtesy of Elias Madai, Rishon LeZion.
Department of Jewish Ethnography photo archive, The Israel Museum, Jerusalem.
Courtesy of Elias Madai, Rishon LeZion. 175

Figure 42: Chiang Min village in Szechwan province, China. 1994.
Photographer: Aran Patinkin, Jerusalem. 178

Figure 43: Newspaper clippings on the search for the Ten Lost Tribes, 1970s–1980s.
Amishav—The Dispersed of Israel Organization, Jerusalem. Photo courtesy of Beth Hatefutsoth, Tel Aviv. 188

Prologue: The Ten Lost Tribes of Israel in the World Today

One day in November 1984, the world woke up to news of a devastating famine in Ethiopia. Televised reports from the field brought into every home pictures of starving children, of dying young and old, of weak, suffering people leaving their villages and walking hundreds of miles in search of food. Long marches of lean and hungry people across barren land became part of reality, and people everywhere mobilized to help the unfortunate inhabitants of the region in a moving show of human compassion. Governments pledged funds, children donated their pocket money, churches and synagogues collected contributions, pop singers organized a worldwide benefit concert and issued special records. And yet, no operation to save the starving was more moving, more daring, than Operation Moses, the airlift of the Jews of Ethiopia to Israel.

The Jews of Ethiopia are an ancient tribe that calls itself Beta Israel—House of Israel. Until recently they have been known by the derogatory name "Falasha," meaning strangers or immigrants, bestowed upon them by their neighbors. The Beta Israel have been living in the remote mountain province of Tigre in northern Ethiopia for centuries, scraping a meager living out of a land that was not theirs, and suffering persecution of every sort. In the mid-1970s, with the overthrow of the ancient monarchy, the ongoing civil war, and the

Figure 1: A venerable elder of the Ethiopian Jewish community

Figure 2: Operation Solomon 1991, Ethiopian immigrants aboard an Israeli Air Force plane.

worsening drought, the conditions of the Beta Israel deteriorated even further. Perhaps ironically, the opportunity to rescue these people presented itself only when the general situation in Ethiopia was on the verge of chaos, with hundreds of thousands of starving people on the move. Under these circumstances the Beta Israel managed to leave the mountains of Tigre, and undertake the long and perilous march into Sudan. From there, often after a lengthy sojourn in refugee camps, they were airlifted to safety in Israel. When the story of Operation Moses was revealed to the media, it immediately captured the imagination of the public, and made headlines in every major newspaper, radio, and television station. Newspapers wrote:

> Modern-day successors of Moses and Aaron found the authorities in the Sudan more amenable than the Pharoah was when they sought to lead out the so-called "lost tribe" . . . In its way as inspiring a story as the biblical Exodus (*The Times*, January 1985).

> Israel extends "a strong hand and outstretched arm"—in the words used to describe the very first Exodus from Egypt—to pluck her own people from the brink of disaster (*The Scotsman*, January 1985).

Amid all the excitement over the heroic rescue, and while the Beta Israel were taking their first hesitant steps in their new home in Israel, questions were raised. Who were these people? When and under what circumstances did they get to Ethiopia? What is known about their history? How Jewish is their Judaism? Their origin was particularly intriguing, and became the source of many inquiries and much speculation. The Beta Israel themselves had no origin stories, but some picked up such stories from their Christian neighbors, including the romantic claim that their forefathers came to Ethiopia in the days of king Solomon. The Queen of Sheba, so tradition relates, was an Ethiopian queen who, on her famous visit to the court of Solomon in Jerusalem, received many gifts from the king, including a son. To safeguard mother and child on their return journey, Solomon sent a retinue of bodyguards, who eventually settled in Ethiopia and became the forefathers of the Beta Israel. Perhaps not surprisingly, this tradition complements the claim of the ancient ruling house of Ethiopia, of being direct descendants of Menelik, son of Solomon and the Queen of Sheba.

Scholars who dealt with the origin of the Beta Israel made other suggestions, including one that they descended from Jewish settlers in Upper Egypt, who drifted farther up the Nile. Their ancestry was tentatively traced to Jewish soldiers who, between the middle of the sixth and the fourth centuries B.C., held a military outpost on the island of Elephantine, near Aswan in Upper Egypt. A large collection of documents written by these soldiers was discovered in archaeological excavations. These documents provide an interesting picture of a rather unique type of Jewish life in that region.

Yet another suggestion to the origin of the Beta Israel, upheld by several scholars, proposed that they came to Ethiopia from Yemen, across the Red Sea, where a short-lived Jewish kingdom that controlled Ethiopia existed in the sixth century, just before the birth of Islam. Others hold that the Beta Israel were local tribes who, through their dealings with Jewish traders who occasionally visited Ethiopia, adopted an archaic form of Judaism, hence their dark complexion and Nilotic features. But no theory has kindled the imagination of the public more than the proclamation in 1973 by Ovadiah Yosef, Chief Sephardi Rabbi of Israel, and reaffirmed by his successor in 1985, that the Beta Israel were none other than descendants of the tribe of Dan, one of the Ten Lost Tribes of Israel.

This surprising declaration by the chief Sephardi rabbi is based on the ruling of the sixteenth-century rabbi David Ben Zimra of Cairo, who in turn based himself on the stories of the mysterious ninth century traveler Eldad the Danite (see chapter 1). This declaration, however, did little to facilitate the acceptance of the Beta Israel into the body of normative Judaism. They had been so completely severed from the Jewish people for so long that their Judaism was of an ancient brand. The Beta Israel kept observing certain customs long abandoned by all other Jews, and were not aware of the religious rulings and modifications made over the centuries. Their separation was so total that until the end of the nineteenth century they regarded themselves as the only surviving Jewish community in the world. In the years since Operation Moses, and especially during Operation Solomon in 1991, the entire Beta Israel community was brought to Israel, where it gradually adjusts to life in its old–new homeland.

The dramatic story of the Beta Israel has all the components illustrating the scope of the issue of the Ten Lost Tribes of Israel. It contains the original exile of the tribes, their dispersal to remote corners of the earth, the occasional reference to them by travelers, and their role in the world today. Here is an issue—over 2,700 years old—that

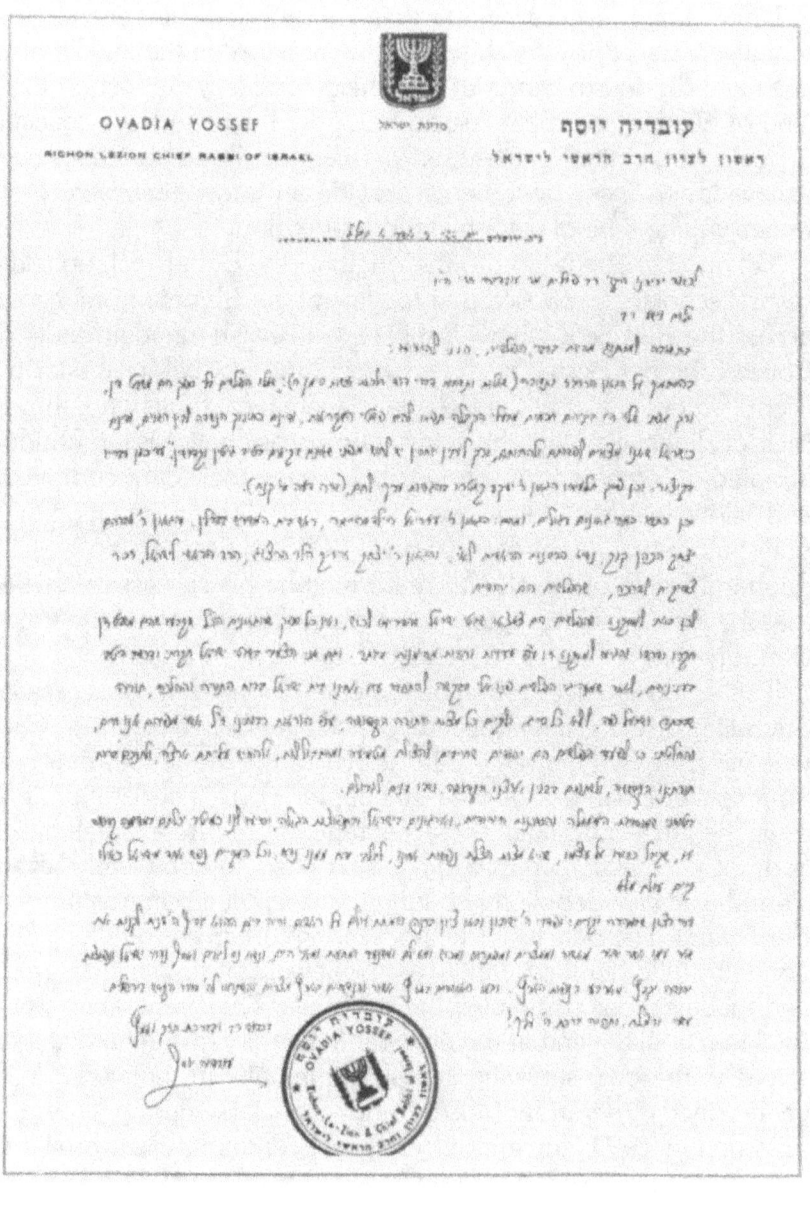

Figure 3: Official declaration by Israel Sephardi Chief Rabbi Ovadia Yoseph that the Ethiopian Jews are from the Tribe of Dan.

Figure 4: Ethiopian immigrants demonstrating.

has been kept alive during all this long period of time. It is an issue that propounds questions such as the relationship between the modern world and its ancient roots, between scientific history and religious beliefs, between reality and myth. These intriguing questions will be explored in the course of this book.

The sudden appearance of the Beta Israel is perhaps the most dramatic event connecting the Lost Tribes with the world today. It is, however, far from unique. Many nations, tribes, and societies around the world are known to claim to this day a Ten Tribes of Israel lineage. To my astonishment, I myself encountered many such claims in various parts of Asia, America, and Europe, and through research, consequently discovered the extent of their distribution. My first encounter, most memorable due to the element of surprise it contained, was in Japan. Many years ago I visited Kyoto to view the famous Gion festival. Solemn rites in Gion Temple are followed by a joyous procession of highly decorated portable shrines carried on the shoulders of young men, which winds its way through the streets of Kyoto. While watching the procession, I asked a Japanese bystander about the nature of the festival. On learning that I was from Israel he became visibly excited, and told me that the festival was a direct continuation of the Jewish rites that used to be performed in the Temple of Jerusalem prior to its destruction. The portable shrines, he said, were copies of the Holy Ark carried by the Children of Israel in the Sinai desert, and the name Gion derives from Zion, a poetic name of Jerusalem. "We Japanese," he ended his dramatic declaration, "are descendants of the Ten Tribes of Israel." In Tokyo I met the venerable Mr. Kobayashi, who left me with the strong feeling that he and the person I had casually encountered in Kyoto were not alone in this belief. The story of the Japanese connection to the Lost Tribes of Israel will be related in chapter 6.

Stories of Ten Tribe descent seemed to follow me wherever I went, and my next encounter with them was in the American Southwest. During a visit to the city of Albuquerque, New Mexico, I entered a shop to look for a piece of silver and turquoise Zuni jewelry. I had already heard rumors of a Native American tradition of Ten Tribe descent, and wondered where I could find out more about it. While admiring the jewelry and chatting with my family in Hebrew, the shopkeeper, a pure American Indian with shiny black hair, copper-colored skin, and high cheekbones, wondered what strange language we were speaking. Upon hearing that it was Hebrew, he invited us to the inner room of his store, and with a solemn tone of voice told us that we were brothers, as his own tribe, the Zuni, had a long tradition of descent from the Ten Tribes of Israel. Moreover, the tribe was waiting to be summoned back to its original homeland. Although the Zuni shopkeeper did not know how this tradition evolved, he assured me that it was an undeniable truth, shared by the entire tribe. Further investigations taught me that the Zuni was not the only Native American tribe that held such a claim, and that the extraordinary belief in ancient Israelite origin was spread all over North and South America. Moreover, it is also shared by the followers of a Christian church born on American soil, the Church of Jesus Christ of the Latter-Day Saints, the Mormon Church. The fascinating subject of the Lost Tribes of Israel in America will be dealt with in chapter 8.

Once on the trail of the Ten Lost Tribes, and of present-day communities that claim to have descended from them, I found that examples positively proliferated. A small advertisement in the *Daily Mail* of London led me to yet another group. The advertisement read: "THE LOST TRIBES OF ISRAEL. Who are they in today's world?" A letter to the address mentioned in the advertisement produced a pamphlet named *The Bible History and Britain*. This pamphlet assured its readers that the Lost Tribes of Israel were not lost at all, but were to be found among the British people. For all practical purposes, claimed the pamphlet, "Britain is Israel." The pamphlet sketched the history of wanderings of the tribes of Israel, from the time they were exiled until they landed on British shores, as part of the large-scale tribal migrations of the early Middle Ages. It also pointed out that the rise of Britain to the status of world empire was a clear sign of its Israelite descent, and suggested that if Britain adhered to the Scriptures, it would overcome its present-day problems and rise again to its rightful position in the world. Thus I was introduced to yet another group of people who believed in their Ten Tribes of Israel origin, this time not a remote group but one that has for long dominated the limelight of world history. The pamphlet also claimed that this opinion has to this day many adherents in Australia, New Zealand, Canada, and Southern Africa, as well as in the United States, Holland, and the Scandinavian countries. The movement that holds these ideas, known as British Israelism, is still active today, although not as active as it was in the last decades of the nineteenth and first decades of the twentieth centuries. Around 1900 it was said to have had two million adherents in Europe and America. A vast number of books, pamphlets, and articles propagating the ideology of the movement were circulated at that time and since. Some were of a quite astonishing nature. In these I learned that the British–Israel movement counts among its successes the boosting of the morale of the British people during both the First and the Second World Wars. It did so by assuring the British public that Britain, descending, as it claimed, from Israel, could never be destroyed. The amazing story of the British Israelites will unfold in chapter 7.

By now I knew that Ten Tribe descent was an honor sought by many groups of people, Jews and Christians alike, although I did not yet know why it was considered such a privilege. I was also wondering if there were communities in the Islamic world who shared this aspiration. Unexpectedly, I stumbled upon the beginning of an answer to this last question in an exhibition of photographs I saw in Jerusalem. These photographs were taken in villages in Pakistan, whose inhabitants claim to be Bani Israel—children of Israel. Having located the photographer, I heard the story of his visit to Pakistan, and of the curious fact that in every village he visited people spontaneously and repeatedly told him of their Israelite descent. The photographer noted that Pathan tribesmen in both Pakistan and neighboring Afghanistan practiced several rites reminiscent of Jewish customs. Several Jewish people who migrated to Israel from Afghanistan reported that such customs indeed prevailed among their Muslim neighbors. A Pakistani friend residing in London assured me that beliefs in Israelite descent were common not only among Pathan tribesmen, but also among all classes of Pakistani and particularly Afghani society, from villagers and nomads to the highly placed. He himself, so he said, had known this tradition since boyhood. "We are not Jews," he stressed, "we are devout Moslems, but are at the same time Israelite by origin." He did not use the term "Ten Tribes" but only Bani Israel—Children of Israel, and could not tell me what their tradition had to say about the circumstances of their arrival in Afghanistan and Pakistan. This I learned by searching libraries for reports of travelers and explorers. The story of the Tribes of Israel among the Moslems of Afghanistan will be told in chapter 5.

Traditions of Ten Tribe descent can thus be traced in all parts of the world today and are relevant to large groups of people. The story of the exiled tribes of Israel has spread to Asia, Africa, Europe,

America, and even New Zealand. People of different races and colors, speaking a variety of languages, practicing different religions and customs uphold it. All three monotheistic religions of the world—Judaism, Christianity, and Islam—have a stake in it. How did it come about that all these different people share an ancient belief in a common origin? How did the tradition spread to such widely separated regions? The search for answers to these questions is the subject of this book.

1

The Man from Cush—Firsthand Account of the Ten Tribes

One day in the year A.D. 883 a man who called himself Eldad the Danite appeared in the town of Qairawan in Tunisia, North Africa, and told a strange and exciting story to the Jews of that town. The story, put in writing by one of his listeners, was sent in a dated letter to the Jewish community of Spain, for them to share the good news. A few sentences from that memorable letter will introduce us to a fascinating person and story:

> To us came the pious man Eldad, from the tribe of Dan, to bring good tidings to the scattered Israel. When he left the land on the other side of the rivers of Cush, he traveled with a man of the tribe of Asher in a small boat, with the intention of doing some commerce with the crew, more especially to buy cloaks and jewelry. A great storm wrecked the boat in the middle of the night, but God prepared a plank for him and his companion, on which they kept floating until they were thrown up amongst the tribe called Amarnum; they are black as a raven, of high stature and are cannibals. They seized at first the man of the tribe of Asher, who was fat and healthy, and devoured him alive. . . .
>
> After having devoured this pious man, they put a collar on Eldad's neck, intending to keep him until he became fat and healthy (for at present he was ill and lean) and gave him food. Thus he remained with the cannibals until God by a miracle saved him. Armed men from an-

other place came upon the Cushites, took them prisoners, and slew them. Amongst the captives was this just Danite, and he remained with these fire-worshipers during five years, then they brought him to the province of Sin, where a Jew paid the price for his ransom—thirty-two pieces of gold.

The story of Eldad reads like a typical adventure story, of the kind told throughout the ages and in all lands. Captured travelers, devouring cannibals, miraculous redemption, are part of this genre of stories common the world over, from Jonah swallowed by the whale, to Ulysses threatened by the Cyclops, to present-day heroes who face monsters and evildoers on our planet and in outer space, stories interwoven with fantastic beings, hair-raising adventures, and last-minute escapes have been told and retold in every type of media, from wandering storytellers to television, to the delight of young and old alike. Compared to some adventure stories, Eldad's account of his travels is rather mild. What is astonishing about it, however, is that Eldad calmly refers to himself as a Danite—of the tribe of Dan—and to his ill-fated companion as a member of the tribe of Asher, two of the Ten Lost Tribes of Israel.

One can imagine the excitement caused by the appearance of Eldad the Danite on that memorable day in the year 883 in the dusty streets of Qairawan. More than 1,600 years had elapsed since the exile and disappearance of the Ten Tribes of Israel. Although their existence has never been doubted, there has not been any communication with them during all that long period. No one knew where they were, and no one dared go search for them. And here, completely unexpected and unannounced, comes a man, flesh and blood, claiming that he himself was a member of one of the Lost Tribes. His very appearance, and the exciting and exotic features he exhibited, must have been considered miraculous. The very name he bore, Eldad, was an ancient biblical name, long out of use among Jews. He communicated in Hebrew, a language used only for the study of sacred Jewish literature, but not anymore a living, spoken vernacular. Eldad claimed to know the whereabouts not only of his own tribe Dan, but also of all other nine Lost Tribes. The Jewish community of Qairawan must have been elated by this first recorded visit of a messenger from the Ten Lost Tribes, and greatly honored to host such a distinguished guest. It is not difficult to envision the lavish banquets given in honor of Eldad, and visualize him telling and retelling his fabulous story to the elders and respectable members of the community. The dignitaries were probably gathered in ornate halls, reclining on low benches and colorful cushions to listen with awe and respect to every word the stranger uttered. The uninvited must have crowded outside, pressing themselves against the doors and windows, in an attempt to catch a phrase, a word, and pass it on to the excited multitudes that filled the narrow streets of the Jewish quarter. The suspicious rabbis first wanted to know whether this wondrous stranger was at all Jewish, and their satisfaction of that fact was pronounced in these words:

> Mar (Mr.) Eldad was full of the Law and the Commandments, and if some one was sitting with him from morning to evening his tongue would not cease from explaining the Law in Hebrew. His words are sweeter than honey and honeycomb.

At a time when the majority of people did not venture out of their own native town to visit a neighboring settlement, names like Cush, Sin, and the Land of the Tatars (Tartars) would have had the bewitching sound of high adventure. The man who not only mentioned them but also said he had been to them and to other mysterious places must have fired the imagination and reverence of all his listeners. Moreover, the names Eldad mentioned were not only faraway, romantic lands, but the actual, if somewhat hazy, locations where their lost brothers, the Ten Tribes of Israel, were residing.

Many questions must have been asked during those memorable days in Qairawan: Where are these mysterious lands? Do the tribes live there together or are they separated from one another? What do they look like, how do they dress, how do they live, in what language do they speak? As the fate of the Ten Lost Tribes of Israel has been an important issue ever since they were exiled and cut off from the body of the Israelite nation, every bit of information, every hint or speculation concerning their whereabouts was bound to create much excitement. High expectations for their eventual discovery and hopes for their return— and with it, the salvation of the Jewish people—were aroused. Was Eldad in fact the carrier of the long-awaited message that the Ten Lost Tribes were about to emerge from centuries of seclusion and join their brothers? Were the many centuries of their separation about to end? Was all this a sign that the Messiah was about to come?

The great excitement caused by the stories of Eldad the Danite is manifested by the fact that several manuscripts carrying different versions of his story exist. The various versions indicate that the story was not written down by Eldad himself, but probably by several of his listeners, some time after they heard it. It is they who gave the story the form of a diary. Eldad's "diary" was so popular that it was one of the first books to be printed. The first printed edition was published in Mantua, Italy, before 1480, only about twenty years after the printing of the very first book, Gutenberg's Bible.

The location of the tribes

Let us return to Eldad's description of the whereabouts of the various tribes of Israel. Eldad classed the tribes into northern, eastern, and southern groups, each group occupying a different region in or on the outskirts of the Near East. The northern group was the largest, and included the tribes of Reuben, Zebulun, Issachar, Simeon, and half the tribe of Menasseh, a strange combination, as these tribes were not close to one another in their Israelite homeland. In fact, the tribe of Simeon was a southern tribe, early incorporated into the tribe of Judah and not belonging to the Ten Lost Tribes at all. None of Eldad's listeners were bothered by this minor deviation, being probably too fascinated to care. According to Eldad the Reubenites now lived "behind the mountains of Paran"—most probably the Caucasian Mountains. Zebulun was their neighbor, and dwelt "in the mountains of Paran, and their tents are planted from the Province of Armenia to the river Euphrates." Issachar "dwells in high mountains near to the land of the Medes and Persians," in Iran. Simeon and half the tribe of Menasseh "are in the land of the Khozars"—the plains north of the Caspian Sea. This group of tribes, then, occupies a vast region that stretches from the Caucasian Mountains and the plains west and north of the Caspian Sea, to the Iranian Plateau.

The eastern group was smaller, being made up of only one tribe and half of another. The tribe of Ephraim and the other half of the tribe of Menasseh dwell in "the Southern mountains in the province of the Mohammedans," meaning perhaps Yemen in southern Arabia.

Figure 5: Title page of *The Book of Eldad the Danite* Constantinople, 1766.

The southern group includes the tribes of Dan, Naphtali, Gad, and Asher, who live together "in the ancient Havilah, where there is gold," referring to the biblical land of Cush, identified with Ethiopia.

The way of life of the tribes

Eldad's characterization of the way of life of the various tribes and of their particular qualities is most interesting. Reuben is described as a pious tribe that possesses the Bible, the Mishnah, the Talmud, and the Agadah. On each Sabbath they study the Law, beginning with a Hebrew text and commenting on it in Tatar.

This is a rather strange description, as Reuben was originally a tribe of cattle herders on the Transjordania plateau, never known for its learning or intellectual pursuit. In fact, the tribe is never even mentioned in the Bible after the period of the Judges, and did not seem to have taken an active part in the life of the kingdom of Israel. How did the Reubenites obtain the Bible, the Mishnah, the Talmud, and the Agadah, compiled centuries after they were exiled and had lost all contact with the Jewish people? This question also did not seem to have bothered Eldad, and probably not his listeners either.

Zebulun, a former coast-dwelling tribe renowned for its maritime skills, was now placed in the high mountains of Paran, where it collaborates with its neighbor Reuben. They go together to war, make together the roads, and divide with one another the spoil.

Eldad has only words of praise for the tribe of Issachar. Having exchanged their original habitat in the plateau of the Lower Galilee in northern Israel with the high mountains of Persia, they have become a most pious tribe.

> No worldly yoke is upon them but only that of heaven, they are not at war with anybody but their energy is devoted to the discussion of the Law; they are at peace with all, and have no enemy . . . They possess much cattle, as well as camels and asses, and also male and female servants. The only weapon they possess is the knife for slaughtering animals. They are men of good faith, and in their hands is nothing stolen or robbed, and even their servants behave in the same faithful way . . . Their judge and prince is called Nahshon . . . They speak Hebrew, Persian, and Tatar.

Of the tribes of Simeon and half of Menasseh who live in the lands of the Khozars, Eldad only says that they are of infinite number; they take tribute from twenty-eight kingdoms, and many of the Muslims also pay them tribute.

The eastern group of tribes are a different matter altogether, and Eldad has few but uncomplimentary words to say about them. They are of a horrid mind and always on horseback, cut the roads, and have no mercy upon men; they have no other means of living than by spoil. They are valiant warriors; one of them will vanquish a hundred.

The southern group is prosperous and valiant:

> They possess much gold, silver, and precious stones, as well as sheep, oxen, camels, and asses. They sow and reap, dwell in tents, and encamp in a land extending four days' journey, pitching their camps only in fertile places. The name of their king is Uziel, son of Malchiel, the name of their prince is Nicolay (!), of the children of Ahliab, and the name of their judge is Avdan, son of Michael of the tribe of Asher . . . When they go to war, the trumpet is blown, and 120,000 horsemen and 100,000 foot-soldiers gather round their chief. Every tribe goes out for a month's service, and remains three months, and when they return after the three months the spoil is divided amongst them all . . .

The story of how these tribes arrived in Cush is dramatic. It all started at the time of the division of united Israel into two kingdoms, Judah and Israel. Jeroboam son of Nebat, first king of the kingdom of Israel, ordered the ten tribes, and in particular the valiant tribe of Dan, to fight against the house of David. Dan refused to shed the blood of its brothers, and had to flee. The Danites first meant to go to Egypt, where they intended to kill all the inhabitants and destroy the country, but their princes reminded them that it was forbidden to return to Egypt. And so they went up the river Pishon until they reached the land of Cush, which they found fertile, with numerous vineyards and gardens. They settled here, and made a covenant with the children of Cush that they should pay tribute to Israel. Thus the Danites dwelled there for many years, multiplying and increasing greatly. They were then followed by three other tribes—Naphtali, Gad, and Asher—who crossed the desert until they came to the territory of the Danites.

This completes Eldad's account of all ten tribes, a description that no doubt warmed the hearts and elevated the self-esteem of his listeners. Here were free and powerful Jewish tribes, who had kings, an army, and much wealth. How can they be compared to the life of the Jewish people, living for hundreds of years in exile, under the yoke of various rulers, devoid of the trappings of a free people? No wonder the stories of Eldad captured the imagination and fired the hopes of generations of Jews to come.

An eleventh tribe

Eldad had a further surprise: an account of an eleventh tribe—the tribe of Moses (Levi). Despite the fact that the tribe of Levi had no territory, being temple servants and intermediaries between the people of Israel and the divine, and is not mentioned in the biblical descriptions of the exile, Eldad devoted a lengthy description to its idyllic and holy life. The tribe of Moses lived secluded from all other Israelite tribes, and kept their holy way of life intact.

> They dwell in beautiful houses provided with handsome towers, which they have built themselves. There is nothing unclean among them, neither in the case of birds, venison, or domesticated animals; there are no wild animals, no flies, no foxes, no vermin, no serpents, no dogs, and in general nothing which does harm; they have only sheep and cattle, which bear twice a year. They sow and reap, there are all sorts of gardens with all kinds of fruit and cereals; e.g., beans, melons, gourds, onions, garlic, wheat, and barley, and the seed grows a hundred fold. They have faith; they know the Law, the Mishnah, the Talmud, and the Agadah, but their Talmud is in Hebrew . . . They have no knowledge of the Tanaim [sages of the Mishnah] and Amoraim [sages of the Talmud] who were active during the time of the second Temple . . . They speak only Hebrew, and are very strict as regards the use of wine made by others than themselves, as well as the rules of slaughtering animals . . . They do not swear by the name of God for they fear that their breath may leave them, and they become angry with those who swear . . . Therefore they live long to the age of 100 or 120 years. No child, be it son or daughter, dies during the life-time of its parents, but they reach a third and fourth generation, and see grand-children and great grand-children with their offspring. They do all field-work themselves, having no male or female servants; there are also merchants among them. They do not close their houses at night, for there is no

thief or any wicked man among them. Thus a little boy might go for days with his flock without fear of robbers, demons, or danger of any other kind; they are indeed all holy and clean . . . They see nobody and nobody sees them, except the four tribes who dwell on the other side of the rivers of Cush; they see them and speak to them, but the river Sambatyon is between them . . . The river Sambatyon is 200 yards broad . . . full of sand and stones, but without water. The stones make a great noise like the waves of the sea and a stormy wind, so that in the night the noise is heard at a distance of half a day's journey . . . And this river of stone and sand rolls during the six working days and rests on the Sabbath day. As soon as the Sabbath begins, fire surrounds the river, and the flames remain till the next evening, when the Sabbath ends. Thus no human being can reach the river for a distance of half a mile on either side; the fire consumes all that grows there. The four tribes, Dan, Naphtali, Gad, and Asher, stand on the borders of the river when shearing their flocks here, for the land is flat and clean without any thorns. When the children of Moses see them gathered together on the border, they shout, saying, "Brethren, tribes of Jeshurun, show us your camels, dogs, and asses," and they make remarks about the length of the camel's neck and the shortness of the tail. Then they greet one another and go their way.

This is not the first time the fabulous and awesome river Sambatyon is mentioned in connection with the Lost Tribes, yet this is the first time its unusual features are described in great detail. For the first time the role of the Sambatyon as an insurmountable barrier is clearly stressed. Interestingly however, it features as a barrier not between the Lost Tribes and the rest of the Jewish people, but between them and the tribe of Moses—viewed as the kernel, the pure essence of the lost Israelite entity. The river Sambatyon will feature again in chapter 3.

Could Eldad have been an imposter?

The stories of Eldad were so astonishing, and perhaps verging too much on the fantastic, that the rabbis of Qairawan decided to consult the highest Jewish authority of the time, Zemah Gaon, head of the rabbinical academy of Sura in Babylon. They sent him a long letter, which has been preserved, in which they related the story of the four tribes of the south, namely Dan, Naphtali, Gad, and Asher, but did not mention the other tribes. The rabbis then expressed their bewilderment concerning the Hebrew language Eldad used, and quoted several strange and unknown words. Nevertheless, they stated that they put him to a test, by showing him the objects to which he gave names which they wrote down. After some time they repeated the same questions, and Eldad gave the same words as before.

The ritual laws mentioned by Eldad, especially those dealing with slaughtering animals, were also cause for suspicion to the rabbis of Qairawan, as they did not conform in all details to those used by law-abiding Jews. The letter quoted Eldad's laws at length, asking Zemah Gaon's opinion. It then related that the Children of Moses were miraculously transported to Havilah as a reward for refusing to sing the song of Zion on the rivers of Babylon, and ended with the story of the Sambatyon.

Zemah Gaon's reply, which has also been preserved, warmly endorsed Eldad and his stories. The Gaon excused Eldad's variations of the law, saying that because of the troubles and misfortunes of traveling, Eldad may have unintentionally reported a halakah (law) in another sense than that usually known. The Gaon also wrote that he believed in the stories of The Tribes and of the Children of Moses, and quoted earlier sources that mentioned them. Zemah Gaon's answer, full of enthusiasm, even elation, expressed his hope that now that a messenger from the Ten Lost Tribes had appeared, and the existence of a prosperous and valiant Jewish existence had been confirmed, the restoration of the Jewish people was near at hand.

Scholars expressed a variety of opinions concerning the real origin and hidden purpose of Eldad, whoever he was. One scholar, for example, described him as a daring impostor crowned with an unexpected success. Impostor or not, searches for the Ten Lost Tribes of Israel had since the appearance of Eldad relied heavily on the information included in his diary. Indeed the Lost Tribes were sought in the plains beyond the Caspian Sea and in the Caucasian Mountains (chapter 4), as well as in Yemen (chapter 3) and in Ethiopia. The proclamation of the Beta Israel community of Ethiopia as originating from the tribe of Dan is its most recent success.

2

Enigma—Where Are the Ten Lost Tribes?

The enigma of the Ten Lost Tribes of Israel is one of the oldest, most interesting, and long-lasting mysteries of world history. It does not lie in the fact that a nation, or a group of ancient tribes, may have been lost. Many have disappeared in the course of the history of the world, without calling for an ongoing search. After all, who, archaeologists notwithstanding, has been looking for the Moabites or Edomites of biblical times, for the Scythians or Tracians of the Greek era? Why is it that many people to this day cannot accept the disappearance of the tribes of Israel, and believe that their fate is not in the same category as that of any other lost nation? Why do so many people insist that these tribes are still alive, under one disguise or another, in Britain and Japan, in New Mexico and Afghanistan? How is it that different people identify themselves as descendants of these tribes?

To understand the enigma, let us explore briefly the ancient history of Israel and the circumstances of exile of ten of its twelve tribes. Let us also read some of the sublime words of the prophets of Israel, and remind ourselves of their message regarding the fate of the Ten Tribes.

Ancient Israel: the beginnings

The ancient Israelite nation was made up of twelve tribes, descendants of the twelve sons of Jacob, the third Patriarch of Israel. The twelve sons and their families went down to Egypt, where their numbers multiplied and the twelve families became twelve tribes. As tribes they came out of Egypt, and wandered in the desert of Sinai on their way to the Promised Land. As tribes they crossed the Jordan River to conquer Canaan, where they eventually settled in territories assigned to each by lot. The tribe of Levi was not allocated a territory, as its members dispersed among all other tribes to fulfill their special role as religious functionaries. Splitting the large tribe of Joseph into two—Ephraim and Menasseh—filled the place of Levi in the count of twelve. Once settled, each tribe developed its own way of life and its own character, alluded to in the prophetic blessings of Jacob and Moses. The tribal sentiment remained very strong throughout the history of ancient Israel, and the slogan "every man to his tent" characterized the turbulent period of the Judges, when tribes were often reluctant to come to the aid of one another, even when endangered by enemies. Only the common threat of the Philistines, and the charismatic personality of David, eventually brought all the tribes together into a United Kingdom of Israel. But this did not come easily. David, who was of the tribe of Judah, had first to depose the house of Saul, the first king of united Israel who was from the tribe of Benjamin, and then to put down several separatist rebellions, including one led by his own son Absalom. David managed to hand down a united kingdom to his son Solomon, who ruled over it for forty peaceful years. The eighty years of combined rule of David and Solomon were the only period in the history of Israel when all twelve tribes were united under one king and operated as one nation. The embers of separatism, however, were not extinguished even then.

Division of the kingdom

Immediately following the death of Solomon in 930 B.C., the kingdom of Israel crumbled under a combination of heavy taxation, harsh administrative regulations, and idolatry in high circles. Under these

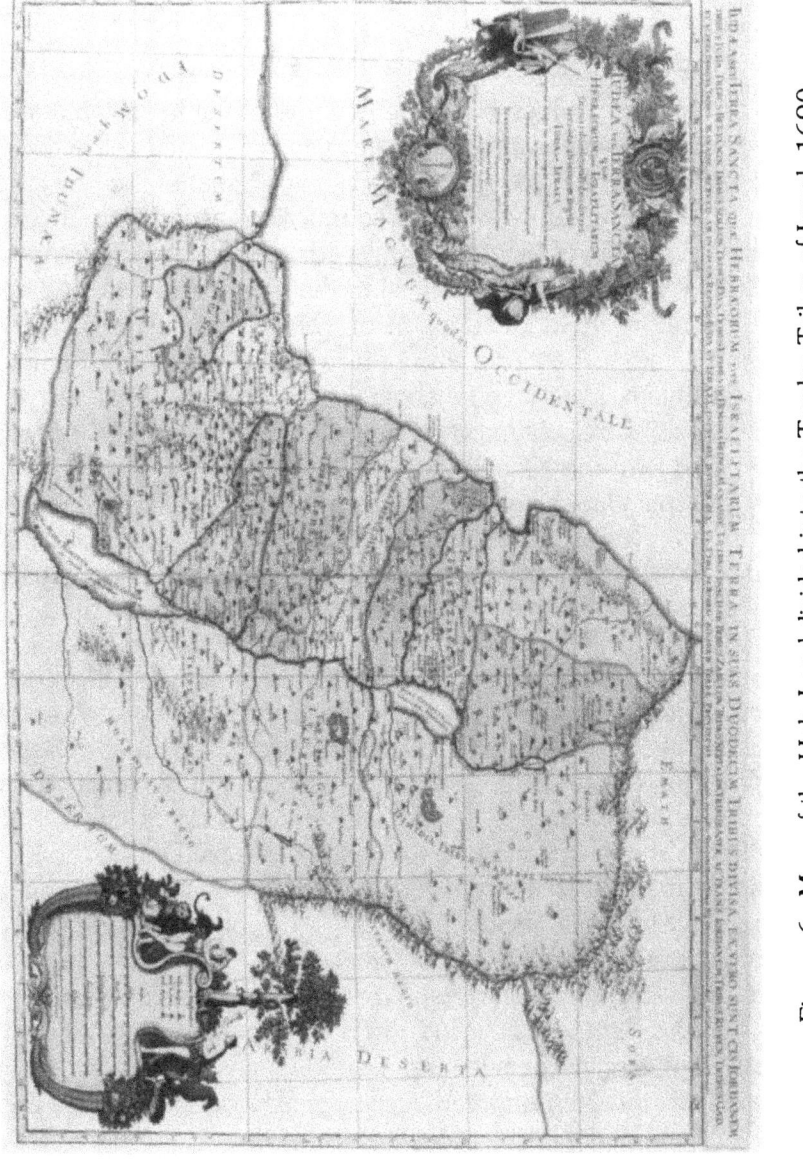

Figure 6: Map of the Holy Land divided into the Twelve Tribes of Israel, 1690.

circumstances, the deeply entrenched tribal sentiments came to the foreground:

> What portion have we in David, neither have we inheritance in the son of Jesse; to your tents, oh Israel. Now, see to thine own house, David. So Israel departed into their tents. [I Kings 12:16]

Ten of the twelve tribes, the large majority of the Israelite nation, seceded to create a separate kingdom, which retained the ancient name Israel. Its first king was Jeroboam son of Nebat of the powerful tribe of Ephraim, a man who harbored rebellious aspirations already in the lifetime of King Solomon (I Kings 11:26–35). Only two tribes, Judah and Benjamin, remained loyal to the house of David, and accepted the reign of Rehoboam son of Solomon over a diminutive kingdom of Judah, centered around the traditional and sanctified capital Jerusalem. Thus it came about that the twelve tribes, descendants of Jacob, were split into two groups: ten forming the Kingdom of Israel, and two, the Kingdom of Judah.

After the split, Judah and Israel became separate political entities, each with its own history, fate, culture, and even dialect. The tribal sentiment remained strong, especially in the kingdom of Israel, where various geographical regions continued to be named after the tribe that lived in them. Rapid succession of kings and ruling dynasties in the kingdom of Israel reflect these strong tribal sentiments and competitions. The kingdom of Judah enjoyed a much higher degree of internal stability, having accepted the dominance of the house of David throughout its history. Both Israel and Judah fought wars with their neighbors, and occasionally against each other, and got involved in international affairs through alliances and coalitions. During the first hundred years of its existence, Israel dealt mainly with its immediate neighbors in Syria, but already in the days of King Ahab, one of the greatest if most notorious kings of Israel, a new force, Assyria, cast its menacing shadow over the region. From its homeland on the upper reaches of the Tigris River in northern Mesopotamia (present-day northern Iraq), Assyria pursued a policy of expansion. The threat of being annexed by Assyria forced twelve small kingdoms in Syria and on the eastern Mediterranean coast to form one of the earliest recorded military coalitions, known in contemporary documents as the Southern Coalition. An Assyrian inscription listing the events of the first six years of the reign of Shalmanesser III, king of Assyria at that time, mentions Hadad king of Damascus at the head of this coalition, with Ahab of Israel (Ahabbu Sir'ialu) in the third place. Notwithstanding, Ahab contributed to the joint army of the coalition 2,000 chariots, more than any other member. The battle between Shalmanesser of Assyria and the army of the coalition took place in 853 B.C. in northern Syria. Its outcome was indecisive, despite an Assyrian claim for a major victory. The Southern Coalition, in which Ahab's successors continued to take part, succeeded, despite several setbacks, to maintain the independence of its members for over a hundred years.

While the Kingdom of Israel was active on its northern frontier, serving as a barrier against Assyrian expansion, the Kingdom of Judah was concerned with its southern neighbor, Egypt. The Egyptian Pharaoh Shishak invaded Judah in 925 B.C., only five years after the death of Solomon and the division of the monarchy. When Assyria rose to dominance, both Judah and Israel tried to maneuver between the two superpowers of the day, Egypt and Assyria, in an attempt to maintain their independence. This dangerous game finally brought about the downfall of Israel.

The end of the Kingdom of Israel

> In the days of Pekah king of Israel came Tiglath-Pileser king of Assyria and took Ijon and Abel-Beth Maachah, and Janoah, and Kedesh, and Hazor, and Gilead and Galilee all the land of Naphtali, and carried them captive to Assyria [I Kings 15:29]

At the same time he carried away the tribes who lived on the eastern side of the Jordan:

> The Reubenites and the Gadites and the half tribe of Menasseh, and brought them unto Halah and Habor and Hara, and to the river Gozan unto this day. [I Chronicles 5:26]

Shortly after these events, Hoshea son of Elah assassinated King Pekah of Israel. Hoshea hoped to withstand the Assyrian pressure by rallying with Egypt, but failed:

> The king of Assyria found conspiracy in Hoshea: for he had sent messengers to So king of Egypt, and brought no presents to the king of Assyria as he had done year by year. Therefore the king of Assyria shut

him up, and bound him in prison. Then the king of Assyria came up through all the land and went up to Samaria, and besieged it three years. In the ninth year of Hoshea the king of Assyria took Samaria, and carried Israel away into Assyria, and placed them in Halah and in Habor by the river of Gozan, and in the cities of the Medes. [II Kings 17:4–6]

Thus came the end of the Kingdom of Israel. In two campaigns, one in 734 B.C., the other in 721 B.C., the Assyrians subdued the kingdom, destroyed its capital Samaria, and, according to the policy of deportation practiced by them in all their conquered lands, carried its population—the Ten Tribes of Israel—into captivity. Since their captivity, the Ten Tribes are hardly ever again in the Bible.

The exiled and the remnants

When reading the biblical accounts of the fall of Israel and the deportation of its people, one gets the impression that the great majority

Figure 7: Assyriam siege on the town of Ekron.
Palace of Sargon at Khorsabad.

of the inhabitants of the kingdom were exiled. But is this realistic? Is there a way of knowing how many were actually deported, and, if any remained behind, find out what happened to them? It is not easy to arrive at answers with a reasonable amount of certainty, as there is no accurate information concerning the numbers of deported Israelites. Ancient sources are usually not reliable in matters of statistics, as they either disregard numbers altogether, or they distort them to serve one purpose or another. While the Bible does not give the number of deported Israelites, some Assyrian inscriptions do. One such inscription (Annals of Tiglat Pileser, line 227) mentions that (an unknown number of) heads of families of the two and a half Transjordanian tribes, as well as 3,000 men from five towns in the Galilee, were exiled in the first deportation. This document, then, does not do much to throw light on the issue. Another source (Annals of Sargon, line 10) gives what seems to be more accurate information, referring to 27,290 people deported from Samaria. If this number refers to the city of Samaria, it is probably exaggerated, as at the height of its expansion the area of the city did not exceed 150 acres, and by the accepted average ratio of 120 inhabitants per acre, its population could have been 18,000 at the most. However, during the Assyrian campaigns the number of people in the city must have greatly swollen by refugees from captured regions of the kingdom, an increase that no doubt was balanced by heavy casualties during the three-year siege laid by the Assyrian army (II Kings 18:9–10). If the number quoted in the Assyrian document refers to the whole kingdom, known to the Assyrians also by the name Samaria, it could not have accounted for its entire population. We may assume that not all Israelites were deported, and that the deportees were for the most part heads of families, probably members of the aristocracy, professionals, and skilled laborers. The majority, especially rural and small-town populations, the old and the weak, were most probably left behind.

If only a minority of the Ten Tribes of Israel were deported, what was the fate of the majority that remained behind in the conquered land? Many no doubt fled to neighboring Judah, which still maintained its independence at that time, and found refuge there. Indeed, archaeological excavations revealed a dramatic increase in the size of Jerusalem in the eighth century B.C., to include areas never occupied before. Lachish, the second largest city of Judah, underwent at that same time a phase of "slumization," the filling up of open areas around the

Figure 8: A city taken by assault and its inhabitants led away captive.

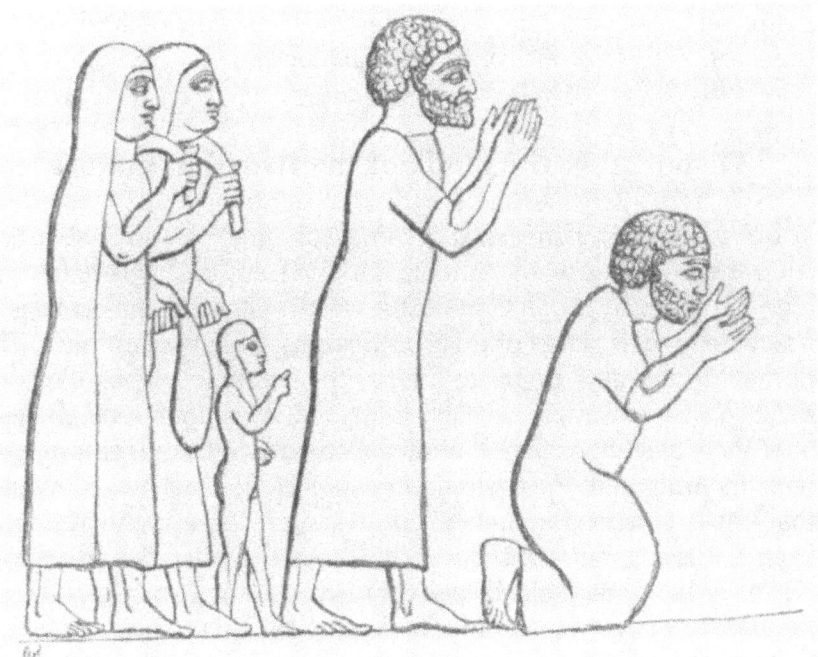

Figure 9: Jewish Captives from the town of Lachish Palace of Sennacherib, Nineveh.

city center with poorly built houses. Archaeology has also pointed to a marked increase in the number of rural settlements throughout Judah at about that time. All this indicates a dramatic growth of population in Judah, which can be explained only as a direct consequence of the influx of refugees from conquered Israel.

Of those who continued to reside in the region that was Israel, some retained their Israelite identity as long as the Kingdom of Judah continued to exist (II Chronicles 30:1–11). They did not, however, become part of the Judean nation. Others, probably the majority, mixed with the foreign peoples brought by the Assyrians from all over their empire to settle in the conquered land (II Kings 17:24). Together, old-timers and newcomers formed a new entity, the Samaritans, that still exists today, centered in the town of Nablus-Shechem in the heart of the former Kingdom of Israel. Still others were open to foreign influences, and with the changing political and religious fate of the region, accepted Hellenistic and Roman paganism, then Christianity, then

Islam. All those who remained in the land thus lost their identity as Israelites, and need not concern us any longer.

Dispersal in the lands of the Assyrian Empire

The Israelites who were exiled became with time the Ten Lost Tribes. After the exile they were mentioned in the Bible only in very few references, for example, in Chronicles, which states that the captives of Israel are in their places of exile "to this day" (I Chronicles 5:26). The phrase "to this day" points to the fourth century B.C. when the book of Chronicles was most probably compiled, some four hundred years after the exile. Other than that they were erased from memory. Perhaps the trauma of the destruction and exile of Israel was so intense that books compiled in Judah centuries after these events refrained from discussing their consequences. Contact with the deportees may not have been maintained, possibly because they soon established themselves in their new homes and assimilated with their neighbors. Only a very limited range of written references of First and the Second Temple period enable us to follow the exiles into their new homes.

Biblical verses dealing with the locations to where the tribes of Israel were exiled are short and cryptic. The first wave of exiles was deported to "Halah, Habor and Hara and the river Gozan" (I Chronicles 5:26), the second and larger wave to "Halah and Habor by the river Gozan and the cities of the Medes" (II Kings 17:4–6). Halah is mentioned in both lists, but its identification has in the past presented many problems, as no ancient place with such a name has been known inside or outside Assyria. However, with the advance of modern research, and especially of archaeological excavations that greatly expanded our knowledge of the Kingdom of Assyria, Halah is now identified with a place known in the Bible as Kelah, and in the Assyrian language as Kalkhu. Kalkhu was a very large and important city, situated on the banks of the river Tigris in northern Mesopotamia, in the Assyrian heartland. For a while it was the capital of the Assyrian Empire, and was embellished by a succession of kings. Its site, known by the local Arabic name Tel Nimrud, has been extensively excavated, and palaces and temples, richly adorned with enormous statues and elaborate and masterful reliefs, have been unearthed. It is rather surprising, then, that some Israelite exiles were brought to this very center of Assyria, and not, as one would perhaps expect, to more remote corners of the empire. Possibly the Israelites so favored were the upper classes, or perhaps the skilled masons and craftsmen, who were put to work in this prosperous metropolis. That some Israelites were actually brought to this Assyrian city is confirmed by an ostracon (a piece of broken pottery used in antiquity as scrap paper) carrying Hebrew names. This humble piece of pottery, written around the year 700 B.C., a very short time after the deportation, is one of the few concrete pieces of evidence for the existence of Israelite exiles in Assyria.

The Assyrians also embellished Kalkhu with spoils of war from the countries they subdued; hoards of carved ivory plaques that once adorned wooden furniture, as well as richly decorated bronze plates, have been unearthed in its ruins. These treasures reflect the distinct artistic style of the Phoenicians, dwellers of Tyre and Sidon and other cities of the East Mediterranean coast, conquered by the Assyrians. Some of these spoils may actually have been brought from Israel, which was at the time within the cultural sphere of Phoenicia. Indeed, carved ivory pieces, very similar to those from Kalkhu, have been unearthed in the ruins of the palace of the Israelite kings in Samaria.

Habor and Hara and the river Gozan are other places of exile mentioned in the Bible. The biblical scribe must have confused these names, as Gozan is a well-known city, while Habor is a river, tributary of the Euphrates, on which Gozan is situated. Gozan on the river Habor had long been identified with a mound known by the local name Tel Halaf. Unlike Kalkhu, Gozan was not situated in the Assyrian heartland. It had been an important center of the nomadic Aramean tribes, who inhabited the regions of Syria and northern Mesopotamia before they fell to the Assyrians around 800 B.C. When the Israelite exiles were brought there to settle, the region and city had already long been under Assyrian rule. Excavations at Gozan produced ostraca and other documents carrying Hebrew names. The names "Paltijau" (Paltiyahu) and "Nirijau" (Neriah), as well as the name of a man from the town of "Samerina" (Samaria), appear in a letter sent to one of the Assyrian kings of the seventh century B.C. From the letter it can be understood that both Paltiyahu and Neriah were officials, Neriah a high official in the ministry of finance. This letter indicates that at least some of the exiles of Israel rose to important positions in the Assyrian administration. An official document from the same time

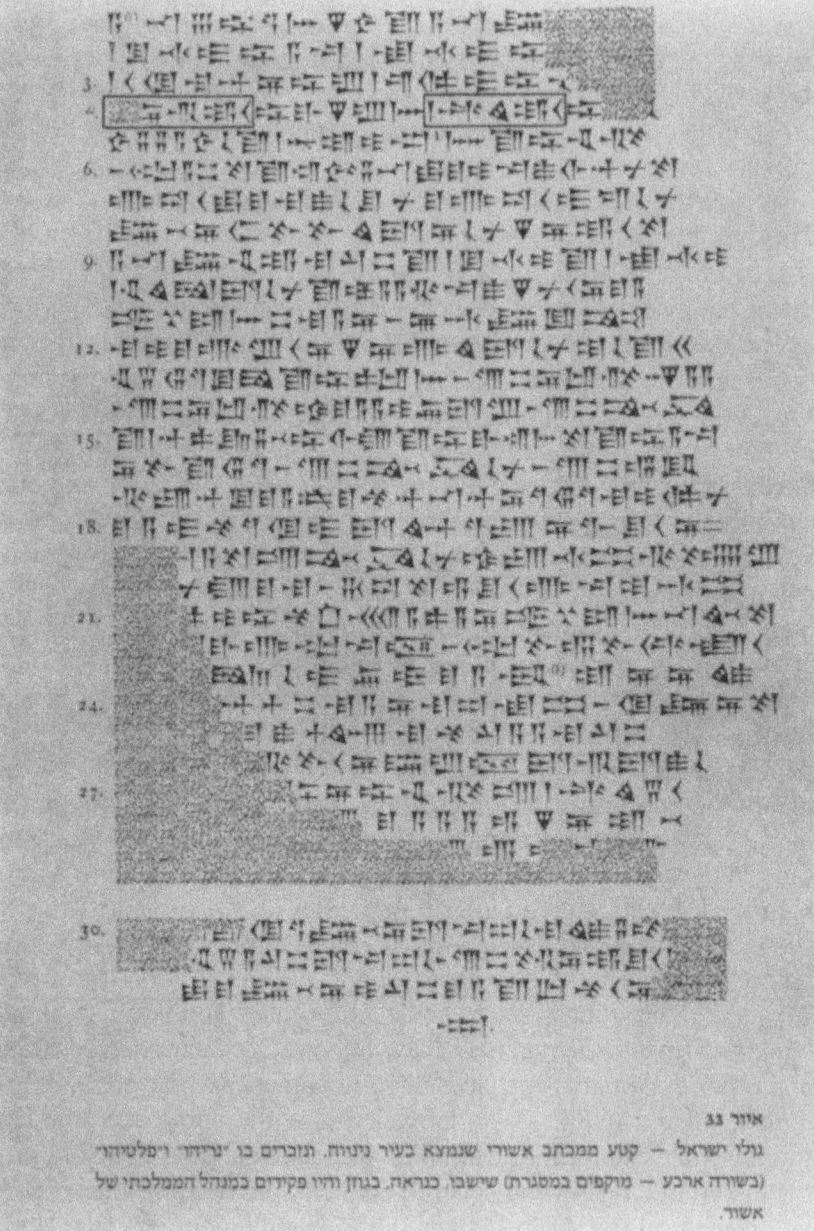

Figure 10: Detail from an Assyrian letter from Tel-Halaf mentioning Neviah and Paltiyahu.

orders a certain person to hand over a woman named "Danaya" (Dinah) to "Usi'a" (Hoshea), both Hebrew names. Other Hebrew names are also mentioned in letters of the fifth century B.C. found in Gozan, spanning a period of about 100 years. They prove that Israelites residing in that city continued to use Hebrew names, thus maintaining their identity for a considerable time after the exile. As for Hara, mentioned only in the first list, no identification has as yet been suggested, as no identical or similar name is known.

The cities of the Medes are mentioned only in the list of places of the second and larger deportation. Media is a large, mountainous region in northwestern and central Iran of today, between the Caspian Sea and Lake Urmia. It was a frontier country inhabited by the Medes—nomadic tribes who continuously harassed the northeastern borders of Assyria. Over the centuries the Assyrians conducted numerous raids into Media, and eventually annexed this region. An inscription commemorating one of these raids, conducted in the days of Tiglat Pileser II king of Assyria, proves that the Assyrians practiced their common policy of population exchange there too. This inscription states that 65,000 Medes had been deported from their country and replaced by peoples from other conquered lands. These newly settled people may have included some Israelites.

Modern research has thus enabled us not only to trace the fate of the Israelites who remained in their homeland, but also to draw a fairly accurate map of the different places to where the exiles had been deported and where they settled. These places stretch from the very center of the kingdom of Assyria to its western and eastern peripheries. However, after the fifth century B.C. the exiled Israelites are not mentioned in any historical record, and seem to have faded into thin air.

The fate of the Kingdom of Judah

The kingdom of Judah was saved from destruction at the hands of the Assyrian king Sennacherib in 701 B.C., and managed to maintain a fragile independence for some 150 years after the fall of the Kingdom of Israel. Its turn came in 586 B.C., shortly after the mighty Kingdom of Assyria fell to its southern neighbor Babylon. The Babylonians under king Nebuchadnezzar pursued the same policy of expansion and mass exile as their Assyrian predecessors. They led a military campaign to Judah, besieged and captured its capital Jerusalem, and led many of its citizens to exile in Babylon. But the Judeans did not remain long in captivity. Forty-eight years after the fall of Jerusalem, Cyrus king of Persia, conqueror of Babylon and successor to its empire, permitted them to return to their homeland and rebuild the Temple in Jerusalem. Not many of the exiled stood up to the challenge and returned to Judah. Those who did, and the small numbers who continued to trickle back to Judah for the next hundred years or so, established the Second Monarchy of Judah and built the Second Temple in Jerusalem. They, alongside the majority of Judeans who remained in Babylon, became the forefathers of the Jewish people.

Why are the Ten Tribes of Israel kept alive?

The strong belief that the Ten Tribes were not really lost, but that they exist somewhere and will reappear, is fueled by divine promises, found throughout the Bible, for their return to their homeland and for their glorious future there. At the heart of the unwillingness to accept their disappearance lies the fact that the fortunes of the two sections of the original nation, Israel and Judah, were historically very different. While the Ten Tribes of Israel, or at least that part of them that was deported to Assyria, were lost and never heard of again, Judah, perhaps because of their short period of exile, continued its existence as a nation and increased in numbers and strength as time went by. The return of Judah to its homeland after the exile was in direct fulfillment of promises pronounced by the prophets, while the Ten Tribes, to whom similar promises were given, vanished. In the words of the prophet Hoshea:

> The children of Judah and the children of Israel shall gather together and put upon them one head and come up from the land. [2:2]

The prophet Isaiah expressed the same sentiment:

> And it shall come to pass in that day that the Lord shall set his hand . . . And shall assemble the outcasts of Israel and gather together the dispersed of Judah from the four corners of the earth. [11:11–12]

The prophet Ezekiel, who lived among the exiled Judeans in Babylon, was ordered:

> Take thee one stick and write upon it, For Judah, and for the children of Israel his companions. Then take another stick and write upon it, For Joseph, the stick of Ephraim, and for all the house of Israel his companions: and join them one to another into one stick; and they shall become one in thine hand . . . Behold I will take the children of Israel from among the heathen, wither they be gone, and will gather them on every side, and bring them into their own land. [37:16–21]

These and other promises were fulfilled in regards to Judah. But what about the other part of the promise, made to the Ten Tribes of Israel? It is true that Israel was repeatedly portrayed in the Bible as wicked and low in religious and moral standards, but so was Judah most of the time. Both were exiled as a divine punishment for their conduct, and both were promised that the purgative measure would come to an end. Indeed an end to the exile had come to Judah, not to Israel. It was difficult to explain why one part of a divine promise was fulfilled, the other not. And thus, the fact that the Ten Tribes of Israel, carriers of prophecies for a return to their original homeland, became Lost Tribes, was bound to create a deep sense of imbalance, a flaw in the perfect pattern of recurrent sin–punishment–redemption. This pattern lies at the very foundation of the moral fabric of the world, as expressed time and again in the Scriptures, and has been ever since the guiding principle of the Western world. History in general, and the history of Israel in particular, as understood in biblical terms, is construed as an expression of a divine design, and if the divine has expressed time and again the promise that Israel will return, then it is bound to return. The seeming disappearance of the Ten Tribes must be a problem of human shortcomings, not a flaw in the divine design. The Ten Tribes must therefore not be regarded as lost. They are there, somewhere in the wide world, waiting for their time to appear and resume their role in world history. This belief, which lies at the heart of the quest for the Ten Lost Tribes of Israel, has had wide-ranging effects. It has encouraged voyages of discovery; it has influenced the interpretation of the origins and way of life of newly discovered tribes and nations; it has given new meaning to historical processes; and it has stood behind repeated messianic movements.

Where are the Ten Lost Tribes hiding?

Past generations of Lost Tribe seekers were, of course, unaware of present-day scientific identifications of the places to which the Bible says the Ten Tribes of Israel were exiled. To identify the names Halah, Habor, Gozan, and Hara, they sought place-names that had a similar sound. Gozan was thus identified with Ghazni, a mountain region in Afghanistan, or with the river Ganges in India. Habor was sought in Khaboor—a river that flows north from the Caucasian Mountains— or in the Khaibar Pass in Afghanistan, or in the Khaibar region in Arabia. The tendency to search the places of exile in distant lands was aided by the prophets of Israel themselves, whose passionate words seemed to have known no geographical boundaries. The prophet Isaiah promised the return of the exiled of Israel "from Assyria and from Egypt and from Pathros and from Cush and from Elam and from Shinar and from Hamat and from the Islands of the Sea." (11:11)

There is no hint that Israel was ever exiled to Egypt or to Pathros— the biblical name for Upper Egypt—nor to Elam in southern Iran or to Shinar in southern Mesopotamia, nor to Cush, usually identified with Ethiopia. Nor is there any mention of a sea voyage that would have taken the exiled Israelites to islands of the sea. Isaiah also promises a return "from the north and from the west and from the land of Sinim" (49:12), Sinim being usually identified with China. The prophet Jeremiah (31:8) was equally vague when he foresaw a return of Israel "from the north country . . . and from the coasts of the earth," and the prophet Amos (9:9) prophesied that the house of Israel will be sifted among all nations before being gathered back to its homeland (9:9). For tribe seekers these hazy geographical definitions presented an actual challenge, and opened up unlimited horizons for speculative search. Tribes were indeed sought, and said to be found, everywhere, including the remotest corners of the earth.

From Assyria to the ends of the world

Following the biblical prophesies, the question arises how, and under what circumstances, did the exiles further disperse from Assyria and Iran, where they had been settled following their deportation, to remote regions all over the world? The answer is neither found in biblical records, which, as mentioned, are silent about the earthly fate of the tribes after the exile, nor in Assyrian records, which do not refer to an Israelite existence after the fifth century B.C. The missing link, the necessary second dispersal of the Lost Tribes beyond Assyria, is to be found in writings and comments of several Jewish scholars and mystics who lived in the turbulent first centuries of the common era.

It is perhaps no accident that the fate of the Ten Tribes of Israel emerged as an issue in rabbinical and mystic circles in the first and second centuries of the common era. Opinions on this matter voiced in those days were instrumental in developing the saga of the Lost Ten Tribes. They laid the foundations for future search around the world.

The first two centuries of the common era were a time of intense political and spiritual turmoil. Rome, which for centuries had been annexing region after region around the Mediterranean Sea, completely subjugated Judah in A.D. 70. The destruction of the country and its capital Jerusalem, and the burning of the Second Temple, which had served as the spiritual center of the Jews for some 600 years, followed a period of about 150 years during which Rome gradually tightened its grip on Judah. This was done through client rulers, the best known of whom was Herod the Great. The destruction of Jerusalem brought an end to the political independence of the Jews, robbed them of their country, and took away their religious freedom. The Jews had to make far-reaching adjustments to cope with the post-destruction situation, and, under the leadership of capable sages, set out to do this difficult task. But even before its destruction, Judah experienced a period of intense spiritual fermentation. On the one hand the encroachment of Rome brought about a growing political oppression, but on the other it facilitated contacts with many foreign lands and exposed the people of Judah to a wide array of religions and values. Foreign commerce enriched the country, and with the accumulation of wealth came the corruption of the upper classes, and the intensification of urban crowding of the lower classes. This was happening at a time when the Roman world itself was undergoing a religious crisis, when alternatives to the official Greek–Roman gods were sought. Mystical practices of the East, such as the cult of the Parthian god Mitras and the Egyptian goddess Isis, preoccupied with ways of coping with death and securing an afterlife, were spreading throughout the Roman empire. The people of Judah, under internal and external pressures, developed a variety of strategies to confront the crisis. The realistic and rational rabbis toiled to interpret and modify the Law of Moses, the basis of Jewish life, in order to provide answers to pressing moral, social, and religious problems. At the same time other, more mystical trends were unfolding. The Essene sect, the views of which had been revealed through its library known as the Dead Sea Scrolls, sought redemption in the desert, where its members were free to pursue eschatological doctrines. The urgent need for redemption felt in those days found a more lasting answer in the movement that eventually became Christianity. Individual mystics, not part of a known movement, were also active in those days, and left a rich body of literature.

Josephus Flavius and the Ten Tribes

It was in such a frenzied atmosphere that the issue of the Ten Lost Tribes and their fate found its place. Being part of the divine scheme of the future redemption of the Jewish nation, it became a source of much needed comfort in turbulent times. The first to voice an opinion on the whereabouts of the Ten Tribes was Josephus Flavius, the well-known, coolheaded Jewish historian of the first century A.D. In his book *Antiquities of the Jewish People*, Josephus relates the circumstances of the return of the exiled Judeans from their captivity in Babylon. He also quotes letters given by the king of Persia to Ezra the Scribe, the prominent leader of the return, granting the Jews of his kingdom permission to return to Jerusalem. Upon receiving this letter, Ezra, so says Josephus, read the epistle in Babylon to those Jews who were there, but he kept the epistle itself, and sent a copy of it to all those of his own nation who were in Media. Many of them took their effects with them and came to Babylon, wishing to go to Jerusalem.

Josephus knew, then, that some of the descendants of the Ten Tribes were in Media, and many of them joined their Judean brothers and returned with them to Jerusalem. The large majority, however, remained behind. He summarizes the situation in his own days by saying that only two tribes (Judah and Benjamin) who lived in Asia and Europe were subject to the Romans, while the Ten Tribes were beyond the Euphrates, and they were an immense multitude, and not to be estimated by numbers. This exaggerated description echoes earlier formulas such as, "I will increase your seed as the stars of heaven and the sand on the shore of the sea" (Genesis 19:17).

In the opinion of Josephus, the Ten Tribes were still beyond the Euphrates in his own days. The notion of the "immense multitudes," first introduced here, became an important element in the way the Ten Tribes were viewed by later generations.

The mystical visions of Esdras the Fourth

While Josephus did not concern himself with the fate of the Ten Tribes but just reported their existence, others were more speculative. Most important from the point of view of subsequent searches for the tribes was Ezra—Esdras in Greek—a mystic of fiery vision, contemporary of Josephus Flavius. It was Esdras who first described the cause and circumstances of the dispersal of the tribes from their places of residence beyond the Euphrates to new localities. His *Visions of Esdras*, written around A.D. 120, is included in the Apocrypha, a collection of books, mainly of mystical character, written over a period of several centuries and left out of the officially sanctified twenty-four books of the Jewish Bible. Esdras, commonly known as the Fourth to distinguish him from other personages carrying the same name, received his visions at a time when the fall of Jerusalem to the Romans in A.D. 70 was a vivid, traumatic memory of the recent past. Esdras voiced a deeply felt sorrow for this tragic event, and expressed his hope for the swift downfall of Rome in revenge for her cruel deeds. His sixth vision, The Man from the Sea, introduces the subject of the Ten Lost Tribes in these words:

> And wherever thou sawest that he gathered another peaceable multitude unto him, those are the ten tribes, which were carried away prisoners out of their own land in the time of Osea the king, whom Salmanasar, the king of Assyria led away captive, and he carried them over the waters, and so came they into another land. But they took this counsel among themselves, that they would leave the multitude of the heathen, and go forth into a further country, where never mankind dwelt, that they may there keep their statutes, which they never kept in their own land. And they entered into Euphrates by the narrow passages of the river. For the Most High then showed signs for them, and

held still the flood, till they were passed over. For through that country there was a great way to go, namely for a year and a half, and the same region is called Arzareth. There they dwelt until the last times; and now when they are about to come again, the Most High will again stay the springs of the River that they may be able to pass over. [Esdras IV; XIII:39-46]

The miraculous crossing of the river Euphrates vividly recalls the crossing of the Sea of Reeds during the exodus from Egypt (Exodus 14:16-29), as well as the crossing of the river Jordan when the Israelites entered Canaan (Joshua 3:12-17). The miracle of the holding of the water emphasizes divine interest in the preservation of the Ten Tribes, and associates their fate with that of Israel in the most crucial moments of its history.

The name Arzareth, the land to which the tribes migrated after having crossed the river Euphrates, has opened up wide vistas for speculative search. Arzareth was sought far and wide, and identified with many localities with remotely similar sounding names. But Arzareth is really not a mysterious place at all; it is a corruption of the Hebrew words *Eretz Aheret*, meaning another land, giving the second dispersal of the Israelites very hazy geographical clues. Being as it may, the double mystery of the miraculous crossing of the Euphrates and the enigmatic Arzareth kindled the imagination of future generations, and became the basis for numerous theories concerning the whereabouts of the Ten Lost Tribes.

3

Jews in Search of Their Lost Brethren

Among the Jews, the enigma of the Lost Tribes was kept alive in stories and legends, as well as in rabbinical discussions. Because of historical circumstances the Jews, who lived in exile since the destruction of their temple, their country, and their independence in A.D. 70, did not venture out to conduct active searches for the Ten Lost Tribes. They kept praying and hoping for their miraculous return, believing that these hidden brethren were immense in numbers, independent, and politically and economically powerful. This belief kindled hope in the hearts of the downtrodden Jews, who for the time being had to make do with finding clues about the Lost Tribes in the Scriptures, with speculating, and with inventing legends about them. Yet at several points in the long history of the Jewish people, a handful of people who attributed themselves to the Ten Tribes have appeared out of nowhere, kindled the imagination of the people, and even caused some to attempt to go and find them.

The sages of the Mishnah and Talmud and the Lost Tribes

In the centuries following the destruction of the Second Temple and the loss of Jewish political and religious freedom, several rabbis and mystics speculated about the fate and location of the Ten Tribes. Bits of hazy and speculative information concerning this matter are contained in the Talmud and in the Apocrypha, as we have met already in the writings of Esdras. Two sages of the Talmud, Rabbi Berechiah and Rabbi Helbo, in the name of the earlier sage Rabbi Samuel Ben Nahman, are quoted as saying:

> Israel wandered into exile in three divisions; the one to the other side of the Sambatyon, another to Daphne in Antioch, and the third was covered by the cloud which descended upon them. [Palestinian Talmud, Sanhedrin 10.6]

Only one name, Daphne in Antioch, seems to have geographic reality. In another version of the same description, Daphne is said to be "of Riblathah" (Psiktha Rabbathi chapter 31). Both Antioch and Riblathah were two famous cities in ancient Syria, over 200 kilometers apart, and built in different periods. Riblathah flourished in the seventh through the sixth centuries B.C. Antioch was founded only in 300 B.C., when Riblathah had already been in ruins some 300 years. While Daphne was indeed a suburb of Antioch, no such name is known in the vicinity of Riblathah. All this shows that when the Talmud and related sources were compiled in the fifth century, information relating to the Ten Tribes was already very vague. However, both quotations indicate that at least a third of the exiled tribes were believed to have gone to Syria. This view was expressed also by Rabbi Hanina, who said (Sanhedrin 93b) that the tribes were exiled to the mountains of Selug, perhaps Seleucia, the name for Syria in the Hellenistic period.

Another third of the tribes are said to have been covered by a cloud, meaning perhaps that nothing was known about them. Yet in another version of the same description, the dark cloud is replaced by "inside the dark mountains," which, in a talmudic legend referring to Africa, are said to have been crossed by Alexander the Great on his way to Carthage (in Tunisia of today). Here then is a reference to a legendary exile to Africa, later developed in the stories of Eldad the Danite.

The river Sambatyon

The most intriguing feature that appears in all variations of the talmudic story relates to the river Sambatyon, which is to become a very important feature in the story of the Ten Lost Tribes. The talmudic sources mention this river by name, in a matter-of-fact way, without attributing any unique qualities to it. For a description of its unusual features, we return to the great Jewish historian Josephus Flavius, who relates how the Roman general Titus set out to return to Rome after his victory over Judah. On his way from Berytus to Antioch,

> He saw a river as he went along, of such a nature as deserves to be recorded in history; it runs in the middle between Arcea, belonging to Agrippa's kingdom, and Raphenea. It hath somewhat very peculiar in it, for when it runs its current is strong and has plenty of water; after which its springs fail for six days together, and leave its channel dry, as any one may see; after which days it runs on the seventh day as it did before, and as though it had undergone no change at all. It hath also been observed to keep this order perpetually and exactly: whence it is that they call it the Sabbatic River, that name being taken from the sacred seventh day among the Jews. [Book VII, chapter V:1]

A contemporary of Josephus, the Roman geographer Pliny the Elder, also mentions this strange river. While describing the marvels of many bodies of water in the world—the standing water called Silas in India, lakes in Africa in which everything floats and nothing sinks, waters that burn like flames in Bithynia, and prophetic springs in Cantabria—he adds that "in Judaea is a stream that dries up every Sabbath."

Both Josephus and Pliny mention the unusual, though not singular pattern of flow of the Sabbatical River. Periodic fountains and rivers are known in the semiarid Near East. One example is the Gihon Spring in Jerusalem that gushes once every several hours and is dry at other times. The opposing descriptions of the actual pattern of the river—flowing for six days and drying up on the seventh or vice versa—indicate that neither Josephus nor Pliny had actually seen the river, but each reported rumors he had heard. The two also disagree as to the location of the river. While Pliny confines himself to a general designation "in Judaea," Josephus places the Sambatyon between Berytus (present-day Beirut) and Antioch (present-day Antakiya), on the Mediterranean coast of Syria.

Neither Josephus nor Pliny connect the Sabbatical River with the Lost Tribes. Neither they, nor the rabbis of the Talmud, have as yet attributed to it any supernatural quality. Its natural if somewhat erratic pattern of flow was so well known that when the Roman general Tineius Rufus asked Rabbi Akiva to prove the cosmic value of the Sabbath, the rabbi used the river Sambatyon as one of his most convincing arguments (the story is mentioned in several midrashic sources; e.g., Bereshit Raba 11:2). Only in the Middle Ages, beginning with the stories of Eldad the Danite, and then in letters supposedly sent by Prester John—a legendary twelfth-century Christian ruler of a kingdom in India, later transferred to Ethiopia—did the river Sambatyon grow into mythological proportions. Prester John reported in one of his letters that between him and the Jewish kingdom, ruled by King Daniel, was a river that carried water and a great quantity of precious stones all week long, and rested on the Sabbath. That was beneficial, because if the Jews were to cross the river, they would cause great mischief to the whole world and no nation could resist them. The location of the Sambatyon was shifted to various parts of the world. It was sought in Africa and in various parts of Asia, all the way to China. The river Sambatyon and the Ten Tribes became inseparable components of the same story.

The fate of the Lost Tribes

The ancient rabbis not only mentioned the Ten Lost Tribes, but also discussed their future fate. The most important debate on this matter took place in the circle of sages surrounding Rabbi Akiva, one of the greatest rabbis who lived in the turbulent second century A.D. Rabbi Akiva was one of the main contributors to the oral religious tradition, compiled in writing shortly after his time to form the Mishnah. He was also a great mystic, and although his mystical teachings have not been preserved, it is known that he and his immediate circle of friends and disciples were engaged in mystical speculations. It was said that he was the only sage who had entered the Pardes—the world of mystical speculations—and had come out sane. Rabbi Akiva was the most important spiritual authority behind the Second War or Bar Kochba Revolt against the Romans in A.D. 132–136. He endorsed Simon bar Kosba, the leader of the revolt, as the Messiah, changed his name to Bar Kochba (Son of a Star), and entrusted to him the hopes of redemption of the Jewish people in that difficult time, some sixty years after the destruction of Jerusalem and the burning of its

Figure 11: The legendary King Prester John.

Temple. One of the debates in which Akiva was involved concerned the question of who will be entitled to life in the world to come, a debate quoted in the Mishnah (Sanhedrin 10:3):

> The Ten Tribes shall not return again, for it is written: And he cast them into another land like this day (Deuteronomy 29:28). Like as this day goes and returns not, so do they [the tribes] go and return not. So Rabbi Akiva. But Rabbi Eliezer says: Like as the day grows dark and then grows light, so also after darkness is fallen upon the Ten Tribes shall light hereafter shine upon them.

Rabbi Akiva's argument here is notable, because on another occasion when a similar debate was held, Rabbi Simon Bar Yohai, the great mystic said to have composed the Book of Zohar—the cornerstone of Jewish mysticism—is reported to have expressed the view that the tribes would not return, while Rabbi Akiva believed they would (Abot of Rabbi Nathan 31). All other rabbis whose opinions on the subject are recorded supported the view that the tribes would return. Rabbi Yehuda ha-Nassi, for example, compiler of the Mishnah and head of the Jewish community in the Land of Israel, said that

> Both have a part in the world to come. And what is the meaning of "and in that day He will blow a big horn and those lost in the Land of Assyria will return"? These are the Ten Tribes. [Palestinian Talmud, Sanhedrin 10:4]

It is a challenging question, which of Rabbi Akiva's opinions came first, and why he changed his mind. Perhaps the change expressed his deep disillusionment after the failure of Bar Kochba's revolt. While preparing for the revolt, Rabbi Akiva may have cultivated hopes for the return of the Ten Tribes, as part of the messianic age. But with the terrible consequences of the revolt—the total destruction of Judah and the mass exile of its Jewish population—he strove to extinguish all messianic hopes in the hearts of the surviving Jewish people, and with them the hope for the return of the tribes.

The reality of the Ten Tribes was thus accepted by both mystic and apocalyptic circles, and by the pillars of normative Judaism. It was expressed even in some of the rulings of civil law, as in the one concerning the collection of loot. Collecting loot, so the ruling goes, does not involve a waste of time that could otherwise be devoted to the study of the Torah. But the need to sort out that part of the loot that belongs to the Ten Tribes and return it to them does involve such a waste of time (Sanhedrin 84b). Concern was also expressed over the marriage of a Babylonian gentile with a Jewish woman "lest he is of the Ten Tribes" (Yebamot 16–17).

In the days when the Mishnah and Talmud were created and formalized, the belief in the existence of the Ten Tribes and in their eventual return was thus firm and unshaken. Considering the crucial impact of the Mishnah and Talmud on Jewish life to this day, it is not surprising that the Ten Tribes were accepted as an actual reality, not lost but only temporarily eclipsed. It was not clear, however, where the tribes resided, and from where they would return. As time went by, as the conditions of the Jews in their lands of exile deteriorated, the belief in a hidden large, strong, and independent segment of the people of Israel grew and was embellished with various legendary ornaments. With it grew the belief that the tribes are certain to return and come to the rescue of oppressed communities. This belief, based on the proclamation of the prophets as well as on the opinion of revered rabbis, became an integral part of life, and sustained many a Jewish community in times of stress. The sudden appearance in the ninth century of Eldad the Danite, who claimed to be himself of the Tribe of Dan, and who told stories of the whereabouts of the powerful and independent Ten Tribes, kindled the ashes of yearning for the eventual return of the tribes into a burning hope for their immediate appearance. Eldad gave the Jewish communities of his time the feeling that their plight is not shared by the majority of Jews, namely the Lost Tribes, who are ready at any minute to come to the aid of their oppressed brothers. From now on, the Ten Tribes became connected with messianic hopes. The drying out of the river Sambatyon, that great mystical barrier, and the appearance of the tribes were announced whenever a false Messiah made his appearance.

Benjamin of Tudela and the Ten Tribes

One of the most famous Jewish adventurers of the Middle Ages was the twelfth-century Benjamin of Tudela in Spain, who attempted to follow in the footsteps of Eldad the Danite and boasted of having traveled far and wide in search of Jewish communities. His diary has been one of the best read books since it was published in 1543. It is certain that Benjamin did not visit all the places he mentioned, and some scholars even go as far as suggesting that he never left Spain. Be it as it may, Benjamin heard rumors that place several of the Ten Tribes in Persia, or to the east of Persia, and has this to say about them:

> There are Jews in Persia . . . who say that in the towns of Nisabur dwell four tribes of Israel, viz. Dan, Asher, Zebulun and Naphtali, being the first exiles who were carried into captivity . . . The extent of their country is twenty days' journey, and they have provinces and great cities in the Mountains, and on one side the river Gozan marks the boundary. They are subject to no nation, but are governed by their own prince, whose name is Rabbi Joseph Amarkala, the Levite. Among them are scholars; others carry on agriculture; whilst a number of them are engaged in war with the land of Cush, by way of the desert. They are in alliance with the Kofar al Torak who adore the wind and live in the desert.

The Kofar al Torak are described by Benjamin as untamed, ungainly, noseless subjects of the fabulous Prester John, identified with Genghis Khan, or who perhaps ruled India or Ethiopia. When they attacked the kingdom of Paras (Persia) the Israelite tribes joined forces with them and came to their aid. The king of Paras became very afraid, and tried to persuade the Tribes not to fight him, being aware of their superiority over him. He also warned them that he would take revenge over the Jews of his kingdom. This warning persuaded the tribes to accept the king's request and withdraw.

Benjamin also mentions the tribes of Reuben, Gad, and half of the tribe of Menasseh, who were called also Jews of Khaibar, or, according to another version, Sons of Rechab. These tribes lived in the faraway country of Thema, twenty-one days' journey from Babylon through the desert of Sheba or al-Yeman (Yemen). They were independent and ruled by their prince Hanan. They fought with their marauding nomadic Arab neighbors and were the terror of the region. Their country was large, their cities big and strong. Some of them cultivated the land, others reared cattle. Yet others spent their lives in the study of the Law, and lived an ascetic life in caves and remote places, where they mourned over the destruction of Jerusalem and prayed for the salvation of the Jews.

An adjacent province was Telmas, ruled by prince Salmon, brother of Hanan. The two brothers were descendants of the royal house of

David. The Jewish population of Telmas numbered some 300,000, living in 200 villages and towns, the chief town being San'a, which was very large and strong. Many of the inhabitants of Telmas were learned, wise, and rich.

Benjamin's diary, which strongly echoes that of Eldad the Danite, was the ultimate source of identifying the Jews of Yemen, living in southern Arabia, with the Ten Lost Tribes. It is interesting that this identification echoes historical evidence based on inscriptions discovered in Arabia, of the existence in the fifth and sixth centuries, prior to the advent of Islam, of a semiindependent Jewish kingdom in the Samin mountains in Yemen, headed by king Joseph Du Nuas. Du Nuas fought against Christian and pagan tribes in Arabia, and forced some of them to convert to Judaism. He carried his fighting across the Red Sea to Africa and for a while subdued Ethiopia. The identification of the Jews of Yemen with the Ten Tribes took hold in Jewish lore, and later travelers indeed attempted, mostly unsuccessfully, to traverse the deserts and find them.

News of Jews in India, Yemen, and Ethiopia

The small Jewish community of Jerusalem in the fifteenth and sixteenth centuries was steeped in an atmosphere of mystical fervor and messianic aspirations, in which hopes for the imminent return of the Lost Tribes held an important place. Several reports and letters containing information on the subject were sent from Jerusalem to several Jewish communities. Much of what these letters had to say about the Tribes echoed the popular and widely circulated stories of Prester John and his legendary Christian kingdom in India, and of the neighboring Jewish kingdom situated beyond the river Sambatyon. They contained also references to the stories of Eldad the Danite, as well as bits of real information about Jews in India, Ethiopia, and Yemen that began to be circulated, but which assumed legendary proportions. These three regions—India, Yemen, and Ethiopia—were since that time at the center of Jewish search for the Ten Tribes.

The earliest report dealing with the Ten Tribes beyond the river Sambatyon was sent by Elijah of Ferrara from Jerusalem to his sons in Italy in 1435. In it Elijah relates news he heard of a mighty Jewish

Figure 12: A family of Yemenite Jews walking through the desert, 1949.

kindgom in India. He mentions the sons of Moses who dwell in an island near the Sambatyon River as well as all the other tribes, recalling the descriptions of Eldad the Danite. A letter from Jerusalem written in 1454 relates that the river Sambatyon had dried up, and the tribes were crossing to wage war with Prester John. The drying up of the Sambatyon and the crossing of four of the tribes that lived beyond it was reported also in a letter written over a hundred years later, in 1563. Rabbi Obadiah of Bertinoro, the famous commentator of the Mishnah who visited Jerusalem towards the end of the fifteenth century, sent to Italy two letters, one in 1488, the other in 1489. In them he expressed much concern over the report that Prester John had the upper hand in this war against the Tribes, and nearly exterminated all the Bene Israel of India—a name appearing here for the first time. Some, however, survived, and, with the help of other Indian kings, managed to grow. During a later war some Bene Israel were taken captives and brought to Egypt to be sold as slaves, but were redeemed by the Egyptian Jewish community. Obadiah saw them with his own eyes and found them dark, but not as dark as the Ethiopians. They believed themselves to be of the tribe of Dan, and said that their country grows pepper and spices. It thus seems that Obadiah indeed met Jews from Cochin in southern India, and that the stories of the kingdom of Prester John and his Jewish neighbors were based in part on the historically documented Christian activities in southern India, and of a Jewish community there. In his second letter Obadiah gives another version of the Bene Israel group: their land lay fifty days' journey from Aden and was surrounded by the river Sambatyon that threw stones all weekdays and rested on the Sabbath, and therefore could not be crossed. They claimed to be the pure and pious Sons of Moses, the unblemished members of the Tribe of Levi. It is not known with whom these second Bene Israel could be identified.

Similar news of the Sons of Moses who lived on the other side of the Sambatyon, while on this side lived the Ten Tribes, is the subject of yet another sixteenth-century letter from Jerusalem. These Sons of Moses did not have the Talmud but only the prophets, the Mishnah, and Maimonides' Mishne Torah, and they were great Kabbalists. This information seems to relate to the Jews of Yemen, and indeed at that time the Yemenite Jews did not have copies of the Talmud, and relied on their correspondence with Maimonides on issues of religious law. They were also known to have been devout students of the Kabbalah. Other information relating to the presence of Jews in the desert of Arabia is attributed to Muslim pilgrims to Mecca. When crossing the desert, these pilgrims were sometimes attacked by a large and very strong tribe called Sons of El Shaddai, because they invoked this name of the Jewish God while fighting. It was reported that these valiant fighters observed the Jewish religion, and were said to descend from the Sons of Rechab, mentioned by Benjamin of Tudela. This story may relate to the Jews of Haban in Southern Yemen, whose long hair gave them a somewhat wild appearance.

Yet other reports from Jerusalem center around the Jewish kingdom of the Falasha, situated in the high mountains of Ethiopia. The Falasha, as the Jews of Ethiopia were called, are reported to have lived in tents and to have been constantly on the move in search of pasture for their flocks. They were thought to have been of the tribes of Dan and Gad. Another angle of the story of the Falasha is related in a letter from 1525, stating that the writer himself met in Jerusalem a man who was captured at sea and after many adventures brought to Alexandria, where he was redeemed. The man reported, strongly

Figure 13: A Jewish man from Haban.

Figure 14: A Jewish woman from Haban.

alluding to the stories of Eldad, that in his native country were a great many people of the tribes of Simeon, Issachar, and two others he did not remember. They were very rich and powerful, and were ruled by a great king, the only Jewish king who had Christian and Muslim subjects. The man added that his people did not have the Talmud, and that their oral law was transmitted in the name of Joshua, son of Nun, rather than in the name of Moses. The sons of Issachar devoted themselves to study, while the others divided their time between the study of the Law and waging war against their Christian neighbors, the kingdom of Prester John (which by now had moved to Ethiopia). He added that once a Portuguese Jew visited them, and told them of the destruction of Jerusalem and the dispersal of the Jews. The Falasha, who never heard about it, tore their garments and wept, and were ready to set out and march with force on Jerusalem. Their prince, however, pleaded with them to wait for a sign from God.

Jerusalem was not the only source of information concerning the Lost Tribes. The Jews of Italy were also active in reporting about this matter, and several of their letters had survived. One letter of 1532 mentions an independent Jewish kingdom in Ethiopia. Another reported that the Sambatyon was now dry on Mondays, Thursdays, and Saturdays, and myriads of Jews had already crossed it and were now camped a thirty days' journey from the Holy Land. However, they were commanded by God to remain there for two years. The writer of another letter claimed that he had seen in Damascus a messenger from the prince of the tribe of Reuben, named Hananel, and even drank a glass of wine with him. The prince, he said, was 250 years old, and had crossed the Sambatyon with numerous of his tribe and of the tribe of Dan. It is interesting that the same king Hananel and the same messenger from the tribe of Reuben, here named David, are mentioned in a letter sent from Safed around 1525. It is very likely that both letters allude to David Reubeni (see next).

Messiahs and the Lost Tribes

All these reports sent from Jerusalem and Italy were part of an atmosphere of messianic expectations that engulfed the Jewish world during the fifteenth and sixteenth centuries, following the persecution and final expulsion of the Jews from Spain. The idea of "the birth pangs of the Messiah," very strong in Jewish lore, associated the coming of the Messiah with times of extreme peril. The Ten Lost Tribes of Israel—those large segments of the nation that were seemingly independent, rich, and strong—were believed to precede the Messiah, and inflict the hoped-for revenge on the oppressors of Israel, Christians and Muslims alike. Rumors of the drying up of the river Sambatyon, the formidable barrier that on the one hand preserved the tribes and on the other prevented their appearance, followed by the crossing of the river by the tribes, were considered "the footsteps of the Messiah." This concept was also applied to historically recorded appearances of tribes and nations that swept parts of the world. Thus, the amazingly swift conquest of Christian lands in the Middle East and North Africa by the Muslims in the seventh century was viewed as "the footsteps of the Messiah." Likewise were the invasions of the Mongols who swept Asia and Eastern Europe in the thirteenth century, and the onslaught of the Turks in the fourteenth and fifteenth centuries, which brought the downfall of the long-lasting Christian Byzantine Empire.

The strong messianic hopes led, at extremely crucial moments in Jewish history, to the appearance of several personalities who proclaimed themselves messiahs, and connected themselves with the Lost Tribes.

David the Reubenite

The prince of the tribe of Reuben, mentioned in one of the letters sent from Jerusalem to Italy, may refer to a mysterious person who called himself David the Reubenite (Reubeni), who appeared in Venice in 1523. His appearance was no doubt connected with the devastating effect the expulsion of the Jews from Spain had on the Jewish world. From his diary, which included an itinerary of his voyages—thought to be more fantastic than real—we learn that Reubeni claimed to have come from the desert of Habor (Yemen), to have gone to Jerusalem where he revealed himself as a member of the Lost Tribes. He then went to Egypt, from where he sailed to Venice. In Venice he reported that he was the son of King Solomon and the younger brother of King Joseph, in whose service he held the position of chief of staff. Joseph's kingdom was located in the "deserts of Asia and Yemen." Its inhabitants numbered more than 300,000, all from the tribes of Reuben, Gad, and half the tribe of Menasseh. They produced spices, pepper, articles of medicine, and other good things. In 1524 Reubeni went from Venice to Rome, riding on a white horse, and was received by Pope Clement VII. Reubeni laid before the pope his plan to join the forces of the Jewish kingdom with those of the Christian world, and together fight the expanding Ottoman Turks who terrorized Europe at that time. Reubeni asked the pope for letters of credence to Emperor Karl V and to King Francoise I, and also to Prester John, whose imaginary kingdom was by then thought to be in Ethiopia. Because diplomatic relations between the Christian and the Muslim world were carried out at that time by the Portuguese, the pope sent requests to the king of Portugal, as well as to the king of Ethiopia, to authenticate the stories of Reubeni. In the meanwhile Reubeni was sent to Portugal, where he aroused strong messianic hopes among the conversos (Jews converted to Christianity, but who secretly continued to keep Judaism). He announced that the time of redemption had arrived, and that they would all go to Jerusalem and take the Land of Israel from the Muslims. The news spread, causing much excitement among the Jews of Europe and North Africa. In 1532 Reubeni, accompanied by Shlomo Molcho, a converso who returned to Judaism and claimed himself a messiah, was received in audience by the Emperor Karl V at Regensburg. The two were arrested. Shlomo Molcho was sent to Mantoba where he was later burned at the stake, and Reubeni was sent in chains to Spain. His whereabouts after that event are not very clear. He died in Spain, probably in 1538.

Shabbtai Zvi

The appearance of the best known of the false messiahs, Shabbtai Zvi of Izmir, in the seventeenth century, is thought to be a late reaction to the expulsion from Spain. His appearance, after having been proclaimed messiah by his pupil Nathan of Gaza in 1665, was heavily tinted with kabbalistic ideas that developed in the wake of the expulsion. In the summer of that year news reached Holland, England, and Germany of the appearance of the Ten Tribes, led by a prophetic and saintly commander who performed many miracles. According to some reports the armies of the Tribes were conquering Mecca, the center of Islam. According to others they were assembling in the Sahara Desert, and according to yet others they were marching into Persia.

At the same time the self-proclaimed prophet Nathan of Gaza sent letters to many Jewish communities proclaiming Shabbtai Zvi a messiah. In one of his letters he stated that Shabbtai Zvi would take without war the crown from the Turkish sultan, and make him his servant. After four or five years he would proceed to the River Sambatyon to bring back the lost tribes and to marry the thirteen-year-old Rebecca, daughter of Moses. These events, and the news of the movements of the Ten Lost Tribes, caused Shabbtai Zvi to be acclaimed messiah by numerous Jews who sold their belongings and prepared themselves to follow him to Jerusalem. The whole episode ended tragically when Zvi was captured by the Ottoman authorities, and in prison converted to Islam.

Jewish messengers to the Ten Tribes

Starting in the nineteenth century, when the situation of the Jews in many countries improved, some began to harbor hopes of reaching the Lost Tribes themselves, rather than being content with stories based on reports of others. Several people ventured out on expeditions, but were honest enough to write true and accurate reports on the peoples they encountered and places they visited rather than follow their wishful desires.

One such messenger was Jacob Sappir, sent in the second half of the nineteenth century from the Holy Land to Jewish communities in India and Australia with appeals for financial support. In the course of his travels he visited Yemen, established the first historical contact with the Jews there, to whom he does not attribute a Lost Tribe ancestry, and also discovered the long-haired and fierce-looking Jews of Haban in southeastern Arabia, whose appearance probably gave rise to stories of the Lost Tribes in that region.

Another famous traveler of the nineteenth century was Joseph Israel (1818–1864), a colorful and adventurous Rumanian Jew, who

Figure 15: A true portrait of Shabbetai Zvi, by an eyewitness in Smyrna, 1666.

so admired Benjamin of Tudela that he decided to follow in his footsteps, and consequently changed his name to Benjamin the Second. The main aim of his travel was to find the Ten Lost Tribes. He started his journey in Istanbul in 1845, from where he went to Alexandria, Cairo, Palestine, Syria, Babylon, Kurdistan, Persia, India, and Afghanistan. He collected invaluable information about the Jews in these places, their number, way of life, professions, customs, and folklore. He encountered in India the Bene Israel community, which he did believe to be of the Ten Tribes as they kept the Sabbath, circumcision, and dietary laws. He did not, however, manage to get to the legendary river Sambatyon. In 1859 he left for North America, where he collected information on newly established Jewish communities there, as well as on the nature of the land and its inhabitants. He died poor and penniless in 1864.

A late emissary in search of the Lost Tribes was Shmuel Yavneeli, who went in 1911 to Yemen as a representative of the Zionist organization to study the situation of the Yemenite Jews, and to encourage them to immigrate to Palestine. It is said that one of his aims was to find the tribe of Dan, the Sons of Moses, and the Rechabites—so frequently mentioned by previous travelers and emissaries as living in or in the vicinity of Yemen. He succeeded in his Zionist mission, but does not report of his other, secret hope.

Voyages to discover the Lost Tribes are not only a thing of the past. In our own day, an organization in Jerusalem named Amishav (my people return), headed by Rabbi Avihail, has been searching and locating people rumored to have an Israelite ancestry. Their emissaries have been to Afghanistan, India, China, Africa, and South America. They convince these people that they really are descendants of the Ten Lost Tribes, and persuade them to immigrate to Israel. From time to time this organization proudly announces to the public that such nations as the Afghans or the Japanese have Ten Tribes roots, and that they set their minds to move to the Promised Land. Such additions to the population of Israel will be very beneficial to the state, claims Amishav, as the Japanese are industrious and excel in production, while the Afghans are fierce warriors and will be welcome in the Israeli army. But despite these enthusiastic reports, to this day the organization has had only minor successes with some remote tribes whom they convinced to openly declare their supposed Ten Tribe descent, and actually immigrate to Israel.

The Ten Tribes in popular legends

Being such a strong factor in Jewish lore, folk imagination created a whole body of legends concerning the Ten Tribes. They all relate that the tribes are independent, have a lot of political, economic, and physical power, are pious and keep all the laws and regulations of Judaism. Another feature often attributed to them for unknown reasons, is that they had red hair, and were thus called "The Red Jews."

Moses Edrei, a Moroccan Jew who claimed to have been of the tribe of Naphtali, reports of a man who visited Ethiopia on his own accord. According to Edrei, in the year 1630 a man went from Alexandria to Salonica, where he heard that a caravan from Ethiopia had arrived. The man beseeched the leader of the caravan to let him join, and was taken to the land of the Sambatyon, where he met the Israelite king Eleazar. Next to the Israelite kingdom were the Pristiani (subjects of Prester John), with whom the Israelites maintained peaceful relations.

Edrei tells also of Rabbi Baruch, a Jerusalemite who was sent in 1646 to collect money for the Jews of the Holy Land. When he came to Persia he was attacked by robbers and was about to be killed by one of them. When he pleaded for his life in Hebrew, the man revealed himself as Malkiel of the tribe of Naphtali. The tribes furnished Baruch with a long and flowery letter from the Children of Moses to the Jews of Jerusalem, signed by their king Ahitub the son of Azaria, and two other dignitaries. The letter, describing their independence and power, lamenting the plight of the rest of the Jewish nation, and explaining that they could not come to its aid because of the river Sambatyon, was brought to Jerusalem, where it was authenticated by nine rabbis. It then passed many hands and changed many places until eventually published by Edrei and later by Jacob Sappir, who added a note of apprehension about its authenticity, mainly on linguistic grounds.

Another legend tells of a Yemenite Jew named Zaddok who resided in Jerusalem, and had a strong desire to find the tribes. He gathered a group of Jews who went along with him. After a while some members of the group returned to Jerusalem and related that they did not know the way to the river Sambatyon, and wandered aimlessly until their provisions ran out. Zaddok insisted on continuing. After more time had passed, Zaddok himself returned and related that he reached the shore of the Sambatyon, where he waited until Friday just before the Sabbath, when he cried out in Hebrew, "Jews, come and take me over." A boat came, manned by giants, who inquired who he was. Upon hearing that he was from Jerusalem they embraced and kissed him and carried him across the river. On Sabbath eve he went to the synagogue, where he told the tribes about Jerusalem and sang them Yemenite melodies. His hosts offered him to stay with them, but he became homesick and worried about his wife and children who were left without support, and decided to return to Jerusalem. Members of the tribes gave him precious presents, and late one Friday afternoon conveyed him across the river. Unfortunately on his way back he was robbed, and arrived in Jerusalem as penniless as he left.

Another legend tells of the king of Yemen who passed by a school of small children just as they happened to be reading the verse, "How could one have routed a thousand, or put ten thousand to flight?" (Deuteronomy 32:30). The king, being sure that the verse was meant for him, ordered the teacher to either erase the verse from the Torah, or prepare himself to be executed. The community decided to appeal for help to the Sons of Moses beyond the Sambatyon, and sent an emissary to them. The emissary reached the river just before the coming of the Sabbath and saw two girls drawing water. He threw a stone, breaking one of the water jars to draw the girl's attention from him, and managed to cross the river without anyone noticing him. When he was discovered in the synagogue and proclaimed that he was a Jew from Yemen, he was accused of having crossed on the Sabbath, but one of the girls testified his innocence. He married her and the two returned to Yemen. At the trial of the teacher the girl proved to the king that the verse was true. A thousand soldiers were brought, whom she killed all at once with a phylactery strap.

Another legend is the story of Baruch, son of Samuel of Pinsk, who was sent in the year 1831 by the Ashkenazi Jewish community in the Land of Israel with a letter to the Children of Moses and the Ten Tribes. The letter contains an appeal for financial support for the community. It also mentions Eldad the Danite, tells of the sufferings of the Jews, relates the appearance of David the Reubenite, and reports that two years previously, emissaries from Palestine to Yemen met a member of the tribe of Dan, who told them of his tribe's wealth and strength, and then disappeared. Baruch went to San'a in Yemen, where he cured the king of a disease. The rabbi of San'a joined him in search of the tribes, taking along a servant named Joseph Ben Zion Modai. After many hair-raising adventures in the desert they encountered a shepherd who claimed to be of the tribe of Dan. They asked to be brought to the tribe, but were delayed for many days in the desert and finally returned to San'a. In San'a, Baruch continued the cure of the king, and was killed by the envious king's physician. His tomb was shown in San'a, as proof of his adventures.

As the crossing of the Sambatyon is an almost impossible task, sometimes one has to get help from animals to find the way to the Ten Tribes. A legend from Poland tells that a certain poor Jew had only one she-goat. One Sabbath eve the goat disappeared, and the man set out searching for her. Although the Sabbath was about to enter, the man went farther and farther into the forest, when he suddenly realized that he was in an unfamiliar surrounding, where the stars, which had just come out to proclaim the Sabbath, were as big as suns. The goat disappeared. The man suddenly saw a very tall man who looked like armor-clad Goliath the Philistine, who nevertheless proclaimed he was a Jew. Many other giants came, all perplexed at the sight of the small man. The first giant picked him up and put him in his pocket, and they all went toward a large and beautiful town. At home the giant put the Jew on the table, and asked to hear him pray to prove that he too was a Jew. The Jew recited the invocation "Shema Israel," and other blessings and prayers. The giant then told him that they were of the Ten Tribes, and that this was the land beyond the Sambatyon. After the Sabbath the giant threw the man in the air. The man found himself near the forest, with the she-goat standing beside him. He told the people of his village of these events, and was proclaimed a *zaddik* (righteous man).

And so the Jewish search for the Ten Lost Tribes of Israel was mainly carried out in the realm of rumors, stories, and legends. The few attempts to actually find the tribes made by several adventurers ended with mishaps and failure. The great barrier—the river Sambatyon—proved most effective, and the Ten Tribes remained closed behind it, their appearance postponed to the times of the Messiah.

4

Mountain Tribes and Plain Tribes—Israel in the Caucasian Mountains and Beyond

While the Jews dealt with the enigma of the Ten Lost Tribes by means of speculative thought, rumors, messianic outbursts, legends, and a few real search ventures, the Christian world, well versed with biblical history and prophecy, was also searching the world to find traces of these long-lost tribes. Their search was much more active, having access by means of military, commercial, and missionary activities to remote corners of the world. The enthusiastic efforts of the Christian world to locate the Ten Lost Tribes was fueled by the desire to convert them and thus bring the final salvation of the world.

Biblical prophecies and historical data, the visions of Esdras, and the appearance of Eldad the Danite were all instrumental in kindling interest in the saga of the Ten Lost Tribes, and in arousing the imagination of generations of Christian dreamers and seekers. Neither one of these sources, however, provided clear geographic information as to the whereabouts of the tribes, and the searchers had to rely on their own interpretations. Eldad seemed to have supplied the most solid geographical background, and, by charting three regions where the tribes were supposed to be living, was instrumental in pointing to areas where the searches could be most fruitful. He directed attention to the Caucasian Mountains and the vast plains of beyond, situated to the north and west of the Assyrian Empire to where the tribes of Israel were historically exiled. He also pointed to the mountains of Arabia and to the upper reaches of the Nile river in East Africa, areas not related to the geography of the exile.

Of the three regions, the first, the Caucasian Mountains and Euroasian plains, was the most promising. Geographically it lies close to Assyria, to where many, if not most of the exiles of Israel were deported. Moreover, it corresponded with the direction of Esdras's description of the second dispersal of the Israelites through the narrows of the River Euphrates to the far-lying land Arzarath, which, despite its clear visionary character, was regarded a valid historical event. The regions to the northwest of ancient Assyria, namely the Caucasian Mountains and the plains beyond—lying as they are in the direction of this "second dispersal"—became early favorites of tribe seekers, promising territories where the tribes, or at least some of them, might still be found.

The vast and varied area of the Caucasian Mountains and the plains beyond were virtually unknown to Europeans until recently, and even today most people have only a hazy idea of their geography, history, and ethnography. The scarcity of reliable information has added much to the mystery and romance of the region. The high and rugged Caucasian Mountains were, and still are, inhabited by numerous tribes of different origins, who found refuge in its almost inaccessible terrain. The great Asian plains, extending from the borders of China to eastern Europe, were home to many tribes, but were also the highway on which numerous waves of invaders marched. A succession of barbarous nomads, originating in eastern and central Asia, swept through these vast plains, and repeatedly threatened the great civilizations of western Asia and Europe. Some were indeed the great destroyers of settled life in these regions, and their names are to this day remembered with terror and awe. Such were the Scythians of the first millennium B.C., and the much later Huns, Tatars, Mongols, and Turks. Each wave in its turn caused enormous losses to life and property, and each was regarded in its day as a tool in the hands of God to punish humanity. After these marauding tribes had stretched to the utmost their strength and resources, they often settled down and mixed with the remnants of the local population.

The people living in the mountains and the plains, whose curious customs and ways of life were only vaguely known, as well as the mys-

Figure 16: Armies of the Lost Tribes from the Caucasus, 1606.

terious tribes who had lived there in the past, became, on account of their geographic location, plausible candidates for Lost Tribe lineage. Not all tribes who inhabited these regions attracted the same degree of attention. Those that did, including some of the wildest and most dangerous of them, were identified as such because they had a particularly attractive and suggestive history, or because they practiced customs that seemed to recall ancient Israelite ones.

This chapter will deal with four of the ancient and contemporary peoples believed to be of Ten Tribe lineage—the Tatars, the ancient Scythians, the Khazars of the plains, and the Mountain Jews of Daghastan in the Caucasian Mountains. Each of these people has a completely different history, and yet they were all believed to have been connected to the Ten Lost Tribes of Israel. Two—the Scythians and Khazars—have long been extinct. The other two—the Tatars and Mountain Jews—still survive today, but have lost the attributes that captured the imagination of tribe seekers. The Scythians and Tatars were not Jewish, and both probably never suspected that they would be connected with the Ten Tribes. The Khazars converted to Judaism, an almost unique occurrence in world history, while the Mountain Jews of the Caucasian Mountains were and are Jews. This last group was an exception to the general practice of Christian tribe seekers, to seek their targets among the non-Jewish peoples of the world rather than among the Jews. The case of the Scythians is particularly interesting, as their connection with ancient Israel developed because they were supposed to have been an indispensable link in the story of the dispersal of the tribes throughout Asia and Europe. Their history was reconstructed to fit that theory. The story of how the remnants of Israel were identified with these four peoples will introduce both the drama of the search, and the methods used by the tribe seekers in their efforts to locate the Lost Tribes of Israel.

1. The Tatars

The Tatars were the first group to capture the imagination of European tribe seekers as possible candidates for Lost Tribe ancestry. This identification was suggested already in the Middle Ages.

The Tatars, a group of tribes related to either the Turkish or Mongolian tribal groups, first appeared on the eastern borders of Europe in the twelfth century. They are mentioned by name for the first time in a group of eighth-century inscriptions in the old Turkic language, discovered near the Orkhon River in Mongolia. Several Tatar tribes, each with its own name, joined the Mongols and took part in the raids and conquests of central Asia, the Caucasian Mountains, the Near East, and eastern Europe between the thirteenth and fifteenth centuries. The Tatars became so confused with the Mongols that the Mongol raids on Europe are known in Russia as the "Tatar Subjugation," while in western Europe they are referred to as the "Mongol Invasion." Eventually the Tatars settled in wide areas of what is today Russia, from Siberia in the east to the Ukraine in the west, with heavy concentrations in the central valley of the River Volga and in the Crimean peninsula that projects into the Black Sea.

Early attempts to connect the Tatars with Israel

The Tatars were the first group of nomadic Asian tribes that came to the attention of Europeans since the stories of Eldad the Danite began to circulate. The diary of Eldad, quite well read in the Middle Ages by Jews and non-Jews alike, became a reference book for the people of western Europe to which they compared the vague and incomplete reports on the Tatars that reached them. Some scholars indeed found enough points of similarity between the Tatars and the tribes to encourage them to declare the Tatars the true descendants of Lost Israel.

The first to mention a connection between the Tatars and the Israelites was Matthew Paris, an English Benedictine monk of the thirteenth century. Paris was a well-informed monk, and his book *Chronica Majora* is to this day considered an excellent source of information on events that occurred in Europe between 1235 and 1259. Without elaborating on the subject, Paris stated that the Tartars and Cumans, two Turkish tribes who lived in the Straights of Caucasus, were of the Posterity of Israel whom Alexander the Great had shut within the Caspian Mountains. Tatar–Israel connection was probably fairly widely circulated and accepted at the time. Another citation to that effect is found in the writings of Thomas Bradwardin (1290–1349), one of the leading mathematicians of the Middle Ages.

Early geographic knowledge and the Tatars

These early citations of Tatar–Israel connections did not develop into a full-fledged identification until the seventeenth century, when Matthew Paris's book was first printed and became widely circulated. These were times of great expansion of geographic and ethnographic knowledge. The discovery of foreign peoples that were never before encountered rekindled interest in the whereabouts of the Ten Lost Tribes, who could now perhaps be found through an actual search in hitherto distant and unexplored regions. The effects of the widening horizons of the period can be witnessed in the writings of one of the earliest geographers, Richard Blome, who based his work on research carried out some years earlier by Monsieur Sanson, "Late Geographer to the present French king" (Louis XIV, 1643–1715). Blome gives his readers quite an accurate geographic description of the lands of the Tatars. Tatary is described as the most northern part of Asia, from the river Volga to the strait of Jesso, which separates it from America (today's Bering Straits), and from the Caspian Sea, the River Gehon (?), and the Mountain of Caucasus unto the Northern (Frozen or Scythian) Ocean.

The Tatars were supposed to still be living under their original tribal names, and to retain their tribal organization. After giving this factual evidence, Blome, in the fashion of the day, proceeded to offer some speculations as to the origin of the name Tatary. His first suggestion was that this name is apparently taken from the River Quarter, or Hoard of Tatar, from whence these people being issued, have overrun and made themselves known in all parts of Asia. Apparently not satisfied with this straightforward explanation, Blome offered a much more romantic and appealing one—a Ten Tribes of Israel ancestry. Blome based his suggestion on grounds that the word Tatar, or Totar, signifies in the Syriac language remnant or forsaken. The Tatars took this name for themselves because they esteem themselves the Remnants of the Jews.

Having introduced this fascinating explanation, Blome set out to give a concise history of the dispersal of Israel, followed by a suggested connection of the Tatars with the Scythians of the first millennium B.C. (see later). Such speculative methods of research, based mainly on linguistics or rather on similarities of sound, as well as disregard for chronology and history, were very common in Blome's days. They were to become the typical methods used by future generations of tribe seekers.

Giles Fletcher and the Tatar–Israel theory

Perhaps the best known propagator of the identification of the Tatars with the Lost Tribes of Israel was Giles Fletcher. He was, in his own words (and spelling) a faithful agent for Queen Elisabeth of Famous Memory at the Pallace of the great Czar of Muschovy, as he describes himself in the preface to his book. As envoy to Moscow in the second half of the sixteenth century, Fletcher had the rare opportunity of becoming acquainted with the lands and peoples of the steppes and mountains near the Caspian Sea, areas that were closed to Europeans at that time, and thus of great romantic appeal.

After suggesting that it is best to inquire and seek for them where it is likely that they are to be found (and truly the likeliest place to find them, Fletcher said, was in or near those Colonies, where they were planted in the first), Fletcher gave eight reasons for identifying the Tatars with the Tribes of Israel. Direct quotations from his book will give the flavor of his argumentation:

> 1. From the Place: The Israelites were transported in the greatest numbers to the cities and Parts of Media. Media, as described by Cosmographers, and more especially by Merchants and other Travelers, lyeth about the Caspian Sea, which the Russe calls the Bachualensky or Chnolensky-More. All the country north of the Caspian and to the Hibernian and Northern Sea is inhabited by the Tatars. By the consent of all Stories written of the Assyrian and Persian Monarchy since the time of Cyrus, Cyrus invaded the Schythian Shepherds, or Tartar people about 200 years after the Israelite deportation who were grown by that time into a great and mighty people.

Fletcher then states that it is most likely that the Assyrians did not settle the Israelites in the best part of Media but rather in remote and barren places in the north and northeast parts of their kingdom, namely in areas now inhabited by the Tartars (or Tatars).

> 2. From the Appellation of the Tartar Citys: Their metropolis is Samarchian, which has many monuments of that nation, where the great Tamarlain had his seat and place of residence. And how little

> differing is Samarchian from Samaria . . . only differing in termination, a thing usual in proper names of Men and Citys . . . They have besides, the Mount Tabor, a great town and well fenced with a strong fort, situate upon a high Hill . . . They have a city called Jericho, seated upon the River Ardoce. . . .

Fletcher adds that the cities of the Tatars are large and fortified, as against the Scythians who are shepherds and live in tents.

> 3. From the distinction of their Tribes: Their tribes are united in one government but may not mix by intermarriage. And this division of the Nation into Tribes, and without commixation of their Kindreds, which was no where else used by any Nation save the Israelites, is still observed and continued among the Tartars most religiously.
> 4. From the number of their Tribes: They are ten in all. . . .
> 5. From the Testimony of the Tartars: They affirm that they received it by Tradition from their Ancestors that they had their Origine from the Israelites who were near the Caspian Sea; by which tradition as by the stories of those times, it is reported that the great Tamarlin would boast himself, that he was descended from the Tribe of Dan.
> 6. From their language: some words, which I have heard repeated by the Ruses, have many Hebrew and Chaldee words.
> 7. From their manner of circumcision.
> 8. From all the Scriptures for their return into their country.

Fletcher assumed that the statement in Revelation 16 that there would be a return from the east through the dried-up river Euphrates must apply to the Ten Tribes. It could not refer to Judah and Benjamin, who were exiled by the Romans to the west and therefore cannot return from the east. Also the returnees are called kings, and this could not suit the Jews, who have no kings and are poor and oppressed. The Tatars, on the other hand, are eastern people and have kings.

Fletcher's eight points are quite amazing to the modern reader, trained to use scientific geographical, historical, anthropological, and linguistic methods, rather than the fleeting impressionistic methods used by the searchers in the past. Moreover, it is possible that Fletcher never visited the lands of the Tatars and did not make firsthand observations of their customs, but based his conclusions on unauthenticated rumors. In the seventeenth century, even well-educated and highly placed people like Fletcher were not bound by scientific or logical ways of thinking, and would easily and creatively weave from disconnected bits of information a colorful, if fanciful, fabric. Similarities of names, seeming connections between peoples who lived millennia apart, free associations of people who practiced ostensibly parallel customs and possessed similar social organizations—these were the tools used to explain a perplexing world that had expanded considerably since the end of the Middle Ages. The same methods were also used in the attempts to locate the Ten Lost Tribes.

Tamarlin and the tribe of Dan

The remarks that the Tatars considered themselves of the Ten Tribes, and that Tamarlin, grandson of Gingis Khan, believed he was of the tribe of Dan, are particularly intriguing, and serve to indicate that Fletcher did not distinguish the Tatars from the Mongol–Turks. Tamarlin, or Temurlenk ("the lame iron man" in Turkish), was not a Tatar, but a Mongol–Turkish prince, one of the greatest conquerors of all times. Between 1370 and 1405 he conducted numerous raids from his capital city Samarcand (Fletcher's Samarchian) westward, conquering vast regions in central and western Asia. Tamarlin was renowned for his cruelty, and did not hesitate to massacre thousands of his enemies and erect towers from their skulls. We have no way of knowing how and why Tamarlin came to regard himself of the tribe of Dan, if indeed he did so. Nor did the Tatars ever regard themselves connected to the Ten Tribes of Israel, and were not convinced by enthusiastic tribe searchers that they were so, as had occurred in other instances. Concise versions of Fletcher's arguments found their way to several later accounts regarding the Tatar–Ten Tribes connection, as to the writings of the eighteenth-century Aaron Hill. Hill summed up Fletcher's eight points, and added new information such as the existence in Tatary of a mount named Zion, a river Yordan (Jordan) and a thousand other names of places that plainly prove a Jewish etymology. He also reported that "Tamarlene or Tam-er-lane the Great . . . would often take occasion to be vannting of his pedigree, affirming that he was really descended from the tribe of Dan in an uninterrupted genealogy."

The search for the Tribes and Christian doctrines

Fletcher became interested in the search for the descendants of the Ten Lost Tribes of Israel not only out of curiosity. His hidden purpose, expressed in his book, was their conversion to Christianity. This purpose is clearly stated in Samuel Lee's introduction to the first edition of Fletcher's book. The book, writes Lee, had two parts: "The First contains an essay upon some probable grounds that the present Tartars near the Caspian Sea, are the Posterity of the ten Tribes of Israel. The Second, a dissertation concerning their ancient and successive state, with some Scripture Evidence of their future Conversion and Establishment in their own Land."

Already in the seventeenth century, then, the hidden purpose of identifying tribes as lost tribes of Israel was to convert them to Christianity. It was hoped that once their Israelite ancestry could be proved and accepted, these tribes would gladly convert. This aim was probably meant to counteract the fact that ages-long attempts to convert normative Jews were not very successful

Alongside the Tatar-Israel theory there were other opinions relating to the origin of the Tatars. The Reverend Samuel refuted the Tatar-Israel theory, and accused Fletcher of having never actually visited their regions, and of not possessing any personal knowledge of the customs and names of the Tartars. According to him the Tartars have nothing to do with the tribes of Israel, but are descendants of the Syrians, who were transplanted in their present home in seven hundred B.C. When Rezin king of Syria made war, in company with Pekah king of Israel, against Judah, Tiglat Pileser subdued Syria and exiled its inhabitants to the river Kur into which the river Araxes empties itself. There they are known today as Usbeck Tartars.

2. The Scythians

The Scythians, often confused with the Tatars and connected with them, were already long extinct when this association was made, and when attention was focused on them as possible descendants of the Lost Ten Tribes of Israel. It is quite extraordinary that an extinct people was assumed to be carrier of a divine, living promise of return to a faraway homeland. The Scythians drew the attention of nineteenth-century tribe seekers, due to their wide geographic distribution and the variety of names under which they were known in different places. They came to play the part of the necessary link between ancient Israel and various contenders to Ten Tribe descent. They became an especially favored link to the British Israelite movement (see chapter 7), as well as to Afghans, Indians, various tribes in southeast Asia and China, and Japanese, all of whom claim a Ten Tribe lineage.

The Scythians being an extinct group, all information about them was gathered from vague biblical references, and especially from the writings of Greek and Roman historians. Very little was known about Scythian culture until the advent of archaeological excavations of their material remnants begun in the nineteenth century, just when the Scythian–Israel theory reached its full bloom.

How did the Scythians become Israelites?

Attention to the Scythians, a nomadic tribe or group of tribes of obscure Asian origin that swept the ancient Near East in the seventh century B.C., was initially drawn by their name. The classical Greeks, who established contacts with them after they had settled in the East European plains of the rivers Danube and Don, knew them by the name Scythians or Skuthai. The Persians called them Sakai or Sakas, and under that name they invaded northern India around 100 B.C., where they created a kingdom that lasted for several hundred years. The name Scythians or Sakai sounded vaguely familiar to Colonel Gawler, an Englishman who served in India, and one of the originators of the British–Israel theory. Gawler suggested that the name Scythian "fairly and without straining, or imagination, is translatable as Isaacites, that is—sons of Isaac." Isaac is indeed sometimes, although very rarely, used in the Scriptures synonymously with Israel, as in Amos 7:9, and thus the Scythians became Sons of Isaac, or in other words—Israel.

To back up this interpretation of the meaning of the name Scythians/Sakai, another line of reasoning was introduced by Gawler, not based on similarity of sound but on a proposed meaning of the name Scythians. In Greek, the name Scythians has no meaning, but according to Greek historians it derived from Skutis, the mythical ancestor of these tribes. In time, the name Scythians became in Greek a common name, denoting wandering peoples in general. The Roman historian Strabo noted that the ancient Greeks classed all the northern nations with which they were familiar under the name of Scythians or, according to Homer, Nomads.

The fact that the Scythians were nomads does not in itself connect them with ancient Israel. A much stronger tie was needed, and indeed was found. In Gawler's words:

> Now in Greek ... Skuthai has no meaning; but if I find a language in which such a word has a meaning which indicates wanderings, I have grounds for assuming that the people to whom that language belongs are the owners or originators of the name. In Hebrew S'cot means booths or temporary dwellings, such as gypsies would use, and the dwellers in them would be Succothites. In Leviticus 23:33-34 I find, "and the Lord spake unto Moses, saying, The fifteenth day of the seventh month shall be the feast of S'cot (Tabarnacles) for seven days unto the Lord ... all that are Israelite born shall dwell baS'cot, that your generations may know that I made the children of Israel to dwell baS'cot, when I brought them out of the land of Egypt." Thus, besides S'cot meaning a temporary abode, we have here the institution of the feast of S'cot to commemorate the wanderings in the wilderness, when the Israelites were S'cothi, or dwellers in booths; and this seems to give the origin of the Greek Skuthai ..."

As in the case of the Tatars, this interpretation is based on similarity of sound. But this was not enough, and several features of the history and customs of the Scythians were investigated to find further links.

The Scythians in history

The Greek historians relate that the Scythians were at first a tiny, despicable tribe living in a small territory, who in time, because of their valor, grew and expanded as far as Mount Caucasus and beyond the river Tanais. Ancient Near Eastern sources, including the Bible, indicate that the Scythians invaded much vaster regions than Diodorus reported. It is historically proven that in the seventh century B.C. the Scythians conducted a series of ravaging campaigns throughout the Near East, to become the terror of the day. They defeated Media in 630 B.C., then pushed their way to the gates of Egypt, threatening every nation on the way. The kingdom of Judah, which still maintained its independence at that time, lay on the route of the Scythian thrust toward Egypt. The contemporary prophet Jeremiah voiced the threat of an imminent invasion of Judah by the Scythians:

> A people cometh from the north country, and a great nation shall be raised from the sides of the earth. They shall lay hold on bow and spear; they are cruel and have no mercy; their voice roareth like the sea, and they ride upon horses, set in array as men of war against thee, O daughter of Zion. [Jeremiah 6:22-23]

But, although in 609 B.C. they marched along the eastern Mediterranean coastal plain, the Scythians did not invade the adjacent Kingdom of Judah. This rather outstanding historical fact was ingeniously interpreted: The Scythians, as sons of Isaac, refrained from devastating Judah because of brotherly relations between the two people. This amazing interpretation became another cornerstone in the Scythian-Israelite theory. The unlikely idea that the beaten and exiled tribes of Israel would turn into the ferocious Scythians within a period of less than a hundred years of their exile was not taken into account.

After years of wild marauding, the Scythians were finally beaten by Darius I, king of Persia (522-486 B.C.), and driven out of the Near East. Some settled in southern Russia where they lived for about four hundred years, until being wiped out in the second century B.C. by the Sarmatians, another invading Asian plain tribe. Others moved farther to the west and settled in the East European plains, where they came in contact with the Greeks. Still others settled east of the Caspian Sea, from where, hundreds of years later, they invaded Afghanistan and India under the name Sakas.

Scythian "prehistory"

If in the recorded history of the Scythians there is nothing that overtly corresponds to the history of Israel, their "prehistory" was felt to hold ample clues for such a connection. According to Greek and Roman historians the Scythians believed that their life as a nation started one thousand years prior to the expedition of King Darius, who drove them out of Persia and Media around 500 B.C. Their beginnings would then date to 1500 B.C., roughly corresponding to the date of Israel's exodus from Egypt, at least according to one theory. Moreover, the Scythian legend that tells that their ancestor Skutis was the son of Jupiter and a half river-serpent mother brought to the minds of the propagators of the Scythian–Israel theory some instances in the life of Moses. As an infant Moses was found in the river by the daughter of the Egyptian Pharaoh, and later in life erected a brazen serpent as a holy image. Furthermore, the Scythians attributed their legal system to a slave named Zamolxis who was educated in Egypt, as was Moses, Israel's legislator. However, the propagators of the Moses–Skutis/Zamolxis connection did not go as far as actually identifying the two. When the Israelites were exiled, they were reduced to the state of the "despicable people" of the Greek historian Diodorus—the Scythians.

As for the habits and customs of the Scythians, the Greek and Roman historians were not very complimentary. They were frequently described as cannibalistic barbarians, although sometimes they were treated more benignly. The Greek historian Herodotos noted that some Scythians were learned; another Greek historian, Epiphanius, reported that their laws and customs were a standard to other nations, while the Roman Strabo mentioned that they abhorred swine. These qualities went well with the image of the Israelites.

Excavationg Scythian remains

Another interesting argument in favor of the Scythian–Israelite connection was drawn from archaeological excavations of royal Scythian burial mounds. These mounds were piled over large underground chambers, lined with wooden planks, and communicated by a deep and wide shaft. The chambers contained the bodies of chieftains, surrounded by slaughtered male and female slaves. Alongside the humans lay dozens of sacrificed horses. The chambers contained many valuables, including hundreds of gold and silver vessels, often of Greek craftsmanship. Many pieces of jewelry were found in women's burials; well-crafted weapons, especially lances with large iron points and numerous bronze or iron arrowheads, in men's. After the burial, the tombs were covered with large mounds of earth and stones, sometimes forty-five to sixty feet high. The level of construction of the chambers, and the elaborate craftsmanship of the objects placed in them, proved that the Scythians were of a higher level than the mere wild nomads they were supposed to have been. This high level, so the propagators of the Scythian–Israelite theory argued, befitted the ancient Israelites.

Reconstructed Scythian history

Having summed up all these clues, Scythian history was reconstructed by tribe seekers in the following manner: The exiled Israelites, known as Isaacites, crossed the river Euphrates and reached a remote and small region in eastern Asia. They brought with them traditions of Moses, founder of their religion, who later obtained the name Skutis or Zamolxis. While in their new home, they became barbaric, but retained some traces of their former values, customs, and achievements. Very quickly the exiled Isaacites, now under their new name Scythians or Sakai, grew in number and strength, and within a hundred years of their exile invaded the Near East and wrought havoc and destruction on the entire region, except on their kin in the Kingdom of Judah. After retreating from the Near East, they scattered in the Euroasian plains, and from there conducted several long-range migrations to Afghanistan and India; as Sakas, and to Europe and eventually to England as Saxons.

And thus the Scythians became the forefathers of all contenders of Ten Tribe ancestry in both Europe and Asia.

3. The Khazars

The Khazars belong to our story not so much because they were considered of Lost Tribes of Israel ancestry, but because their very existence was an important factor in developing the story of the tribes, and in granting it credibility.

Who were the Khazars?

The Khazars were most likely a Turkish tribe, or group of tribes. They are first mentioned by name in historical records of the end of the sixth century A.D., following a lengthy and apparently peaceful process of infiltration to the plains north of the Caucasian Mountains, between the Caspian Sea and the Black Sea. Their name, spelled Khazar in Greek and in Arabic, Kuzar in Hebrew, and K'osa in Chinese, seems to derive from the Turkish *Qazmak* meaning "to wander," or *quz* meaning "the northern side of the mountain." Their origin and early history are not very well known. Nevertheless quite a lot of information concerning their tribal organization, nomadic way of life,

Figure 17: Derbent Pass

social customs, and especially their involvement in the military and political affairs of the regions surrounding their kingdom, is contained in the works of several Arab, Byzantine, Armenian, Georgian, Chinese, and Hebrew writers. By the year A.D. 700 the Khazars were firmly established in the lower valley of the river Volga and in the Crimean peninsula, and maintained relations with the Byzantine Empire and with the territories of the Slavs on the river Dnieper. The Khazars and Arabs met in battle several times. The Khazars were first defeated, but in A.D. 653 managed to take the strategic Derbent Passage, known as Bab al-Abwab, Gate of Gates in Arabic, between the Caucasian Mountains and the Caspian Sea. In doing so the Khazars managed to check the thrust of the Arabs to the north and west that threatened eastern Europe. So important was the Battle of the Derbent Pass that historians equal it to the Battle of Poitiers in France (A.D. 732), in which the armies of Charles Martel checked the advance of the Arabs in western Europe.

Having established themselves in the region, the Khazars began to cultivate relations with their western neighbor, the Byzantine Empire. Two Byzantine monarchs married Khazar princesses, who were baptized and received Christian names. Emperor Justinian married Theodora; Emperor Constantine V married Irene, whose son was Emperor Leo IV, known as the Khazar (775–780).

The conversion of the Khazars to Judaism

Around A.D. 740 the Khazars took a most unusual step and converted to Judaism, an act corroborated by several Arab and Jewish sources. The long and detailed description of the Khazars, their country, their manners and way of life, their economy, and their political organization, written by the Arab geographer Istakhri around the year 920, includes the following passages:

> Their king is a Jew . . . The Khazars are Muslims, Christians and Jews, and among them are a number of idolaters. The smallest group is the Jews, most of them being Muslims and Christians, though the king and his court are Jews. The predominating manners are those of the heathen. Their legal decisions are peculiar, being according to old usage contrary to the religion of the Muslims, Jews and Christians . . . The king has seven judges from the Jews, Christians, Muslims and idolaters . . . The Khazars have a city called Samandar between the capital [Atil in the delta of the Volga] and Bab al-Abwab . . . Their king is a Jew . . . The slaves found among the Khazars are idolaters . . . As to the Jews and Christians among them, their religion condemns the enslavement of one another, like the Muslims. . . .

Several Arab writers report on the date and circumstances of the conversion of the Khazars to Judaism. Mas'udi (943–947), in his work *Mural al-Dhahab* [Meadows of Gold], relates that

> In this city [Atil] are Muslims, Christians, Jews and pagans. The Jews are the king, his attendants and the Khazars of his kind. The king of the Khazars had already become a Jew in the Caliphate of Harun al-Rashid [786–809 A.D.], and there joined him Jews from all the lands of Islam and from the country of the Greeks [Byzantium]. Indeed the king of the Greeks at the present time has converted the Jews in his king-

dom to Christianity and coerced them . . . Many Jews took flight from the country of the Greeks to Khazaria . . . An account is given of the Judaizing of the Khazar king which we do not mention here. We have already mentioned it in a previous work.

Unfortunately, it is not known to which previous work Mas'udi refers, as none of his known works contain a description of the Khazar conversion. Another Arab author, Dimashqi, wrote in 1327 that Ibn-al-Athir tells how in the days of Harun al-Rashid, the emperor forced the Jews to emigrate. They came to the Khazar country, where they found an intelligent but untutored race and offered them their religion. The inhabitants found it better than their own and accepted it.

Several sources attribute the conversion of the Khazars to a religious debate. The Muslim Spanish writer Bakri (1094) was the first to report it, having copied it perhaps from one of the Arab geographers, maybe even from Mas'udi's lost work. Bakri reports that

> The reason for the conversion of the king of the Khazars, who had previously been a heathen, to Judaism, was as follows. He had adopted Christianity. Then he recognized the wrongness of this belief and began to speak with one of his governors about the concern with which he was filled. The other said to him, O king, the people of the book form three classes. Invite them and inquire of them, then follow whichever is in possession of the truth. So he sent to the Christians for a bishop. Now there was with him a Jew, skilled in debate, who disputed with the bishop, asking him, What do you say about Moses, son of Amram, and the Torah which was revealed to him? The other replied, Moses is a prophet, and the Torah is true. Then said the Jew to the king, He has admitted the truth of my creed. Ask him now what he believes. So the king asked him and he replied, I say that the Messiah, Jesus the son of Mary, is the Word, and that he has made known the mysteries in the name of God. Then the Jew said to the king of the Khazars, He confesses a doctrine which I know not, while he admits what I set forth. But the bishop was not strong in bringing proofs. So he invited the Muslims, and they sent him a learned and intelligent man who understood disputation. But the Jew hired someone against him who poisoned him on the way, so that he died. And the Jew was able to win the king for his religion.

Much better known is the somewhat later record of Yehuda Ha-Levi, one of the most famous Jewish poets of Muslim Spain, who gives a detailed account of a religious debate that led to the conversion of the Khazars in his *Book of the Khozars*. Yehuda Ha-Levi attributes the reason for the conversion of the king of the Khazars, devout in the religion of his forefathers, to dreams. The king had several dreams in which an angel told him that his intentions were acceptable to God, but his deeds were not. The king sent for a Christian, then for a Muslim, and finally for a Jew, and each in his turn explained the basics of his religion. Ha-Levi's description of the actual act of conversion is intriguing:

> The Khazar revealed the secret of his dream to the general of his army. Now the dream had repeatedly told him to seek the work pleasing to God in the mountains of Warsan. So both of them, the king and the general, set out for the mountains, which are in a desert by the sea. They came by night to a cave where certain Jews rested all the Sabbath and, being seen by them, were admitted to their religion and circumcised there in the cave. Afterwards they returned to their own country. Though their hearts were inclined to the religion of the Jews, they concealed their faith till they had devised means to reveal their secret little by little to certain intimates. Finally they became numerous and avowed what they had not before disclosed. Thus prevailing over the rest of the Khazars, they induced them to become Jews. . . .

Correspondence between Spain and Khazaria

Perhaps even more interesting is the correspondence between Hisdai Ibn-Shaprut of Cordoba, a high-ranking Jewish civil servant in the court of 'Abd el-Rahman III (912–961), the Moslem caliph of Spain, and Joseph, king of the Khazars. The letter of Hisdai, written not later than the year 961, was preserved, as were copies of Joseph's reply in two versions, one long, one short. Another document, with excerpts of the reply of Joseph, came to light in the Cairo Genizah (a repository of old books and documents, too sacred to be thrown out and kept in the synagogue attic). In his letter Hisdai informs Joseph that he has often heard that the Khazars were Jews, and had long wished to contact them. The opportunity now arose, through the good services of two Jews who accompanied a diplomatic embassy sent to Cordoba by "the king of G-b-lim," perhaps Emperor Otto I of Germany. Hisdai describes his home country Andalusia and his own position there, and asks many questions about Khazaria: How did the Jews get there? How did the Khazars convert? How did they perform the religious rituals? Do they conduct war on the Sabbath? Has Joseph any information regarding the end of the world? King Joseph's reply contains answers to some of Hisdai's inquiries, not to all. He relates that the conversion of Bulan king of the Khazars was motivated by a dream, which was then followed by a debate between representatives of the three religions. Joseph also tells Hisdai that from the spoils of war taken by the Khazars in a battle south of the Caucasus, they built a tabernacle on the biblical model, and that at a later stage, in the days of king Obadiah, rabbinical Judaism was introduced. Joseph describes his country, and invites Hisdai to visit. It is possible that Hisdai actually accepted the invitation, but no account of his visit to Khazaria is known.

Although several scholars had cast doubt on the validity of all three letters, or perhaps only on one or the other, the discovery of the excerpt in the Cairo Genizah has reinstated the validity of the correspondence. There can be no doubt that news of Jewish Khazaria reached Spain, and some people from Khazaria visited Toledo in the twelfth century as reported by Abraham Ben-Daud.

The Jewish kingdom and the Jewish world

News of the existence of a Jewish kingdom in Khazaria had a profound impact on the Jewish world. It has been suggested that the account of Eldad the Danite was based to a large extent on information on Khazaria that circulated in Spain and North Africa. Eldad mentions explicitly that the tribes of Simeon and half of Menasseh "are in the lands of the Khazars," while Reuben, Zebulun, and Issaschar live in adjacent lands, which can be identified with regions directly occupied, or being under the influence of the Khazars. These tribes are described as nomads, in correspondence with the way of life of the Khazars. It has also been suggested that all other tribes are to be located in the regions of the Khazars rather than in Arabia or in Africa, on account of their nomadic way of life, occupation with warfare, and subjugation of their neighbors. Some scholars have even gone as far as suggesting that Eldad was himself a Khazar, basing their argument on a possible Greek etymology to several words in Eldad's vocabulary, which proved an affinity with Greek-speaking Byzantium. The suggestion that Eldad's stories reflect the reality of Jewish Khazaria makes more sense than the opposing one that assumes the Khazars originated in the Ten Tribes, a theory proposed for example by the Reverend Charles Forester. Forster bases his arguments solely on the validity of the diary of "Rabbi Eldad the Danite," the title rabbi having been added by Forester, perhaps to heighten the prestige of Eldad.

The kingdom of Khazaria was gradually weakened in the tenth century by continuous Russian raids, and seemed to have lost its independence at the beginning of the eleventh century at the latest. During the period of decline, many Khazars converted to Islam or Christianity, but some, who remained Jews, migrated westward, and are historically documented in several East European countries and cities, including Kiev. According to one sweeping theory, the original and dominant stratum of East European Jewry is of Khazar origin.

4. Jews of the Caucasian Mountains

The very high and rugged Caucasian mountain range extends between the Black Sea and the Caspian Sea. Throughout history these mountains served with greater or lesser effectiveness as a barrier between the Near East south of it and the vast plains of Eurasia to the north. Because of their extremely rugged topography, the Caucasian Mountains have always been a place of refuge for various tribes and peoples ousted from other, more hospitable regions. A wide array of languages, often unrelated, were and still are spoken by the inhabitants of the mountains, who also practice a variety of customs and religions. Indeed, the Caucasian region is perhaps the most varied ethnic and linguistic region in the world. Today the southern slope of the Caucasian mountain range and its immediate vicinity is divided between three independent republics and Georgia, Azerbaijan, and Armenia—while on the northern slopes are the autonomous republics of Daghastan, Chechnia, and several others which are incorporated within Russia. Tribe-seekers who happened to visit this most varied and difficult region, as well as others who heard descriptions of it from others, found suitable candidates for Ten Tribe ancestry among its heteroge-

Figure 18: Caucasus Jews in traditional costume, 1905.

neous population. They based their identification on the geographic location of the mountains in relation to the "second dispersal" of Esdras, as well as on customs practiced there, which they assumed were similar to those of the ancient Israelites.

The Mountain Jews of Daghastan

Daghastan lies in the eastern part of the Caucasian Mountains, west of the Caspian Sea, its name in the local, Turkish–Persian language meaning "Mountain Country." The mountains of Daghastan are high, dissected by steep and narrow valleys that create a wild landscape, and are very difficult to penetrate. They are inhabited by more than thirty small tribes, each of which has tried to this day (and tried much more fiercely in the past) to protect its cultural and political independence. In the middle of the nineteenth century the region was still to a large extent an unknown territory to Europeans. It was the scene of ongoing strife between its three neighboring empires of the day—Persia, the Ottoman Empire, and Russia, each attempting to extend its boundaries in the direction of the Caucasian Mountains. None of these contesting empires was able to penetrate deep into the mountains, and the tribes, who in fact ruled the region, were continuously conducting fierce raids against each other, as well as against the garrison armies of the various empires.

Into this forbidding territory entered in the nineteenth century European tribe seekers. Contrary to the usual practice, they were attracted not to any of the numerous local tribes and peoples, but to the local Jews, an ancient community known as Mountain Jews. Unlike the peoples of the plains, for the most part extinct when tribe seekers became interested in their possible connection with the Ten Tribes, the Jews of Daghastan were a living entity, who could be visited and studied firsthand. The best known of the tribe seekers in this region was the Reverend Jacob Samuel, a Jew by birth, who, after having been converted to Christianity, became in the 1830s "senior missionary to the Jews for India, Persia and Arabia." Samuel extended his efforts into Caucasia through sheer chance, as he relates:

> Being in Teheran in the month of March 1837, prosecuting my missionary labours in Persia among my brethren of the seed of Abraham, I paid my respects to His Excellency Graf Simoneich, ambassador extraordinaire to the court of Mohammed Shah. In conversation . . . His excellency informed me that about five years previously the Russian government had sent a commission into Georgia to investigate the character and circumstances of the Caucasian Jews. The Individuals sent returned without being able to give any satisfactory account of the object of their inquiry.

The Russian ambassador there and then offered the task to Samuel, who accepted it with enthusiasm, being convinced that if the remnants of the tribes were to be found anywhere, the Jews of Daghastan would be the ones. Armed with letters from the Russian and British ambassadors, Samuel entered the country in times of trouble, and his research efforts were often intercepted by soldiers of the contesting empires. Regardless of the difficulties, Samuel visited various parts of Daghastan and produced his report in book form.

Samuel observed that the Jews of Daghastan were an ancient tribe, having lived in these regions "from time immemorial." As there are no historical records on how they reached Daghastan, Samuel, after inspecting their way of life and customs, became convinced that they were descendants of the Ten Lost Tribes of Israel. Interestingly, Samuel felt that had the inquiry been carried out before the invasion of the Persian king Nadir Shah in the middle of the eighteenth century, it would have been more profitable, as the Mountain Jews would have been less affected by the contact with the Jews of Persia. Also, since the time of the Russian conquest of Daghastan at the beginning of the nineteenth century, Polish and Russian Jews arrived there and brought modern manuals and customs of Judaism. Both these events have reduced the characteristic antique customs of the people.

Notwithstanding, Samuel was so extremely impressed by the archaic habits and ways of life still practiced by the Jews of Daghastan, living as they did among their wild tribal neighbors, that he became convinced that this kind of existence had a purpose. This way of life, reflected Samuel, fulfills the prophecy "lo, the people shall dwell alone, and shall not be reckoned among the nations" (Numbers 23:9).

Samuel was honest enough to report that the Jews of Daghastan themselves did not claim to descend from the Ten Tribes of Israel, although he himself became convinced that they were. As for them, they only began to consider themselves as such years later, towards the end of the nineteenth century, probably under the influence of Russian Jewish scholars who visited them time and again to study their customs.

As the Jews of Daghastan did not themselves have a tradition of Ten Tribes descent, Samuel turned his attention to the Lesghians, the wildest of all tribes, described by European travelers as "wild, savage bandits," whose religion was a "curious compound of Islam, Christianity and paganism." These Lesgians, asserted Samuel, affirmed themselves to descend from the tribe of Dan. On these Lesghians Samuel wrote that their physiognomy and character are very similar in many respects to those of the Jews.

Resemblance of physiognomy, a clearly impressionistic detail, is here added to the arsenal of methods of Ten Tribe identification. As for the close associations between the Lesghians and the tribe of Dan, Samuel refers his readers to Jacob's description of this tribe in his blessing: "Dan shall be a serpent by the way, an adder in the path, that biteth the horses' heels so that his rider shall fall backwards" (Genesis 49:17).

Indeed, comments Samuel, the Lesghians, who are the terror of the surrounding provinces, exterminate the nomadic Cossacks exactly in the way specified in the prophetic description of Dan. Samuel does not relate how and why the Lesghians connect themselves to the tribe of Dan, but reports that they acknowledge the Jews to have been the original inhabitants of the mountains. This interesting observation points to the great antiquity of Jewish existence in these regions.

Samuel did not pursue the claim of the Lesghians, but, contrary to their own disregard of the matter, tried to find clues to his identification of the Jews of Daghastan with the Ten Lost Tribes. He based this view on the religious customs of the Mountain Jews of his days, which, to his mind, echoed an ancient, pre-exilic form of Judaism. Being a former Jew, Samuel could compare the customs he observed with those practiced by the rest of the Jewish world and found that most indicative were their festivals, all of which had an exclusive nature aspect rather than the common religious aspects.

On Passover: At twilight of the eve of the festival, the master of the house takes a kid or a lamb, slaughters it, receives its blood into a basin and sprinkles it on every door post (Exodus 12:7). The animal is then roasted and eaten with bitter herbs in the most retired part of the house, by all males of the household . . . These Jews are the only ones in the world who observe this instution in its primitive requirements, while all other communities have substituted the sacrifical lamb for a portion of roasted meat.

Samuel also noted that they do not read the Passover Hagaddah which they do not know, nor have they a cup of benediction over the wine. They eat unleavened bread for six days, as in Deutoronomy 16:8, do not conduct a minute search after traces of bread, and do not change their utensils to ensure that no trace of leaven remains in the house, customs common among all Jewish communities. They are the only community in the world to observe Passover in such a fashion.

The Feast of Weeks (Shvu'ot) is thus celebrated:

From the beginning of (the Hebrew month of) Nissan to the sixth day of (the Hebrew month of) Sivan the elders collect certain tithes of the people. On the sixth day of Sivan the elders ascend to the top of a mountain and there deposit their gifts. The people then come up, burn incense and sing the affirmation of the unity of God. They read several portions of the law, then kindle a fire and throw into it a sheaf of barley from the last harvest. They celebrate only one day of festival, and only in connection with the reaping of the harvest by the Israelites when in their own land, not the giving of the law.

The Feast of Trumpets on the first day of the Hebrew month of Tishrei is not regarded by the Jews of Daghastan New Year's day.

> They assemble and blow a ram's horn, read portions of the law and abstain from work. They do not consider it a day to confess sins, nor prepare for it for a month before. They do not practice casting away the sins nor dress differently than in any other day.

On the Day of Atonement on the tenth of Tishrei

> everybody, including the cattle, abstains from food from evening to evening. They do not observe the atoning sacrifices.

On the Feast of Tabernacles (Succot) on the fifteenth of Tishrei they live in huts and consider it a feast of great rejoicing.

> On the eighth day is the feast of gathering the harvest. Everybody carries a pitcher of water. Stalks of corn are gathered into a sheaf which they deposit in a building used for sacred purposes. After chanting and reading of the law, the water is poured out towards the houses, to bless them, and towards the enemy to curse them. They do not celebrate the Feast of the Law (Simchat Torah) nor carry the four branches and fruit.

As for other religious observances

> they do not observe strict rules of slaughtering animals. They have no scruples to boil or fry meat with butter, but strictly abstain from boiling a kid in butter or milk (Exodus 23:19). They do not use separate dishes, pots or cutlery for meat and milk. They have no priests nor Levites. Their holy books consist of the Five Books of Moses only.

The picture presented by the Reverend Jacob Samuel is indeed of a unique Jewish community. The antiquated details of the Law of Moses as observed by them, the archaic aspects of their festivals, the fact that they do not celebrate Hanukah—a festival initiated in the second century B.C.—indicate that the Jews of Daghastan are indeed an ancient community that was early severed from the main body of the Jewish people and had not been exposed to the gradual modification of the Jewish religion over the millennia. But is this enough to consider them descendants of the Ten Tribes? Probably not, if only

Figure 19: Caucasus Jews in traditional costume, ca 1920.

because they celebrate Purim, a festival originating in Persia in the fifth century B.C., hundreds of years after they were exiled. This fact has led modern historians to consider the Jews of Daghastan a branch of Persian Jewry, and to attribute their early migration into the mountains of Caucasia to the historically recorded persecution of Jews by rulers of the Sasanian Dynasty of Persia in the fifth century A.D. Indeed, the Mountain Jews speak a language related to old Persian, mixed with some Turkish and Hebrew. The Lesghian tradition that Daghastan was formerly Jewish adds credence to the antiquity of the Jewish community there. It also indicates that many of the Jews of that region, as well as the majority of the local heathen tribes, accepted the Islamic religion after Daghastan was conquered by the Moslems in A.D. 644.

It should be added that the Jews of Daghastan did not have any clear tradition on the circumstances of their arrival in the region and sometimes claimed to be descendants of Judeans exiled by Nebuchadnezzar and sent to Daghastan in exchange for military aid supplied by the local chiefs. They gradually accepted a Ten Lost Tribe descent, offered by the Reverend Jacob Samuel and later tribe seekers. The first to

Figure 20: The Agronov Family, Derbent, 1920.

mention that they claimed such a descent was Jehuda Tchornei, a Russian Jew who visited Daghastan several times between the 1860s and the 1880s in search of Jewish antiquities. In interviews he conducted in the 1860s in fifteen communities of Mountain Jews, only three claimed Ten Tribe descent. As time went by, more and more Daghastani Jews, including the chief rabbis, adopted this belief, and today it is widely accepted by the community. Be it as it may, since the 1970s the majority of the Jews of Daghastan have migrated to Israel, perhaps in fulfillment of the biblical prophecies of the return of all exiles, prophecies that have been the basis of all Ten Tribe searches.

5
Lost in the Land of Assyria— The Patans of Afghanistan

The tribes of Afghanistan and neighboring Pakistan are devoted Muslims, who nevertheless claim to have originated in ancient Israel. This is not the only surprising thing in the story of the Afghan tribes, as the Afghan-Israel connection is threefold. Local tribal traditions of descent from ancient Israel have been elaborated by European explorers and scholars of the eighteenth and nineteenth centuries, who developed a new history that connected the Afghans not with Israel in general, but specifically with the Ten Lost Tribes. Present-day Jewish tribe seekers, who see in the Afghans excellent contenders for Ten Tribe descent, had adopted this new history, which has been accepted by some Afghans.

Modern Afghanistan and its people

The modern state of Afghanistan was created by the British in 1893. Land-locked in central Asia between Iran in the west and India in the East, Afghanistan has several geographic zones. The flat northern section, part of the vast Asiatic steppes, is separated from the semiarid plains of the south, the largest section of the country, by the high and forbidding Hindu-Kush mountain range. From time immemorial this inhospitable region was a crossroads between the Near East, Central Asia, India, and China. This region has been traversed by waves of invaders, conquerors, and settlers from all directions—Dravidians, Indo-Aryans, Greeks, Scythians, Arabs, Turks, and Mongols. Each wave left its residue in the region's overwhelming mosaic of tribes who speak different languages, and whose fierce hostility towards one another has led to frequent and ferocious tribal battles. The area occupied by the Afghani tribes does not coincide with the modern state of Afghanistan, and many live in neighboring Pakistan. The dominant tribal group among the Afghans is the Pushtun, forming about sixty percent of the population of Afghanistan. The Pushtuns inhabit the south and east of the country, with the capital city Kabul as their center, as well as sections of Pakistan. The Pushtuns, who speak an Indo-European language known as Pushtu, are divided into three groups—the Durranis, who have always formed the social and political elite of Afghanistan and who occupy the region around the town of Kandahar, the Ghilzays, and the Pathans. Other tribes who speak Indo-European languages are scattered in the Hindu-Kush Mountains and in the semi-arid regions to the south. Turkic-speaking Uzbeks and Turks, the most recent migrants into Afghanistan, inhabit the northern steppes. Afghanistan is now a Moslem country.

Islamic traditions connecting the Afghans with ancient Israel

Several Afghani tribes have an old tradition that they are Bani–Israel, sons of Israel, descended from King Saul. According to their belief these traditions originated in pre-Islamic times, and were transmitted orally over many centuries. They were put down in writing for the first time in the seventeenth century at the latest, and were since repeated in several books written in both Pushtu and Persian. These traditions are known in several versions. The following is a summary of one of the versions, as compiled by Bellew, a British physician and officer, and great propagator of the Afghan–Israel connection.

Figure 21: Members of the Durani Tribe.

The Afghans and the House of King Saul

All Afghan history begins with Sarul (Saul), son of Kais (Kish) of the tribe of Benjamin. The events of the time of Saul's kingship over Israel as related in the Afghani histories closely follow the biblical account, including, for instance, his enmity with David and his visit to the witch at Andor. But with Saul's death the similarity with the Bible ends, and the Afghani tradition introduces new personalities, unknown to the biblical authors. King Saul, the Afghani tradition claims, had two sons—Berekia and Irmia—born after the death of their father on Mount Gilboa to two different mothers, both of the tribe of Levi. These two sons, born on the same day, were brought up by David, whom they loyally served in very high positions—Berekia as prime minister, Irmia as commander-in-chief of the army. Berekia's son Asaaf and Irmia's son Afghana rose under King Solomon to the same high positions as their fathers, and Afghana even supervised the building of "Bait-ul-Mukadas"—the Temple of Jerusalem. As time went by, their descendants grew in number and prominence, and were among the defenders of Jerusalem during the siege laid by Bukhtu-u-nasr—Nebuchadnezzar. Many members of the family of Afghana (the Afghan tradition does not concern itself anymore with the descendants of Irmia) lost their lives in defense of their religion, and those who survived were deported from their homeland to different parts of the Babylonian empire. After a while they revolted against their captors, and escaped to the inaccessible mountain retreats of Ghor and Faroza, east of the town of Herat in Afghanistan. There they fought with the local heathens, and eventually became masters of the region. With time their number increased, they spilled out of their mountain hideouts, and by force of arms extended their borders to the regions of Kabul, Kandahar, and Ghazi. All the while they kept the Taur'at—the two tablets of the Law of Moses. With the advent of Islam, they converted to that religion and became devout followers.

According to this tradition the Afghani tribes, who call themselves Bani–Israel, claim to have originated from the two tribes Benjamin and Levi, who together with Judah formed the kingdom of Judah. They insist that in ancient times they were observant Jews, who kept the Law of Moses for many centuries after they were exiled from Jerusalem. This tradition, which does not relate in any way to the Ten Tribes of Israel, most probably reflects the existence in Afghani-

Figure 22: An Afghan of Damoun: or Man of the "Beni Israel".

stan of a Jewish population that arrived from Persia, an ancient center of Jewish postexilic existence. The Jews of Persia, or at least some of them, were related to the house of King Saul, as reflected in the genealogy of their two most illustrious members, Queen Esther and her uncle Mordecai. Mordecai is referred to in the Book of Esther (2:5–6) as

> the son of Jair, the son of Shimei, the son of Kish, a Benjaminite. Who had been carried away from Jerusalem with the captivity . . . Whom Nebuchadnezzar the king of Babylon had carried away.

It is very likely that here lies the origin of the Afghani claim to ancestry from King Saul. With the gradual advent of the Muslim armies into the region since the tenth century, Jews converted to Islam either by will or by force, but kept the memory of their Israelite origin, and perhaps also several customs that are still practiced among Afghani tribes. Jewish medieval sources mention the existence of a Jewish community in several towns in Afghanistan until the Mongol invasions of the thirteenth century. There is no further indication of Jews in Afghanistan until the nineteenth century, when Persian Jews, escaping persecution, established a community in the town of Herat. The fact that the Afghani tribes recognized their Israelite origin did not ease the life of the Jews that lived among them. The Afghanis always made a clear distinction between themselves, Bani–Israel, and the Jews, whom they despised and often persecuted.

The Afghans as Ten Tribes—European speculations

The Afghan tribesmen who call themselves Bani–Israel were drawn into the issue of the Ten Tribes of Israel when European nations, especially Britain, developed in the course of the eighteenth and nineteenth centuries both a political and a cultural interest in India and its neighboring regions. A handful of Englishmen who served the colonial interests of Britain in the region became enamored with the traditions and sagas of local peoples, studied their languages, and translated into English a large body of literature, including the traditional histories of the Afghani tribes. The earliest among these colorful and adventurous Englishmen was Henry Vasittart (1732–1770), British governor of Bengal and a noted scholar and linguist, who was the first to present Afghan history to the English public. Vasittart translated a Persian abridgment of the *Asrarul Afghinah* (The Secrets of the Afghans), a work originally written in Pushtu by "Husain, son of Sa'bir, son of Khizr, the disciple of Hazrat Sha'h Ka'sim Sulaimane, whose tomb is in Chunargur." Such a long list of ancestors and teachers is common in the Islamic world, to authenticate the information and lend it credence and prestige. Vasittart's translation was published in 1790, to which Sir William Jones (1746–1794), a noted orientalist and pioneer of Indian studies, wrote an introductory note. Sir William, or "Asiatic Jones" as he was fondly known in his time, served as a judge in Calcutta between 1783 and 1794. He was accomplished in several oriental languages, including Persian and Sanskrit, and translated Hindu and Islamic codes of law, poetry, drama, and fables into English. He was the founder and first president of the Asiatic Society in Calcutta, and editor of its publication *Asiatic Research Series*. In his forwarding note to Vasittart's translation Sir William wrote:

> This account of the Afghans may lead to a very interesting discovery. We learn from Esdras that the Ten Tribes, after a wandering journey, came to a country called Arsareth, where, we may suppose, they settled; now the Afghans are said by the best Persian historians to be descendants from the Jews; they have traditions among themselves of such a descent; and it is even asserted that their families are distinguished by the names of Jewish tribes, although, since their conversion to Islam, they studiously conceal their origin . . . A considerable district under their domain is called Hazareh or Hazaret, which might easily have been changed into the word used by Esdras. I strongly recommend an inquiry into the literature and history of the Afghans.

Sir William was thus the first to suggest a connection between the Afghans and the Ten Lost Tribes of Israel, the link between the two being the mystical visions of Esdras. The reputation of Sir William as a scholar encouraged others to follow his recommendation, and opened new vistas for tribe searchers. Inquiries began into the name and identity of various Afghan tribes, with the idea of establishing contacts between them and the Lost Tribes of Israel. Attempts were also made to trace the route and the circumstances of the wanderings of these tribes, and their eventual arrival in Afghanistan. Numerous books and papers were written during the nineteenth century on the subject. Interestingly, not everybody followed Sir William's enthusiastic speculation, and opposing voices were also heard. The Honorary Mountstuart Elphinstone, a high-ranking British civil servant in India and ambassador to the Afghan court at Kabul in 1808, was one who was not impressed. Not having been granted permission to proceed to Kabul to take his position as ambassador, Elphinstone was obliged to remain in Peshawer, and passed his idle time collecting information on Afghanistan. The result of his inquiry was a voluminous book, published in 1815, which immediately won great fame and for many years was regarded as the most important source of information about Afghanistan. In this book Elphinstone referred to the Afghani traditions of origin, but did not take them at all seriously. He remarked cynically that "if we consider the easy faith with which all rude nations receive accounts favorable to their own antiquity, I fear we must class the descent of the Afghans from the Jews with that of the Romans and British from the Trojans." Elphinstone notwithstanding, a growing number of tribe searchers clearly preferred Sir William's version, and several books set out to refute Elphinstone's remarks and endorse Sir William's. The Reverend Charles Forster was among the most fervent supporters of Sir William. The title of the last chapter of his voluminous book, most of which introduced its readers to ancient inscriptions newly discovered in the Sinai, Egypt, Babylon, Assyria, and Persia, is "A new Key for the Recovery of the Lost Ten Tribes." In it Forster not only defended Sir William's opinions, but also attempted to give a clear map of the localities of the different tribes in Afghanistan.

The great propagator of the Israel–Afghan theory was Henry Walter Bellew (1834–1892). Bellew was born in India to a British officer of the Bengal army, and studied medicine in London. Upon completing his studies at the age of 21 Bellew returned to India in 1855 and was appointed assistant surgeon in Bengal. A year later he joined Major Henry Lumsden on his mission to Kandahar in Afghanistan. That was the beginning of a distinguished thirty-year career, during which Bellew carried out various medical and political assignments and retired as deputy surgeon-general of India. Bellew, a brilliant man with an exceptionally keen sense for languages, became fluent in Persian, Pushtu, and several other tongues spoken by Afghani tribesmen, and even published a grammar book and dictionary of the Pushtu language. He traveled extensively among the Afghan tribes of what was known then as the Northwest Frontier, administering medicines and medical advice to the remote and backward population, and teaching them basic hygiene and disease prevention. His name became a household word in the region. With all his medical work, Bellew found time to make penetrating observations of the country and its inhabitants, and to write several books in which he put before his readers a summary of his impressions and studies. He published his theory of the relationship between the Afghans and the Ten Tribes of Israel in 1862. Bellew was the only one among the tribe seekers who addressed himself to the confusion of terms Bani–Israel and Jew. Having asserted that the Afghans indeed referred to themselves as Bani-Israel, Bellew wondered how they, who wanted no part with the Jews, could associate themselves with the kingdom of Judah and with the Judeans deported after the destruction of Jerusalem. Bellew's answer to this problem was that it was simply a matter of confused and faulty transmission of oral traditions that resulted in mistaken dates, events, and circumstances. He decided to leave aside the Judean–Jews part of the tradition, and concentrate on the Israelite–Ten Tribe identification of the Afghans, and on their journey and arrival in their new home in Afghanistan. Sorting out these problems, confessed Bellew, took him many years of pondering and research, and only in 1880 was he ready to present his reconstructed version of Afghan history.

The two exiles

In two lectures delivered in Simla in India to an audience of British officials and their families in 1880, Bellew presented a grand theory, combining his new understanding of the Scriptures, Afghan traditions, and various other sources. Bellew started by defining the exile that uprooted the Israelites, namely the ancestors of the Afghans, from their homeland in Israel. Historically, there were two waves of exile to Assyria—the first in the days of king Pekah, the second twenty years later in the days of king Hoshea. Bellew named the first wave the Pekahan exile, the second the Hosean exile. The captives of both waves were brought to the same regions of Halah, Habor, and Hara on the river Gozan; those of the second, the Hosean, also to the cities of the Medes. Bellew identified Halah, Habor, and Hara with Alamut, Abhar, and Hara, three towns in Persia, in the region south of the Caspian Sea and northwest of Teheran, capital of modern Iran.

The cities of the Medes were, according to Bellew, around the ancient Persian city of Rai, east of Teheran. All Israelite captives were thus concentrated in what today are northern regions of Iran. But from now on the two waves of exile had different fates.

About ten years after the second, Hosean exile, the Medes revolted against their Assyrian overlords, a revolt that triggered the collapse of the Assyrian empire. The captives of Israel, so Bellew argued, could not have remained in their places of exile, and escaped. This was the escape referred to by Esdras and also by the Afghan traditions, although the two sources do not agree on the direction it took. Esdras described an escape through the narrows of the river Euphrates, meaning probably in a western or northwestern direction. But, argued Bellews, Esdras referred only to the ten tribes that were carried away prisoners from their own land in the time of king Hoshea—namely to those of the Hosean exile. The Pekahan exiles, those deported first, took, in Bellew's view, an opposite route of escape, and proceeded along the great caravan route from Teheran to Mashed (ancient Rai, according to Bellew), where some Israelite captives were concentrated. From there they continued to Merv, to arrive in the mountain country surrounding the river Oxus, the region called Ghor in the Afghan traditions. This is the very country to which the Afghans claim their ancestors fled, and where they first settled in their newly adopted country. In these wild mountains the Pekahan Israelites lived for hundreds of years in solitude. When they grew in number and strength, they absorbed many of the earlier inhabitants of the regions, especially, suggested Bellew, the Pushtun and other tribal groups speaking the Indian branch of the Indo-European languages. Thus all these tribes became part of the Israelite heritage, not by actual descent but by accepting the customs and habits of the Pekahan Israelites.

Afghans and Scythians

So far, in his attempt to reconstruct the ancient history of the Afghans, Bellew based himself on Afghani traditions, which he correlated with Esdras's escape of the exiled Israelites. At this point he deviated from these traditional sources, and introduced a new element—the Scythians. While Bellew was conducting his searches in

Afghanistan and constructing his theories, other tribe seekers developed the notion that the Scythians were a most important, even crucial link between the Lost Tribes of Israel and people in various parts of the world, ranging from the eastern limits of Asia, to Europe and even to the Americas. Bellew was no doubt aware of the developments in the Scythian theories, and offered his modest contribution to their exploits in the region of his interest—in Afghanistan. The Scythians were instrumental in explaining the circumstances of Israelite migration to Afghanistan, because of the geographic realities of Central Asia. Bellew realized that the forbidding mountain province of Ghor would be an unlikely choice for any people traveling on the main trade route from west to east in search of a new homeland. As there is no evidence that the fleeing Pekahans were pursued by anyone, the wide and open Turkmen steppe would have been a much easier and more attractive region in which to settle. And this, argued Bellew, is exactly what happened. While some Pekahan Israelites did in fact settle in the Ghor, the majority did not stop there but continued northward, along the easy routes toward the more attractive steppes. In these regions the Israelites

> soon adopted the only mode of life suited to the character of the country, and naturally reverted to the nomad habits of their forefathers in the wilderness of Sinai—the remembrance of which was kept alive in Israel by the ordained commemoration of the Feast of Tabernacles—and there built for themselves the old familiar booths or Succoth.

They were hence known to the Greeks as Succothai or Skuthai, and the modern Europeans as Scythians.

And thus the Scythians were none other than the Pekahan Israelites, who adapted to their new surroundings while reviving their ancient, nomadic way of life. But Bellew was not yet satisfied, and introduced another group of people to the story—the Tatars. With time, said Bellew, when the Scythian/Israelites of the steppes grew in strength, they conquered and vanquished their neighbors but married their women, thus acquiring Tatar blood and features. As Tatars they spread all over the Asian steppes, from the borders of China to southern Russia, and also invaded Afghanistan. These Tatars were not, however, simple barbaric tribes of the steppes, but true Israelites who came to Afghanistan to join their brothers who had settled in the Ghor mountains years before. They left their legacy in Afghanistan in the form of three tribes—the Kakar, the Katti, and the Safi—who consider themselves distinct from the Afghans, and yet each claims independently to be Bani Israel. A fourth tribe, the Ghizli of Turkish origin, also withholds the same claim. Because Bellew believed the Scythians and Turks were related by virtue of their common homeland in the central Asian steppes, the Turkish Ghizli tribe could also be included among Israelite descendants.

According to this sweeping theory, then, all Afghan tribes, regardless of their origin, descent, date, and circumstances of arrival in Afghanistan, were to Bellew Israelites of the Pekahan exile.

Matching Israelite and Afghani tribes

Having established the Israelite ancestry of the Afghans, the task at hand was to try and relate the various Afghani tribes to the tribes of Israel. Bellew made several contributions to this particular issue by trying to clarify the origin of the two most important tribal names in the region—Afghan, the general name of a large group of tribes, and Abdali, a tribal appellation of tribes who lived in and around Kandahar and toward Herat. Bellew, who no doubt knew of the Afghani ancestor Afghana, nevertheless suggested that Afghan was simply a distortion of Pekahan—Israelites of the first exile. Bellew suggested that the name Afghan was often written as Aphakhan. The plural of Pekah is Pekahan—which would mean those belonging to Pekah. In the spoken dialects this plural word would be Apakan or Afghan. The name Abdali, suggested Bellew, derived from the name of the Israelite tribe Naphtali, whose land was invaded by Tiglat Pileser of Assyria and its inhabitants taken captives in the Pekahan exile. The fact that other European writers identified the Abdali with the Aphtali tribes of the White Huns did not disturb Bellew. After all, he said, the White Huns themselves descended from the Scythians and were thus of Israelite origin. The name of the tribe of Naphtali could well have been preserved among them.

Although Bellew mentioned a possible link between the Afghani tribe Ashezi and Israelite Asher, he did not elaborate on the matter and carried his attempts of identification no further. In fact, quite surprisingly, in his latest book published in 1891, Bellew seemed to have abandoned altogether his previous belief in a connection between the tribes of Afghanistan and the Ten Lost Tribes. He now suggested that the Afghan tradition that they originated in the early Israelites probably echoes a Jewish population that lived in the area until the advent of Islam. As for the origin of the Afghans, or at least of their name, this he claims to have found in Armenia.

Despite Bellew's retreat from the Afghan–Israel theory, it was much too attractive, and others continued where he left off. The similarity of the tribal name of Eussof-Zye or Yousuf-Zye to Joseph, for one, has been noted by many. The Yousuf-Zye, dwellers of an extensive area between the river Indus, the Hindu–Kush Mountains, and the river of Kabul was identified not so much with Joseph but with his sons (zye), the two tribes of Ephraim and Menasseh. The Reverend Charles Forster suggested that the Isaguru who live east of the Yousuf-Zye—a tribe of great antiquity mentioned by the second-century geographer Ptolemai of Alexandria—should be identified with the Israelite tribe of Issachar, while the region called Zeblestan, west of the Yousuf-Zyes, is the country of the tribe of Zebulun.

It is a matter of interest that several Afghani tribes in the near past harbored traditions that connected them with the Ten Tribes in general or with specific tribes of Israel, although the original Afghani traditions knew nothing of these tribes. It therefore seems reasonable that several Afghani tribes adopted speculations made by enthusiastic Europeans, who, in the course of their work in Afghanistan, searched for the Lost Tribes. As far as could be established, all these claims are fairly late, one of the earliest being recorded as late as the end of the nineteenth century, a hundred years after the beginning of the European search. Ghulam Haidar, commander-in-chief of a Durrani tribal ruler, told Sir Thomas Hungerford Hoditch, a British army engineer who served in Afghanistan in 1894–1895, that the Durranis believed they were the modern representatives of the Israelites deported from Samaria. Jews of Afghanistan who migrated to Israel in the early 1950s related even more specific identifications. Abraham son of Benjamin of Herat told Izhak Ben-Zvi, second president of the state of Israel:

> According to the tradition current among the Afridis, they are descendants of the Israelites, more particularly, the sons of Ephraim. They grow beards; the older among them did not hide the fact of their Jewish descent, but the younger generation have suppressed this fact which, if

Figure 23: A Eusof-Zye or Afghan of "The Tribe of Joseph".

disclosed, would render them most unpopular in the present political mood of the country. According to my information, there lived in the country stretching from Baluchistan to Kuwait some ten to twenty thousand brave warriors, usually camelmen, who traced their descent to the tribe of Benjamin, as do the Wassili. On the other hand, the Jajio professed to be descended from the sons of Gad, and the Shinwaris from the tribe of Simeon. The total number of tribesmen tracing their descent back to the Israelites must be in the neighborhood of half a million. The Afridis are a formidable race of mountaineers . . . with deep dark eyes and of an unusual oriental beauty of countenance. They are very independent and submit to no alien rule, even the official authority of Afghanistan or the government of India. Each tribe is governed by its own reigning chieftain, and hoists its own banner, but there is a principal chieftain for each of the three major tribes, whose sway is absolute.

Other informants had similar recollections, and added details of interest. Hiya Zaurov, a man who had connections with the highest echelons of Afghani society before migrating to Israel, was told by Gulam Nebu Khan, a cabinet minister, that the Afghans were descendants of the tribes of Israel, and that the royal house was of the tribe of Benjamin. This same information was heard by Michael Gol, one of the elders of the Afghani Jewish community in Tel Aviv. As a child he participated in a reception held by the Jewish community of Herat in honor of king Habib Ala Khan. The king asked the community elders to which tribe they belonged, and was answered that they did not know. But we know, said the king, we are from the tribe of Benjamin, descendants of King Saul and his sons Jonathan, Aphgan, and Patan.

And thus, eight of the Ten Lost Tribes of Israel, most surprisingly including Benjamin, one of the two tribes of the kingdom of Judah exiled to Babylon about 160 years after the exile of the Ten Tribes of Israel, were believed to be living on Afghani soil. There is no explanation as to why the tribes of Reuben and Dan were left out.

Matching place-names

Local place-names, like names of tribes, were also used to prove Afghani–Israelite connections. Bellew suggested that Hazor, the largest and most important city in the land of Naphtali, be identified with

Hazarah in Afghanistan. The reason for this identification was Bellew's belief that the Naphtali–Pekahans, our Abdali–Afghans, on recovering their freedom and acquiring possession of the new country, should name it after some favorite place in their home country; or, perhaps after the place where their leaders lived. Sir William Jones identified the same place, Hazarah, with Esdras's Arsareth.

The Sulleiman Mountains, now in Pakistan, with their most prominent peak Sulleiman's Throne, and the name Solimannec by which the Arabs call the Afghans, drew much attention. It was almost self-evident that all these names had to be connected with King Solomon. Other memories of this king were evoked by the name Kabul, capital of Afghanistan, identified with Kabul in the land of Galilee that Solomon gave to Hiram king of Tyre (1 Kings IX:13). An obscure locality by the name of Siooona Dang has been identified with none other than Zion.

On the physiognomy of the Afghans and the Jews

Another way of establishing a connection between Afghans and Israelites was by a very elusive feature—resemblance of physiognomy. Almost every traveler among the Afghans noted a resemblance between the Afghans and the Jews, including the cautious Elphinstone, who, when visiting the Pathan tribes at Rajpoutana, noted that the upper classes were stout and handsome, with hooked noses and "Jewish features." While observing several groups of wandering shepherds, he was struck in particular by the girls, who also possessed aquiline noses. William Moorcraft, who, as a veterinary surgeon employed by the East India Company, daringly explored the Himalayan Mountains and surrounding regions in search of a Turkmen pony to improve the Arab horse, also observed similarity of physiognomy. In his diary he reported that when passing the Khaibar Pass he noted that the Khaibaris were tall for mountaineers and of a singular Jewish cast of features. The Reverend Dr. Joseph Wolff, remembered from his accounts of the Jews of Daghastan, passed through the Peshawar region in 1843 on his way to his mission in Bokhara. On the way he and was wonderfully struck with the resemblance that the Yousauf-Azeye and the Kaibaree, two of the tribes of Afghanistan, bear to the Jews. Dr. Wolff also suggested that the Kaffre Seeah Poosh, dwellers

Figure 24: Afridis

of the region known then as Kafiristan in the remote valleys of the Hindu–Kush mountain range, were descendants of Israel. The Kaffre tribes, idolaters (Kafirs in Arabic), until Islamized by force as late as 1895, intrigued many European travelers, who saw in them descendants of Alexander the Great and his soldiers, believed to have reached this remote area. Wolff described some of the singular rites of the Kaffre as the worship of gigantic human figures carved in wood and stone. Indeed, several such statues, large but not gigantic, are displayed in the little-known Ethnographic Museum of Florence, Italy. Kafiristan is the very country that Peachy Taliaferro Carneham and Daniel Dravot, gentlemen at large, set out to conquer and rule in Rudyard Kipling's unforgettable *The Man Who Would Be King*.

Sir George Rose quoted a testimony of an officer on the staff of the commander-in-chief in India:

> It is dated from Head Quarters Camp, Munikiala, 20th January 1852. Having been just through a part of Afghanistan Proper, although now part of our dominions, I cannot help writing to you how I was struck with the Jewishness of the people, the moment we crossed the Indus; and not only their appearance, but every possible circumstance tends to convince me that they are the descendants of the Ten Tribes.

Bellew too found a remarkable similarity between the Afghan physiognomy and the Jewish type, noting that this was more notable among the nomad tribes who dwelt among the inaccessible mountains of the Sulleman range and in the hilly regions of the country. This was natural, suggested Bellew, for in these localities the people are more segregated than their brethren who dwell in the towns and cities of the plain, amid a very mixed population with whom they contract connections leading to the alteration of their distinctive features. But even there, with all the racial mixture, the distinction of the Afghan race is so marked and different from those that dwell among them that they can be easily recognized at a glance. Perhaps this persistence of the type of feature is the result of their custom never, but in exceedingly rare instances, to give their daughters in marriage to any but of their own race.

It is significant that so many informants mention a Jewish physiognomy referring to a tall stature, stout body, and aquiline nose. What type of Jew did they have in mind when comparing it to the physiognomy of the Afghans—a Sephardi or Ashkenazi Jew of Europe whom these informants may have encountered in England, or perhaps one of the different Jewish types they perhaps saw during their Asian travels? They certainly could not have had in mind the stereotype of a Jew with a hooked nose of common European caricatures.

Similarity of habits and customs

Another important clue suggested by Bellew to prove the connection between the Afghans and the Israelites is their similar "moral characteristics." As against their physical beauty, the Afghans, like the Jews,

> are remarkable for their impatience under restraint, their instability of disposition, want of perseverance, and their love of freedom and consequent defiance of self-constituted authority. These traits in their character, coupled with their want of respect and loyalty towards their rulers, have acquired for them a notoriety for turbulence and lack of unanimity amongst themselves, which is quite proverbial among neighboring nations, who stigmatize them as a rebellious, stiff-necked, and degenerate people.

Several religious customs observed by the Afghans that are reminiscent of the Laws of Moses are much more intriguing. Some are tribal customs, mentioned in the Pukhtunwal, the old Afghani code of law. However, the laws of the Pukhtunwal have been so greatly modified by the Muslim Shari'a law that it is difficult to establish whether any custom is truly native Afghani, or whether it was introduced by Islam. Nevertheless, several customs are often quoted as proofs to the Afghan-Israel theory; first and foremost are those relating to sacrificial offerings on particular occasions. The Afghans smear the blood of the sacrificial animal over the lintel and side posts of the door of the house, to avert sickness and misfortune. There is a great similarity between this practice and the Biblical Passover celebration, which involved sacrificing a lamb and smearing its blood on the doorposts (Exodus 12:21–25). Because the Ten Tribes of Israel were early separated from the Jewish nation, and were not aware of postbiblical rulings that put an end to private sacrifices, the Afghan practice was considered a very strong clue to the connection between the Afghans and the Ten Tribes of Israel. Indeed, this could have been most convincing, were it not that the sacrifice of an animal and the use of its blood to avert danger were common among pre-Islamic Arabs and is still common today among all Muslims. Present-day Arabs and Bedouins sacrifice an animal on happy occasions such as the building of a new house or tent or a wedding, as well as in cases of sickness and other calamities. They eat its meat, and smear its blood on a certain object, such as on the blanket that forms the door of the tent. Afghan practices therefore fall in the realm of well-recorded Near Eastern customs, practiced from ancient time to the present, and have no specific connection with ancient Israel. The same is true of the Afghan custom of the scapegoat, which is very similar to the biblical practice (Leviticus 16:21–22). When a village or an encampment is struck by disaster, the Afghans transfer the sins of the community on the head of an animal and drive it into the desert to the sound of yells, shouts, and the beating of drums. Transferring evil on a scapegoat and then killing it is a well-known custom practiced throughout the world, as vividly proved by Sir James Fraser's *The Golden Bough*. It does not necessarily indicate an Afghan–Israelite connection.

Other practices that resemble those of the ancient Israelites are less striking, and could well represent customs of a much more general character, or be vestiges of Jewish customs preserved from pre-Islamic times. To the first category belong the Afghan practice of stoning a blasphemer of God to death outside the limits of the camp (Leviticus 24:14–16), and the equal division of portions of land among families of the tribe by lot (*pur* in Hebrew—which Bellew suggested was similar to the Persian *pucha* or *parra*—was incorporated into the Hebrew during the period of the Babylonian exile), as in Numbers 33:54. Other such practices are the strict retaliation on the aggressor in cases of injury—an eye for an eye, a tooth for a tooth, as in Leviticus 24:17–21; and the obligation of the younger brother to marry the widow of his dead elder brother, as in Deuteronomy 25:5.

In the second category fall customs reported by Jews of the Afghan community who migrated to Israel in the early 1950s. According to them—and their reports were verified by researchers who visited the Pathan tribes in Pakistan and Afghanistan in the 1980s—the women in some tribes light candles on Friday afternoon, sometimes hiding them under reed baskets. Matrimonial purity required by the laws of Moses is observed by some tribes; and infant boys are circumcised in some tribes on the eighth day after birth, unlike other Moslems who postpone this ritual to a much later date. Other testimonies are more dubious, being based on visual impressions: The men of most tribes grow beards and do not shave their sidelocks; some men wear shawls similar to the talith; one informant saw an embroidered design on the back of the cloaks of several tribesmen, which reminded him of a Hanukah lamp. That certain customs can be preserved in secret for hundreds of years has been attested to by the conversos, Jews who were forced to convert to Christianity in fifteenth-century Spain and Portugal. To this day they secretly light candles on Friday night, bake *mazzot* for Passover, and keep customs that they themselves do not understand. The Afghani case may be similar, representing Jewish conversos to Islam.

The Afghan–Israelite connection is alive today

The belief in the Afghan–Israelite connection is not only a subject of antiquarian interest, but has proved to be relevant to present-day Afghanistan, Pakistan, and Israel alike. In 1984 a mission was sent from Israel to Pakistan to study the Pathan traditions of their Israelite origins. The expedition, initiated by the Amishav organization for the discovery of the scattered tribes of Israel, visited some fifteen villages in the dense Pathan region between Pashawer and the Khaibar pass, and traveled also to the Gilgit region in the far north of Pakistan, close to the Chinese border. It reported that the belief in an Israelite ancestry is still very strong among the Pathan tribesmen, who otherwise are devout Moslems. They also continue to practice seemingly Jewish customs, alongside the customs of their own code of law, the Pakhtunwal. The Amishav organization and its followers believe that the Pathans are indeed descendants of the Ten Tribes of Israel, and suggest taking practical measures to reconvert them to Judaism and even bring them to Israel. However, when viewed with less enthusiastic eyes, the Afghan story seems to be a blend of local traditions probably originating with the Jews of Persia, hypothetical historical reconstruction by highly motivated European explorers, and customs that are either widely practiced or are vestiges of Jewish customs distorted during the ages. It is of interest that the Jewish community that once existed in Afghanistan before being converted to Islam still exerts its strange influence on the inhabitants of that country and on those who study them.

6

The Tribes in the Land of the Rising Sun—Israel in Japan

It was a lovely day in the month of June when I was first introduced to the notion that the Ten Lost Tribes of Israel existed in Japan. The sun was shining brightly, and Kyoto, the ancient capital of Japan, was celebrating its most important festival of the year—the Gion Festival. The streets were bright with colorful paper lamps and streamers, gently swaying in the light breeze. Vertical fabric shop signs attached to slender bamboo poles added to the atmosphere of color and joy that enveloped the city. Women dressed in their best kimonos, men in dark summer robes, girls with large colorful ribbon bows in their hair, and boys in short loose jackets were lining the streets. They anxiously awaited the great event of the day, the procession of portable shrines about to pass through the streets of the city. At the sound of distant, shrill music, the crowd tensed. Young men tightened the bands of cloth tied around their heads, loosened their muscles the best they could in the dense crowd, stripped the upper part of their bodies and showed signs of growing impatience. When the procession finally arrived, the young men flung themselves into the street, and fought for the right to join the mass of sweating men who carried the portable wooden shrines on their shoulders. They were pushing and kicking until some of those who had been carrying the heavy weight became obviously exhausted, and with faces streaming with sweat, gave

Figure 25: Gion Festival in Kyoto, with portable shrines carried along the streets, 1879.

up and receded into the crowd. The procession continued, carried on the shoulders of fresh and vigorous young men who kept replacing the tired ones, and being replaced in their turn. The crowd was exhilarated, cheering to the slowly moving shrines and to the men who carried them.

At last the procession came to an end and the onlookers, with much bowing and leave-taking, began to disperse. One could sense a feeling of great yet restrained satisfaction, as if the people had participated in some moving experience, as if they had all been through an ordeal, and survived it. There were not many non-Japanese on the street, and now that the main event was over, my presence attracted some attention. I exchanged greetings with the people standing next to me, who were curious and wanted to know where I had come from. Upon hearing that I was from Jerusalem, a man, Mr. Yamaguchi as he introduced himself, asked me if I knew the significance of the Gion Festival. I had to admit that except for realizing that it was one of the oldest and holiest celebrations of the Shinto religion, I was ignorant of its meaning. Mr. Yamaguchi was surprised. How could you, he wondered, having come from Jerusalem, have failed to notice the similarity between the portable shrines carried in the procession we just saw and their prototype, the portable shrine carried by the Children of Israel on their way from bondage in Egypt to freedom in the Land of Israel. The Israelite portable shrine, said my new friend, was kept for many centuries in the Temple in Jerusalem, and was later taken into exile alongside the people of Israel. He also promised me that while the whole world thinks that Israel had disappeared and is talking of the Ten Lost Tribes, the Japanese know better. Their tradition tells that their ancestors came to Japan from the west, and that they descended from the exiles of Israel. The best proof for this is the Gion Festival itself with its portable shrines, and its very name, which is a corruption of Zion, the poetic name of Jerusalem. We Japanese, exclaimed Mr. Yamaguchi, are none other than your distant brethren, the Ten Tribes of Israel.

With this revelation, strengthened by Mr. Kobayashi of Tokyo, who preferred to remain vague on the subject, I began to look for the roots of this strange belief. I found that the origin and culture of the Japanese people have for long aroused the interest of western scholars and enthusiasts. Indeed, among these early students of Japanese history were some who attempted to find parallels between it and the sacred history best known to them—namely that of the biblical Hebrews. They connected the Japanese people with various people of the Bible, but mainly with the Lost Tribes of Israel.

Brief history of Japan relevant to the Tribe issue

To understand how a connection was made between Israel and Japan, something about the unique history of Japan in the last several hundred years must be related. The first non-Japanese inquiry into the origin of the Japanese people was made by Engelbrecht Kaempfer (1651–1716), a German physician and traveler, who entered Japan in 1690, some fifty years after that country had almost completely closed itself to the outside world. In 1606, after many years of civil warfare, Ieyasu Tokugawa, one of the lords of feudal Japan, succeeded in overcoming all other lords. He reduced the emperor, the sacred direct descendent of the sun-goddess, to the role of a mere figurehead, and confined him to his palace in Kyoto. Tokugawa took the title Shogun (overlord), and ruled Japan with an iron fist from his capital Edo (modern Tokyo). He disposed of or reduced the power of the lords who opposed him, and distributed their confiscated land to members of his family and to his retainers, thus gaining the everlasting but concealed hatred of some, and the dependence and support of others. By then the Spanish and the Portuguese, aided by their superior navigation and worldwide connections, gained a foothold in Japan and conducted all its foreign trade to their great advantage. Their missionaries succeeded in converting to Christianity several Japanese, who then served the interests of their co-religionists. In response, Tokugawa constricted Spanish and Portuguese religious and commercial activities, banned Christianity, and brought foreign trade almost to a halt. In 1635 the Japanese were forbidden to make overseas voyages, and those abroad were not allowed to return home. Four years later, in 1639, Portuguese ships were completely barred from Japanese waters. Japan entered a self-imposed period of seclusion from the rest of the world. This policy enabled the Tokugawa Dynasty to maintain political, economic, and cultural stability for some 250 years. A heavy curtain fell on Japan, with only one opening—a limited Dutch trading station on the island of Dejima near Nagasaki. Once a year the

Dutch, who gained the favor of the shogun by their perseverance, honesty, and avoidance of missionary activities, were allowed to bring in foreign goods, supplies, and relief personnel, and obtain Japanese goods for export.

Very few Europeans managed to enter Japan during the Tokugawa period, and those who did were confined to the Dutch trading station. Engelbrecht Kaempfer not only managed to enter Japan, but, because of his friendly manner and medical skills, won the confidence of the Japanese authorities and was granted permission to travel in Japan and even to visit Edo twice. While traveling Kaempfer saw much and learned much, and eventually produced a monumental volume describing what he saw.

Being confronted with a foreign and completely unknown country, Kaempfer was intrigued by the origin of the Japanese people. He learned that the Japanese believed themselves to have been born on the sacred islands of Japan as direct descendants of the gods. He also heard that the Japanese were aware of a European theory that claimed they originated in Chinese rebels who were expelled from China. The Japanese agreed that there were migrations from China to Japan, but placed them at a relatively late date in their history, 453 years after the reign of their first emperor. Kaempfer paid little attention to the Japanese claim to celestial origin. He likewise rejected the Chinese origin. Kaempfer, who believed that language held the clue to the origin of nations, studied Japanese and observed that this language was entirely pure, and free from all admixture with the languages of China to the degree that there was room to endorse its original descent. He also noted that the Japanese people differed from the Chinese in many other respects such as in religion, civil customs, ways of life, food and dress, and inclination of mind. If then the Japanese are an "original nation," where did they originate? Like all Europeans of his and of later ages, Kaempfer had only one reference source that dealt with the origin of nations—the Bible. He did not identify the Japanese with the Ten Tribes of Israel—this would come only later—but suggested that they originated in ancient Babylon, and that their language was among those created after the destruction of the Tower of Babel.

We do not know how Kaempfer's views of the origin of the Japanese were received in Japan, but for Europe his book was the chief source of information about that remote and mysterious country for over a hundred years. It also influenced the speculative thought of the true hero of the Japan–Israel connection—Mr. N. McLeod.

McLeod and the Japan–Israel theory

Mr. McLeod, an obscure person whose first name is even unknown, was a Scottish missionary who arrived in Japan in 1867, in the last turbulent years of the Tokugawa rule. McLeod remained in the country for several years, eyewitnessing the collapse of the 250-year-old shogunate regime, and the beginning of the modern era of Japan. While powerful families in southern Japan were conspiring to overthrow the shogunate and restoring the rightful reign of the emperor, western powers, especially the United States, were trying to negotiate the opening of Japan to foreign relations and trade. The shots fired by Commodore Matthew C. Perry of the United States Navy in Yokohama Bay in 1853 dealt the deathblow to the shogunate regime. In 1867 a new emperor ascended the throne. He assumed total control of the country, deposed the last shogun, and initiated the period of Meiji Restoration. In a very short period Japan was transformed from a medieval, feudal country to a modern state.

All these exciting events occurred in front of McLeod's amazed eyes, and greatly impressed him. He traveled throughout the country and got to know the Japanese people and their culture, and was familiar with current events. McLeod, a dedicated missionary, constantly compared the occurrences he observed in Japan with his ultimate source of knowledge—the Bible. He was convinced that the revolutionary era he was witnessing had to have an ultimate reason, and came to believe that the Japanese people could be none other than the Ten Lost Tribes of Israel. McLeod, who presented his startling theory in a slim volume, did not suggest that he heard an indigenous Japanese tradition of a Japan–Israel connection, and he should therefore be considered the inventor of this original idea. So intrigued was McLeod by this novel notion that he published at his own expense a slim and poorly printed volume which he intended as a preparatory to a work of twelve volumes, with illustrations. That work should have been similar to Kaempfer's, but would contain a more accurate and detailed account of the history of the Japanese, and a description of their Jewish origins. McLeod did not accomplish his grand intentions.

Apparently his views did not meet with enough enthusiasm, and financial support was not coming forth. Nevertheless, McLeod's original theory gradually seeped into Japanese society, was accepted by some, and adopted by several modern-day tribe seekers. Several books have been written since McLeod's days to prove his theory.

McLeod's observations and interpretations

McLeod's first observation was that the Japanese population was made up of three distinct groups: the Ainu who dwelt in the north of Japan and who were of the Caucasian race; a group of Malayan descent that dwelt mainly in the southern island of Japan and which he named the Diminutive Race on account of their slender stature, and the Japanese proper. This threefold division was the main reason why McLeod refuted Kaempfer's suggestion that the Japanese were all refugees of the Tower of Babel episode.

Archaeological research demonstrated that McLeod's observations were correct, and that indeed three groups of people arrived in Japan at different periods. The ancestors of the Ainu came from northern Siberia in the Ice Age, over a land bridge that connected Japan with the Asian mainland. The bulk of the Japanese arrived from Siberia some six to seven thousand years ago by boats across the Japan Sea, and the Malays arrived from southeast Asia and the Pacific Islands at intervals over a long period of time. Having made these correct observations, McLeod proceeded to explain the origin of the three groups of people in terms familiar to him through his religious biblical education. The threefold division suggested to him the biblical division of humanity between the three sons of Noah—Shem, Ham, and Japheth. The Ainu, claimed McLeod, descended from Japheth, and came to Japan shortly after the dispersion of Babel. The Diminutive Race of dark, although not black, are sons of Ham, who also came to Japan some time after the dispersion of Babel. The third group, the largest in Japan, descended from Shem. This makes them Semites, more specifically of the Jewish race—the Ten Lost Tribes of Israel.

To prove this, McLeod gave a sketch of the history of ancient Israel up to the exile, and then of the circumstances of the escape of the Ten Tribes from Assyrian bondage as related by Esdras. The escaping Israelites, argued McLeod, took with them their women and children, their flocks and their herds, and traveled right through Asia, a journey that took them a year and a half—as related by Esdras. On this journey, suggested McLeod, the Israelites may have used wooden carts of the type still to be seen in Japan in his days, which were drawn by oxen none other than the Bulls of Bashan.

When the Israelites reached Korea, they divided in half. One half turned southward to China, and eventually conquered it. To this event McLeod produced an extraordinary proof: The same breed of sheep imported from Palestine that can be seen in Smithfield market in London can be bought in China. The other half of the Israelites were now on the coast of Korea, preparing to cross over to Japan. The year was 663 B.C. or somewhat later, as the Israelite exile occurred in 721 B.C. The chronology was crucial, insisted McLeod, because the Japanese samurai had an ancient tradition that they came from a far country situated in the west of Asia. Under their leader Jin mu Tenno they called a council of war and agreed among themselves to proceed to the east and seek out and conquer some unknown country. This they did, said McLeod, and landed in Japan around the year 660 B.C. There was no doubt in McLeod's mind that the Israelites on the shores of Korea and the Japanese samurai who crossed the sea and conquered Japan were one and the same. Jin mu Tenno is known also as Jimmu Tenno—Tenno meaning Emperor of Heaven—who was the first emperor of Japanese legend. He was a direct descendant of the gods, five generations removed from Amaterassu, goddess of the sun and special protectress of Japan and its imperial family.

McLeod must have been familiar with the earliest Japanese mythical-historical text, put in writing in the eighth century A.D., which describes an expedition to the east led by Jimmu. But that description referred to the mythical expedition of Jimmu from western Japan eastward to the region of Yamato, southwest of Kyoto, the earliest center of Japanese power. It should be noted that the mythical arrival of Jimmu Tenno from out of Japan, as suggested by McLeod, runs contrary to deep-seated Japanese sentiments. According to their belief their own country was created by the gods, and they themselves descended from the gods who personally came down to Japan to create the Japanese people and establish their royal house. In tradi-

Figure 26: Alleged march of the Israelites to Japan.

tional Japanese thinking their first emperor could not possibly have been an outside invader.

McLeod provides an ancient illustration of people in a boat, which he regards as an actual illustration of the crossing of Jimmu Tenno from Korea. This illustration provided McLeod with a wealth of proof for the origin of the boat passengers:

> The princes are clad in an ancient armor of Assyria and Media and shod like the ancient princes of Israel with badger skins; they wear the tachi or Persian sword, and some have ancient Israelite unicorn-shaped spears; others have the spears formerly worn by the ancient Median infantry . . . The bow of Jin mu Tenno's Samurai was a formidable weapon . . . and if Jehu used a similar bow it would be quite easy to send an arrow through a man's body . . . the Assyrian bow (is) an exact facsimile of the Japanese bow.

The exiled Israelites landed, according to McLeod, on the Awa Shima Beach, off the island of Kyushu.

> Jin mu Tenno and his Samurai did as the Israelites were ordered to do when they took the Holy Land, exterminated those who resisted them and spared the weak race in the south.

Then they erected a temple on the Awa Shima Beach, and to the present day the inhabitants of Kyushu make pilgrimage to this place. Soon afterward they built another temple at Ise, to this day the holiest shrine of the Shinto religion of Japan. This custom of building temples, reflected McLeod, is exactly

> As Jeroboam and their forefathers the Israelites did of old, erected high places at Dan and Bethel for the main purpose of securing the loyalty of the ten tribes, so did their descendants even long before they had conquered the north of Japan and Yezo . . . Awa Shima and Ise were then the Dan and Bethel for the north and south of Japan.

The conquest of Japan was not an easy matter. The Israelites had to fight the Ainu race, which held sway over most of Japan. By all accounts, reports McLeod, the Ainu made a strong resistance:

> For the most of them were powerful men like the Japanese wrestlers, and were armed with bow and club; but they could not longer stand against the sturdy warriors of Jin mu Tenno, who were all in the prime

of life and previously laboured in building the Casteleted cities of the Medes, and who had just made a journey of about 18 months and who were armed to the teeth with the arms and armour of Assyria, Media and Jewry.

The fierceness of the battle is even reflected in the very name of the Ainu, says McLeod, being formed of two Japanese words—AA meaning contempt, Inu meaning dog. This name was given to the Ainu by the Japanese samurai, ruling class of the Jewish race "who call all gentiles dogs." Eventually the Ainu were defeated and driven out of the extreme south of Japan. But their defeat was far from complete and they remained very powerful. They absorbed many cultural features brought over by the Jews, such as the tabernacle-shaped houses, in fulfillment of Noah's prophecy regarding Japheth: "He shall dwell in the tents of Shem" (Genesis 8:27).

At this stage of his mytho-historical reconstruction, McLeod left the realm of the distant past and dealt with the recorded history of a period not far removed from his own, to which he gave a no less startling interpretation. The defeated Ainu, suggested McLeod, took the form of the Tokugawa rulers, regained their power and again subjugated Japan for the period of 250 years preceding McLeod's arrival. McLeod viewed the seizure of power by the Tokugawa shoguns and the subjugation of the samurai who opposed him, strictly an internal Japanese matter, as another round of confrontation between the Ainu and the Jewish race. In this round the Ainu had the upper hand, managing to subdue and completely overpower the descendants of Jin mu Tenno. Japan was converted into one vast prison for the Jewish race. This tragic state of affairs started to resolve itself shortly before the arrival of McLeod in Japan: "In 1862 the Jewish hostages were allowed to return from Edo to their separate provinces."

In 1867, the year of McLeod's arrival in Japan, a new emperor ascended the thrown, and under the throne-name Meiji, deposed the last shogun and initiated the Meiji Restoration along western lines. The battle of Fushima, fought in 1868 between the Tokugawa shogun and rebelling princes, was, to McLeod's mind, the first stage in the battle of Gog and Magog, which will be fought in the Far East. McLeod identified the two great typhoon storms and the large fires that raged in Japan exactly at that time with the fires of Magog (Ezekiel 39:6). He also found a remarkable resemblance between Japan and the locality of the last stage of the Gog and Magog battle as described in Ezekiel 38–39. "When this last battle will be over," prophesized McLeod, "it is probable that China, Japan, and Korea will again be united under the power of the Jewish race, with the emperor of Japan at their head. The emperor can without doubt claim to be the head of the house of Ephraim and also heir to the united throne of Israel and Judah."

Ways of identifying the tribes

Having outlined past and future events, McLeod now discusses the means by which the Jewish race is to be identified:

> Whenever and wherever Jews are sought, the following signs are commonly looked for: They will be exercising circumcision; they will all have the prominent features and high noses of the Jews, and, being of the tribes of Judah and Benjamin, would be tallest and strongest of all the Jews; they should at once be known as Jews; they should speak Hebrew and have Jewish names; they shall be scattered all over the earth.

But, says McLeod, these are not the signs to be sought, because the ten tribes rejected the statures and covenant of God, went after the heathens, and were not circumcised. They lost their language because of their period in exile, and in captivity were given non-Jewish names such as Daniel; the ten tribes were not really scattered: The tribe of Judah was dispersed over the four corners of the earth (Isaiah 11:12), while exiled Israel remained together (Jeremiah 30:10). Also, when found they will not be known as Jews, but will be identified by the sign of the curse that was upon them and their seed forever. This was stated in Deuteronomy 28 and repeated in Isaiah 66:19: "And I will set a sign among them and I will send those that escape of them unto the nations."

Now all the curses of Deuteronomy came about in Japan, and McLeod listed them in detail:

> Fires occur in cities more than in any country in the world; there are bankruptcies of businesses; the fields have been cursed for ages; the children are covered with eruptions, a disease they inherit from their parents; pestilence has made a fearful havoc; people are underfed and weak, and in no other country in the world are so many people to be

found ailing; the water is bad with worms and overflow of manure; madness and astonishment of the heart prevail alongside distress and suicide because of the great poverty; spurious and obscene literature and theater plays are common; the wives and daughters of samurai families hold festivals in temples where the harlots worship; as far as money is concerned, foreign nations are the head and Japan the tail. Even songs of the pure Jewish Race in Japan, heard in Shinto temples in Kyoto, are simply howling and lamentations, in fulfillment of Amos 8:10: "and I will turn all your songs into lamentations."

Identification by the fulfillment of the biblical curses is McLeod's original contribution to the means used by tribe seekers to locate the Lost Tribes of Israel. McLeod strengthened his identification by the common technique of similarity of sound. He provided a long list of Jewish or ancient Middle Eastern place-names, objects, and customs and their equals in Japan. For example: Acaldema = field of blood, a pit outside Kyoto, into which bodies of criminals are thrown; Samurai = Samaria, soldiers of fortified mountain cities; Ark = tabernacle-shape; Torii entrance gate to temples = the cloudy pillar that showed the way to the Israelites in the desert; The headband worn by the Empress Jingo Kogo = a Median priestly crown; Women wear scarlet on holidays, as Saul clothed Hebrew women; Shinto priests wear linen caps and dress and worship with heads covered, as did Jewish priests; women and men dance separately, never together, conforming with Jewish customs. In the same vein, all fruits and trees are of Palestinian origin; all vessels are of Jewish and Assyrian origin.

McLeod discusses also the issue of resemblance of physical countenance. To the reader's amazement he testifies that although in his day he has found the Jewish race few in number compared with the aborigines of Japan, yet each one can be easily picked out as they have all the visage of lost Israel. Although McLeod does not describe this visage, he assures the reader that these members of lost Israel in Japan differ from the English Jews, who are taller and fairer and stronger. They are rather like the Ashkenazi Jews, who are actually descendants of the 12,000 of the ten tribes who have returned to the Holy Land with Judah and Benjamin and are thus the true representative of lost Israel. Indeed, remarks McLeod, "the emperor looks much like the von Epstein family of rich bankers of Warsaw and St. Peterbourg."

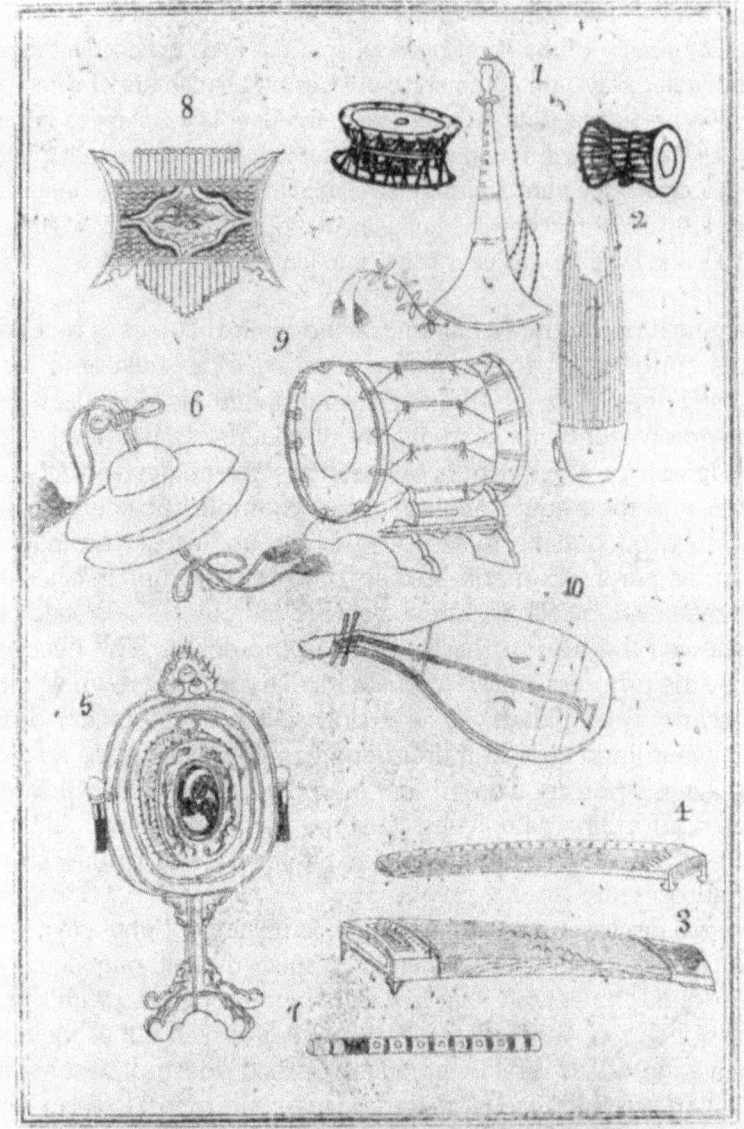

Figure 27: Jewish temple musical instruments envisioned as Japanese instruments.

Figure 28: The Japanese emperor.

The Japanese and the Japan–Israel theory

McLeod presented his notion of the connection between the Ten Lost Tribes of Israel and the people of Japan in a most elaborate way. It is perhaps not surprising that this missionary, brought up in strict nineteenth-century Protestant Scotland, having received a religious education based on the Bible, would rely on the Bible as his sole guide to the understanding of the strange Japanese world with which he was confronted. His vision of a Japan–Israel connection is almost understandable. The real enigma of the Japan–Israel story is why the Japanese, or at least some of them, accepted McLeod's outlandish ideas. Japan is far removed from any biblical connection. Indeed the epoch-making Meiji Restoration brought Japan closer to the west, but while adopting western political and economic systems, technology and way of life, the Japanese were reluctant to adopt its religion. Although the ban on Christianity laid in the seventeenth century was lifted, there was only a trickle of conversions, and the traditional religions of Japan—Shintoism and Buddhism—remained strongly entrenched in Japanese life. Furthermore, one of the essential teachings of Shintoism is the mythological connection between the emperor of Japan and the gods of the land. This idea had a growing appeal in the days of the Meiji Restoration, when the emperor was again assuming an active role as head of state, and even more so in the times of growing nationalistic feelings in Japan, leading to World War II. Ideologically Japan had no need for alternative roots in Israel. And yet Christianity was slowly gaining a foothold in Japan, and the Bible became known among growing circles of the population. To encourage the conversion of the Japanese to Christianity, the Missionary Society of London issued a small pamphlet proposing that the extraordinary success of Japan in the Japan–Russia war of 1903, and the signing of the Anglo–Japanese Alliance of 1909, were proof that the Japanese were descendants of the ancient Israelites, and inheritors of its blessings. Contrary to McLeod, who based his identification of the Japanese with the Ten Tribes of Israel mainly on the fulfillment of biblical curses and calamities, the Japanese were now being identified with Israel by proof of success.

Identification by success lies at the heart of the British–Israelite theory (chapter 7), which claims that God's recurring promises for the dominance of Israel are in the process of being fulfilled, and any nation that visibly demonstrates increase and supremacy is a direct descendent of Israel. The inclusion of Japan in the ranks of the blessed, along with Britain and the Unites States, perhaps attracted some Japanese to the novel idea of a Japan–Israel connection, and indeed since the 1920s Japanese authors published several pamphlets and books expressing similar ideas. One such book, written in 1934 by Bishop Juji Nakada of the Holiness Church Movement, attempted to prove the superiority of the Japanese race through the authority of the Holy Scriptures. He interpreted the biblical verse "For the Lord God is a sun and a Shield" (Psalm 84:12) as referring to the strong relationship between Japan, whose emblem is the sun, and the Jewish nation, whose emblem is the Shield of David.

More elaborate were the ideas of Dr. Zen'ichiro Oyabe, who believed that the Japanese originated in the Israelite tribes Gad and Menasseh, who, being anxious to preserve intact the purity of their Israelite faith, left Canaan and headed eastward under the leadership of the prophet Elijah on his heavenly chariot. This happened about 240 years before the first emperor of Japan, Tenno Jimmu, held the solemn ceremony of his enthronement, and indeed the word Mikado, the ancient title of the Japanese emperors, derived, to Dr. Oyabe's mind, from the name Gad. Moreover, the meaning of the name of this first emperor himself, Tenno Jimmu, is "Divine Valor," a characteristic trait of the tribe of Gad. The descendants of the Gadites and the Menasseites settled in Japan, and left their memory in Japanese surnames such as Cado, Tsuchimikado, Nakamikado, Omikado, and Menasseh, and in the name of a village, Menashe, in the province of Yamato. Oyabe also believed that the regalia of King Solomon, carried away by the Babylonians, reappeared among the imperial treasures of Japan that are kept in the temple at Ise. One item in this treasure is the sacred mirror, another is a small golden jar. When opened by one of the emperors, white smoke arose from the jar, which contained pulverized rice. This rice, according to Oyabe, is the manna, that mysterious food that nourished the Children of Israel in the desert of Sinai on their way to the Promised Land. It is of interest that according to Jewish legend a jar of manna was among the treasures hidden under the Temple in Jerusalem.

Dr. Chikao Fujisawa, professor at Nihon University, proclaimed similar ideas. Dr. Fujisara gave a strange list of characteristics that, he believed, Shintoism and Judaism had in common: They were both a national faith, both were originally polytheistic but developed into monotheism, both hoped for the realization of world peace and universal brotherhood, both abstained from proselytizing, and both did not detach religion from politics because the spiritual and the material alike are manifestations of the Holy.

Ikuro Teshima, founder of the Makuya sect, which strongly identifies with Israel, had his own views about the relation between the Japanese and the ancient Israelites. Teshima, a follower of the Nestorian Church known in Japan as The Luminous Religion, connected the Japanese, whose ancient origin was outside of Japan, with the Israelites, through the place-name Taka-ama-hara—the Plain of High Heaven—identified in several places in Japan. This name derives, so Teshima says, from Takhla Makhan, a plateau in Central Asia, from where people migrated along the Silk Route both eastward, to China and then to Japan, and westward to Palestine. Thus the Japanese did not descend from the Israelites, but rather both had the same primeval origin. As proof of this startling theory Teshima quoted Dr. Tanemoto Furuhata, an authority on the study of blood, who believed that the types of blood and serum of Japanese people are closest to those of the inhabitants in Palestine. He suggested that the Israelites migrated to Japan in the form of the latecoming Hadas tribe, one of the many western tribes that crossed over to Japan at one time or another. This Jewish or Israelite tribe was most important to the development of Japan. Its members, said Tashima, have introduced to Japan their financial skills and also such typical Jewish crafts as cultivating silk cocoons and weaving silk, horse breeding, falconry, whale fishing, and bronze casting. Through them the royal house of Japan had strong Jewish connections. Moreover, upon close examination of the facial features of the Imperial Family, one notices Jewish features, so much so that it was found that the Prince Ayamoro Konoe, the late Premier of Japan, looked like a European Jew. This also explains, in Teshima's view, many details of Japanese life, such as the use of certain Hebrew words in Japanese children's songs, and the typical long Jewish noses on masks used in certain folk rituals. His belief in the strong connection between Japan and Israel led Teshima, who added the Hebrew name Abraham to his Japanese name, to became a true and warm friend of Israel, and to establish the Makuya, "Tabernacle," sect, which maintains an ongoing and supportive relationship with the State of Israel.

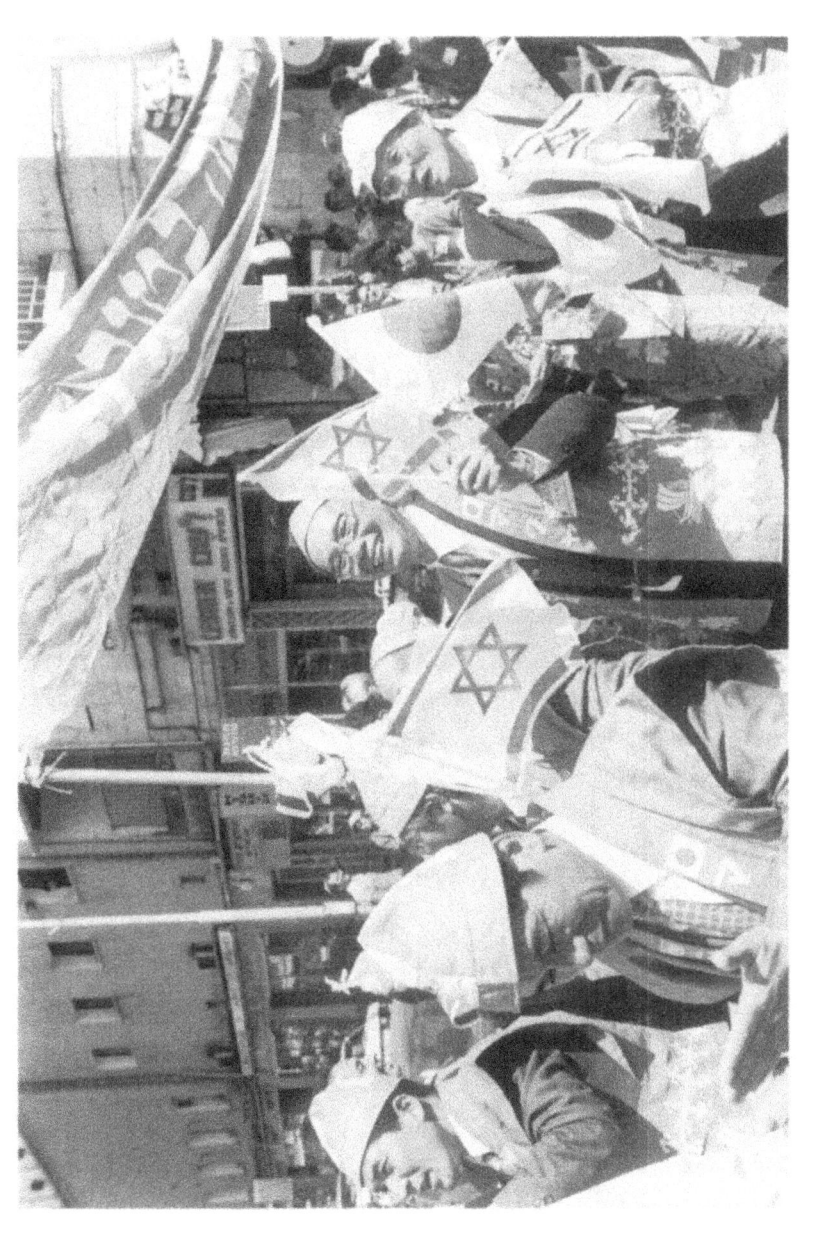

Figure 29: Professor Avraham Tashima, head of the Makoya sect, 1973.

Figure 30: Japanese pilgrims of the Makoya Sect in Jerusalem, 1986.

Several Jews and Israelis warmly accepted the Japan–Israel connection, and at least one, Joseph Eidelberg, responded in a book of his own. Eidelberg repeated several of the points of connection between the Japanese and the ancient Israelites mentioned above, and presented an original suggestion that the migration of the Japanese from the Asian mainland under Tennu Jimmu was none other than the Japanese version of the exodus from Egypt. Eidelberg relies mainly on sound similarity of place-names and words between Japanese and Hebrew—from biblical to modern—as well as archaic Aramaic.

7

The Thrust to the West— How the Israelites Got to Britain

In the personal column of the *Daily Telegraph*, there appeared one day a small advertisement:

> The Lost Tribes of Israel. Who and where are they in today's world? For free literature, write to: Identity Information, Freepost, Glasgow G12 8BR.

A letter to that address produced a pamphlet named *The Bible History and Britain*. On its cover was a map of Great Britain with the name ISRAEL printed over it in bold letters. The pamphlet, published by a group known by the name British Israelites, gave its readers a concise version of their belief that the Ten Tribes of Israel have never been lost. In fact they migrated to the British Isles, where they became the ancestors of the people of Britain. The pamphlet also claimed that this "prophetic persuasion" that flourished in Britain in the nineteenth and early twentieth centuries was still thriving in "Great Britain and Ireland, in the white Commonwealth, namely Australia, New Zealand, Canada, and Southern Africa, as well as in the United States, Holland, and the Scandinavian countries, in which countries it has many adherents." Moreover, the name British itself is ample testimony of its Israelite connection, as it derives from the Hebrew "brit ish"— meaning man of the covenant.

Proof by success: the motto of British Israelism

British Israelism is a movement that, around 1900, captured the imagination of about two million people in Europe and America. It developed in the nineteenth century, in an attempt to explain the amazing fact that Britain had risen to an unexpected height of economic and military success. Throughout the nineteenth century, Britain's economy, molded by the Industrial Revolution, expanded further and further. Much of the country's wealth was allocated to the building and strengthening of its naval and military supremacy, and to the creation of a vast empire. This Victorian period, a time of great optimism in Britain, was also an era of religious and moral conservatism, that encouraged the development of several fundamentalist Christian movements. British Israelism was one such group. This group drew on the longstanding strong sentiments of the British toward the Bible. Having read the Bible with great care, and taking it to be the only reliable source of wisdom, the British Israelites believed they discovered in it the explanation to the unique success of Victorian Britain. The British Israelites were aware of the enigma of the unfulfilled promise for the return of the Ten Tribes of Israel on the one hand, and were wondering about the seemingly unaccountable and therefore somewhat disturbing circumstances of the great success of contemporary Britain on the other. To solve this dual problem, they came up with a simple, neat, and creative idea that combined the ancient past with the present—Britain was Israel. The Lost Tribes were never really lost, claimed the British Israelites, and should not be sought in remote parts of the world. The solu-tion to their disappearance was simple. One had only to look inward and find the tribes, or rather their descendants, right within, in Britain itself.

The British Israelites thus uncovered the hidden design behind the events and circumstances of their own time. To their thinking, the phenomenal military and economic success of nineteenth-century Britain could not be explained by earthly processes. It had to have a higher reason, and, true to their fundamentalist views, they found it in the one and only valid reference source—the Bible, which contains ample promises and vivid descriptions of the success that will come to the chosen people—the Israelites—in the future. Indeed, these promises were originally conferred upon Israel, but they were wholly and clearly fulfilled in Britain, proving that the two were one and the same. By virtue of its success, the British nation proved that it drew upon itself the divine promises. The fast and amazing rise of Britain from a nation of five million peasants in the sixteenth century to a world power that ruled over the vastest empire in world history, could be explained only as the fulfillment of God's promises to Israel through its direct descendants—the British. Success became the best proof that Britain was the true inheritor of the divine promises, and thus the British obtained ancient and honorable roots in Israel. The seemingly dormant enigma of the Lost Tribes of Israel, and the promise for their return to a glorious fate, took a surprising political twist. It was used as an ideological basis not only for explaining the contemporary world, but for promoting a sense of national pride, even nationalistic sentiments, among the British.

To establish the validity of this extraordinary theory, the ideologists of British Israelism set out to construct a historical framework, making use—or rather misuse, as their opponents pointed out time and again—of a body of historical, anthropological, and archaeological data. They aimed to demonstrate how the Israelites migrated from the Near East to the farthest extremes of Europe, and how they became British.

Early Notions of British-Israelite Connections

The British Israelite movement was not the first to suggest hidden connections between Israel and Britain. Such notions had been in vogue long before the formation of a complete ideological framework and of an official organization for its propagation. Although explicit formulations of such notions are scarce, those that exist are enough to indicate the particular inclination of the inhabitants of the British Isles toward the Bible, and their claim that this entitles them to a unique position among the Christian nations. Such were the sentiments that eventually gave birth to British Israelism.

Protestantism, introduced to England by Henry VIII in the sixteenth century, was instrumental in making the Bible accessible to the people, who could not read it in Latin as was ordered by the Catholic Church. The Protestant Church encouraged efforts to translate the Bible into the English vernacular, efforts that culminated in the popular and much cherished King James Bible, published in 1611. But attempts to translate the Bible into English had been made already several hundred years earlier, when England was still Catholic. In the 1380s the priest John Wycliff and his disciples translated the Bible in its entirety from the Latin translation known as the Vulgate. At that time this act was considered a severe offense against the church. The contemporary church historian Thomas Fuller wrote of one of the translators that he could not decide whether to admire him for "his ability that he could, his courage that he darest or his industry that he did perform so difficult and dangerous a task."

Interestingly, already in the fifteenth century a connection was explicitly suggested between promises made to Israel and the fate of Britain. William Tyndale (ca. 1494–1536), the first Protestant who translated the New Testament and sections of the Old Testament into English, viewed England as a covenant nation, like ancient Israel. He believed that the Reformation was an opportunity to renew that covenant, and benefit from the fulfillment of the divine promises that will be manifested by temporal prosperity. Tyndale thus unwittingly prophesied the creation of the British Israel movement several centuries later.

Puritanism, that unique English version of extreme Protestantism that ruled England in the sixteenth and seventeenth centuries, carried the biblical fervor, centered in particular around the Old Testament, to new and extreme heights. The Puritans, who viewed themselves as descendants of ancient Israel, adopted biblical names, used Hebrew phrases in everyday speech, and went as far as consulting the Bible in military and political affairs. John Sadler, a Puritan, man of law, noted scholar, and member of parliament, studied the English constitution and found in it many parallels to biblical law. Although Sadler did not say so explicitly, he implied that such similarities could be explained only by a direct line of transmission from Israel to Britain. Sadler expressed ideas that eventually came to fruition in 1653, when the English parliament adopted the law of Moses as the constitution of England. Sadler was a friend of Oliver Cromwell, Puritan ruler of England, and it is possible that he shared his views of a connection between Britain and Israel with Cromwell. This is perhaps the reason that Cromwell viewed favorably the petition made by Manasseh Ben Israel to admit the Jews back to England. In fact, Sadler actually mentioned the petition in his book. The motivation for

Manasseh Ben Israel's petition may sound strange to us today, but it was well grounded in the climate of the time.

Manasseh Ben Israel and the return of the Jews to England

The Jews were expelled from England in 1291, and for hundreds of years no Jew was granted permission to return. The expulsion from England was neither the first in the history of Europe, nor the last. The most traumatic such episode took place in 1492, when the large, ancient, and well-established Jewish community of Spain was ordered to evacuate the country within three months. The exiled Jews found refuge in Portugal and in countries around the Mediterranean. Later, when Portugal forced its Jews out, some moved to Holland, which toward the end of the sixteenth century freed itself from Spanish rule. The Jewish community of Amsterdam grew in number and wealth, maintaining active commercial relations with its co-religionists around the world, to the benefit of its host country. Manasseh Ben Israel, the venerable rabbi of sixteenth century Amsterdam, received news that the Ten Lost Tribes had been discovered in America (chapter 8). This good news prompted him to approach Cromwell with the claim that, because the Jews were not allowed to settle in England, England was actively obstructing the advent of the Messiah. The Messiah would come, according to biblical prophecies, only when Israel would be scattered all over the world. Cromwell, a devout Puritan well versed in the Bible, supported Manasseh Ben Israel's petition, and in 1655, despite parliament's hesitation, opened negotiations toward the return of the Jews to England. While the negotiations were going on, the English–Dutch war broke out, followed by the English–Spanish war, and the fulfillment of Ben Israel's vision was postponed.

Saxon–Israel and Celtic–Israel connections

The origins of the belief in hidden connections between Israel and Britain can be found in a much earlier period, in the Saxon era. The Saxons believed that the pedigree of their Queen Matilda, of the Saxon line of Edgar Aetheling, was traced to the Patriarchs of Israel. Such notions were probably related to the spread of Christianity among the Saxons, the more literate among whom undoubtedly read the Vulgate. That they actually were well versed in the Bible, and even in later Jewish literature, finds proof in a rather surprising way. In the seventh century there lived near Whitby monastery in Northumbria a humble herdsman known by the name of Caedmon. This man, on whom God bestowed the power to compose religious verse, is the first known English poet of the Christian era. Four of his books—*Genesis, Exodus, Daniel, and The Sufferings of Satan*—have survived. The books *Genesis* and *Exodus*, poetic renderings of complete chapters of the first two books of the Bible, abound with details not found in the original Hebrew text. A meticulous study of these details revealed that they are based on postbiblical Jewish literature of the first centuries of the first millennium, not many years before the date of Caedmon's compositions. Caedmon's deviations are based mainly on the Midrash—explanations of the Bible through legends—which is part of the Talmud, as well as on Hebrew liturgical poetry. It is not known in what way, or by whom, this Jewish literature found its way to seventh-century England. It must have been introduced through the church, as there is no record of a Jewish community in England at that time.

Perhaps already in these early days the English developed their special relationship with the Scriptures, and found, or rather invented, contacts between pre-Saxon, Celtic England and ancient Israel. To this type of presumed connections belongs the story that Joseph of Arimathea, a disciple of Jesus, who offered to bury Jesus in his family sepulchre, migrated to England, and lived, preached, and was buried in Glastonbury. Another legend tells of a boat that landed on the shores of Ireland carrying the prophet Jeremiah and a young girl of Davidic descent, who was to become the ancestor of the British ruling house. The same boat brought also the stone on which Jacob laid his head while dreaming of the ladder that connected heaven with earth. This became the Stone of Scone, placed to this day under the coronation chair of the British monarchs.

These early beliefs, as well as those of the Puritans and others in later periods, were only nebulous inclinations, not actually translated into concrete identification of the British with the Ten Lost Tribes of Israel. This idea was a later creation, first propagated by the flamboyant, self-declared prophet Richard Brothers, who paved the way to the crystallization of these vague ideas into the powerful ideology of British Israelism.

Richard Brothers: the mad prophet

Richard Brothers was a remarkable character who lived the stormy life of a self-made prophet. Pope's lines, "Virtue's self may too much zeal be had/The worst of madmen is a Saint run mad," may well apply to the fate of this singular personality. Brothers was not the originator of the ideas that later became known as British Israelism, but he was the person who formulated them with great force, and popularized them among the common people of England.

Born in Newfoundland, Canada, in 1758, Brothers came to England as a boy and joined the British navy, where he became a lieutenant. He fought in several naval battles, and after the signing of peace treaties with the American colonies, with France, and with Spain, he retired and joined the merchant marine. His eccentricities were first noticed when he married in 1786 and left his wife on the wedding night to rejoin his ship. He then moved to London, where his truly bizarre nature began to unfold. He rented a room in one Mrs. Green's house, but had no money to pay his rent, because he obstinately refused to take an oath to the Crown required in order to collect his meager pension. His landlady brought him to court, but did so quite reluctantly, being so impressed by his behavior. "Mr. Brothers," testified Mrs. Green, "lodged in my house two years. I never saw a more pious, just and generous man. The last twelve months he never went over the threshold." The Guardians of Westminster, before whom he was tried, were also greatly impressed. "His appearance," wrote one of them, "prejudiced me greatly in his favor. He seemed about thirty, tall and well-formed, and in his manner such mildness and gentility." His gentle appearance apparently did not foretell his developing madness, reflected in the wild ideas he already held at that time. Brothers was put in a poorhouse, was later able to rent another room, again failed to pay the rent for the same reason, and was imprisoned. This pattern would have repeated itself, had Brothers not proclaimed his mad views, which eventually led to his confinement in an asylum.

Richard Brothers: prophet to the Jews

Brothers's views were formulated during his long periods of seclusion, when he shut himself up in his room with his Bible. He saw visions of Satan walking through the bloody streets of London, doomed by God to be destroyed completely. Brothers prayed fervently, and after thirteen days succeeded to avert God's anger and save the city. This vision recurred, to be averted again in the same manner. Brothers also deciphered the code of biblical arithmetic, and calculated the time for the coming of the millennium. He believed that the world would last 7,000 years, which in heavenly terms equals one week. As the six weekdays are followed by the Sabbath, likewise 6,000 years will be followed by a millennium of peace, due any minute. Through his contemplation of the approaching millennium, Brothers became aware of the place of the Jews in the divine scheme, and of the problem of the Ten Lost Tribes of Israel. If the millennium was indeed at hand, the Jews and the Lost Tribes alike would soon return to their homeland. But where were those tribes? After some deliberation, and for unexplained reasons, Brothers declared they were in Britain, and proclaimed that when the moment came, thousands of British families would discover their forgotten origins and start on their way to their ancestral Promised Land. Brothers knew who was the leader who would guide this great multitude of Jews and Israelites to Zion, and then rule the entire world from Jerusalem. He did not have the slightest doubt that "I am the Prophet that will be revealed to the Jews to order their departure."

In 1794 Brothers proclaimed his ideas to the world in a book, which revealed a very tight schedule for the great occurrences he foresaw. On July 1, 1795, he was to march into Istanbul at the head of the Israelite army, and on November 19 of that year he was to be crowned in Jerusalem as king of the world. This timetable left very little time for preparations. Three months after his first book he published a second part to his book, which contained the following astonishing passage:

> The Lord commands me to say to you, George II, King of England, that, immediately on my being revealed to the Hebrews as their Prince, and to all the Nations as their Governor, your crown must be delivered up to me, that your power and authority may cease.

Interestingly, except for this proclamation, Brothers did nothing to organize for the coming events, no doubt relying on the divine power to do the work for him.

The amazing success of Richard Brothers's ideas

Brothers's ideas gained immediate success among the common people of England, a success that can be explained only against the background of the stormy events of the time. The French Revolution of 1792 was now in the third year of its reign of terror. England, trembling at the possibility that the slogans of freedom and the rule of the guillotine would spread across the Channel, wondered if it was wise to intervene in France and restore the old order. Into this frenzied atmosphere of disorder and unrest came a man who promised an immediate and everlasting solution to all problems, solutions not based upon human whim but upon the most solid of foundations—the Bible. Brothers's publications became immediate best-sellers. Simple people, small tradesmen, craftsmen of all sorts, ladies of fashion, royal dukes, and even clergymen congregated around his lodging to catch a glimpse of the new prophet and hear his voice. Brothers had attracted several distinguished disciples, such as Nathaniel Halhed, a member of parliament and orientalist of fame, and William Sharp, an engraver of European reputation. On his engraving of Brothers's portrait Sharp wrote: "Fully believing this to be the man whom God has appointed, I engrave his portrait." Foreseeing the great demand for pictures of Brothers upon being crowned, shrewd Sharp made two plates of the same engraving.

Brothers no doubt had a natural talent for public relations. He ordered every one of his followers to publish in print a testimony of his belief. In the years 1794–1795 an endless string of pamphlets was printed, bearing such names as *A Testimony concerning Richard Brothers*; *A Testimony concerning the Spirit of Truth*; *Corroborating Proof from the Holy Scriptures of the Truth of the Chronology of the World*; *Prophecies Fulfilled*; *Crumbs of Comfort for the People*. There were also such publications as *The Lying Prophet Examined in his False Predications Discovered, being a Dissection of the Prophecies of Richard Brothers*, but they were pitifully few. Newspapers carried debates and caricatures, and Brothers was the most talked about person in England.

But soon the government intervened. Brothers himself may have been a harmless lunatic, but the government feared that the tumult he aroused might be used by supporters of the dreaded French Revolution. Brothers was arrested, declared insane, and confined to an asylum. His devout supporter Halhed immediately demanded his release, and moved in the Commons to have Brothers' books put before the House. The move was not seconded, nor was a second move made a month later, to have Brothers's case heard again before a full House. Brothers remained in the asylum for eleven years, in the course of which he failed to keep his appointments in Istanbul and Jerusalem, and lost most of his disciples. Nevertheless, the untiring Brothers continued to write and publish. The most curious of his late publications contained an imaginary description of Jerusalem. Obviously Brothers was still hoping to go to Jerusalem, which needed a total reshaping for the role it was about to play. It is amazing that even then, when Brothers was confined and almost abandoned, his publisher George Riebau still called himself "Bookseller to the King of the Hebrews." After eleven years in the asylum Brothers was released, a disillusioned man. For the remaining years of his life Brothers was tended to by his loyal supporter John Finleyson.

Brothers is nowadays all but forgotten, but during the brief period of his prophetic activity he kindled interest in the fate of the Lost Tribes of Israel, and helped spread the notion that they were to be found in Britain. He thus prepared the ground for the creation, many decades after his death, of British Israelism.

The ideology of British Israelism

Richard Brothers's ideas were carried on by his friend John Finleyson, a Scottish lawyer, who in 1849 published a book in which he set out to discover the hidden Hebrews, who were destined to proceed to the Holy Land and build the New Jerusalem. Finleyson, being perhaps more generous than his master, believed that

> Nearly all the Germans, English, Lowlanders of Scotland, Easterlings of Ireland, are the descendants of the Hebrews. But two thirds of France

are also so, as well as the Persians and those of the Barbary States, one half of the Russians, Poles, Swiss, Italians, Spaniards and Greeks are so, and they abound in the Turkish Empire and adjoining states, and even in China, Japan and Ethiopia, nearly all the North Americans are so. . . .

He added to the list also the Mexicans and Peruvians.

Ralph Wedgwood, who, independently of Brothers and his followers, had published already in 1814 a book in which he explained the events of his own times, and in particular the victory over Napoleon, in the light of the prophecies of the books of Daniel and Revelations, had more exclusive views. The book included a special chapter devoted to the "Evidence that the British Empire was the peculiar possession of the Messiah." To Britain "The Bow of Ephraim, which has bode in strength—Messiah's promised Possession and Naval Dominion." Wedgwood was thus the first to explain Britain's rising position in the world in the light of biblical promises, and he therefore insisted that Britain, and Britain alone, was the beneficiary of divine guidance. In this sense he was a true forerunner of British Israelism.

John Wilson, an Irishman, son of a radical Kilmarnock weaver, was truly the creator of British Israelism as an organized movement. From 1840 until his death in 1871, Wilson toured Ireland and England, delivering lectures on the identity of the North European nations, and of England in particular, as the descendants of the Lost Tribes of Israel. He published his lectures in a book that won great popularity and enjoyed numerous reprints. Wilson suggested that the modern nations of Europe, and especially the English nation, lineally descended from the lost son of Ephraim, and thus they not only contain the main body of Israel but are literally that people.

This idea of an actual, physical continuation of Israel was a daring deviation from the accepted Christian dogma that the church, and through it all Christians, were the spiritual inheritors of Israel and thus entitled to the benefits of all promises. Now it was up to Wilson and his followers to prove that a direct connection between ancient Israel and Britain was at all possible, and to do just that they began to study the movements of the various tribes that migrated to Britain and created its present-day population.

Figure 31: The Four Past Great World Empires and the fifth (indestructible) Stone Kingdom.

"Our Scythian ancestors identified with Israel"

This title, the name of an article by Colonel Gawler, Keeper of the Crown Jewels at the Tower of London, sums up the ideas developed by the British Israelites in their attempt to find the missing link between Israel and Britain. Ingeniously, this link was believed to be found with the Scythians, those Central Asian tribes, whose history, the opinions of Greek and Roman historians who wrote about them, and the way in which they were connected with the ancient Israelites have already been described (chapter 4). In an ingenious way the British Israelites managed to tie these Scythians/Israelites with the Britons.

The Scythians were known to different peoples by a variety of similarly sounding names. "The Persians," says the Greek historian Herodotus, "call all the Scythians Sakai." Other writers called them Sakans, Saccassani, or Saccassuni. Gawler added to this list the name Saxons, although historically, the Saxons were a Germanic tribe that crossed over from the European continent to Britain during the early centuries of the first millennium, and became a dominant component in its population. Gawler added to the list also the name Scots, as yet another variant of Scythians. For the Scythian–Scottish connection Gawler quotes an Irish legend that "they were called Scoti from their leader Ebur Scut, or Ebur the Scythian, latinized Scoti."

Paradoxically, the Israelites, through the Scythians, were assumed not only to be the ancestors of the Saxons and Scots, but also of the Celts, the ancient people who inhabited the British Isles prior to the invasion of the Saxons and other Germanic tribes. This identification was based not on the Scythian connection, but on the similarity of the ancient name of the Celtic Welsh—Cymbri—with the Cimmerians, nomadic Central Asian tribes who roamed the areas later occupied by the Scythians. The expanding Scythians dealt them a virtual death blow and inherited their territory. The British Israelites connected the Cimmerians with the Khumri tribe mentioned by the Assyrian, and suggested these Khumri, or Cymbri, were none other than descendants of Omri king of Israel, after whom the Assyrians named the entire Israelite nation. And thus both the Cimmerians and their conquerors the Scythians were viewed as issue of the same Israelites, and they both were ancestors of the various tribes that inhabited Britain. The Scythians, sons of Isaac, became the Saxons and the Scots; the Cimmerians, sons of Omri, became the Celts.

But this is not yet the end of the story, as the Celts were believed also to be connected specifically to the Israelite tribe Gad, and through them to the Germanic Goths. This identification was made by way of the Getae, another tribe that invaded Britain. The Getae are mentioned in several ancient sources as being close to the Scythians, sometimes even interchangeable with them. When Darius king of Persia led his expedition against the Scythians in 500 B.C., he is said to have encountered the Getae on the southern bank of the river Danube, and the Scythians on the northern bank. During the expedition of Alexander the Great, however, the people on both banks of the Danube were referred to as Getae. Both the Roman historian Strabo and the Roman poet Virgil described these Getae as hairy, unshorn, clad in skins, inhuman, sturdy, stern, wearing long side breeches and mantles (like our Irishmen, remarked Gawler). Pliny the Elder, another Roman historian, says that they used to paint their faces (as did our Britons, noted Gawler). The British Israelites identified the Getae with the Goths, not only on the similarity of the name, but, as Gawler suggested, because the "finest turned arches" employed by the Scythians to construct their burial mounds were "the direct ancestors of the Gothic arch and the Gothic style of architecture." The arrival of the Getae/Goths in England is based on the ninth century historian Nennius, who wrote that "three vessels from Germany arrived in Britain. They were commanded by Horsa and Hengest, brothers, the sons of . . . Folegule of Geta, who, as they say, was the son of god."

The Getae/Goths had been identified with the Israelite tribe of Gad because of the marked similarity of names, as well as by the Hebrew meaning of the name Gad, as in Genesis 30:11: "And Leah said a troop commeth (in Hebrew, ba gad), and she called his name Gad." "Now," says Gawler, "Bagach in Irish is warlike . . . Bagad in Welsh is multitude," and as both Irish and Welsh are Celtic languages, here is proof that the Getae/Goths/Gad were the ancestor of the Celts.

The tribe of Dan also became a great favorite of the British Israelites, who traced its wanderings far and wide throughout Europe, and eventually brought it to England. Dan was not only a judge of his people (Genesis 49:16) and thus very wise, but his people were also enterprising both on land and on sea. Members of the tribe mixed with the Phoenicians, intermarried with them, and took part in their seagoing trade. Wherever one traces the footprints of the Phoenicians, says Gawler:

There, or in close proximity, on the name of some place, river or province, the name of Dan is imprinted, as they did in their earliest independent conquest of Palestine. We have, then, on the Red Sea Dongola; in Greece Calydon, the Eri-dan, Make-don; the Danube, Dan-astris (now Dniester), Dan-apris (now Dnieper) and the Don . . . From Dan-astris, follow it to its source, where we pick up the Vistula, at the mouth of which is Dan-Zig at the shores of the Co-dan Gulf (now the Baltic), across the dannemora, opposite the Gulf of Finland; across the North Sea to the Humber, where we find the river Don, and go south to Doncaster. Then we find a whole country Dannonia, now Devonshire, and from thence we may cross to that undisputed head-quarters of the Dannans, the North of Ireland, anciently called Scotia, where we find an immense per centage not only of the names of places, but of the popular surnames, with the prefix Don, as Dundalk and Donaghadee. This last place, if not the earliest, is one of the earliest reputed settlements of the Tauth de Dannan: it has a sound remarkably Hebrew, and transliterated becomes Danhaghedee, "Dan is my witness." From ancient Scotia we pass over to modern Scotia, or Cale-don-ia, whose namesake we had in Greece. Here, among the host of others, we have Dumfries, Dumbarton (in these the letter n becomes m before the libial), Dundee and Aberdeen (mouth of the Don), and the river Don.

Gawler adds that there can be no doubt that Denmark is the land of the descendants of the tribe of Dan, and that the Danes actually claim as an ancestor or leader a renowned warrior named Dan.

The names of the other tribes of Israel, and in particular those of the house of Joseph, could not be readily found among the European tribes, and a direct descent from the Scythians or the Cimmerians or any other ancient tribe could therefore not be worked out. And yet, because they could not be left out of the picture, their identification with the English had to be based on methods more intricate and ingenious than simple similarity of names. John Wilson relates how he was struggling over the true meaning of the phrase "His bow abode in Strength" included in Jacob's blessing to his son Joseph (Genesis 49:24). Being at a loss for a satisfying explanation, he turned his attention to his children, who were pasting into their scrapbooks. They told him that they were collecting pictures of the battles of Crecy, Poitiers, and Agricourt, which the English won by putting to good use their superior longbows. In a flash of light Wilson understood the connection between the obscure biblical passage about Joseph and the English bow, and proclaimed the English descendants of the lost sons of Ephraim.

There is no need to point out that all these reconstructed names, events, dates, and places are mixed and mingled, and completely taken out of order and context.

Nationalism and biblical ancestry

In the early phases of the development of British Israelite ideas, the reconstruction of the tribal migrations that brought Israel to the west was not confined to the British Isles, but embraced all of northwestern Europe. In fact, the first official organization, the "Anglo-Ephraim Association" founded in 1871, was, despite its name, strongly "Teutonist" in its views. But before long, British national feelings began to object to the inclusion of the nations of the Continent in the Israel connection, mainly because of unrest and war in Europe, from which Britain was attempting to dissociate itself. While Europe was busy fighting, thus demonstrating that it had no place in the divine scheme, Britain was gaining in economic, naval, and military power, and building its empire. The British had proven that they were the true heirs of Israel, and were under no obligation to share this privilege. The all-European Anglo–Ephraim association was gradually losing ground to increasingly pro-British organizations that were formed in the late 1870s in Britain and Ireland. To strengthen the exclusivity of Britain under the covenant, the Bible was searched for revealing passages, which were given new meanings. Hoshea's prophecy that Israel will change its name (1:9) was understood to refer to the name Britain, as was Isaiah's reference to its dwelling in the islands of the sea (24:15). Promises for great strength (Micha 5:8), and extension beyond the former limits (e.g., Isaiah 49:19), were explained as pointing to the British Empire. Reference to the symbols of Britain—the unicorn and the lion—was found in Numbers 24:8–9, while promises that Israel shall possess the gates of her enemies (Genesis 22:17; 24:60) were seen fulfilled in Britain's possession of the important straits of Gibraltar, Aden, Singapore, and Hong Kong. For this reason Britain should also possess Istanbul, argued Dr. Wild, an ardent British Israelite.

While the Continent was losing favor in the eyes of the British Israelites, the Unites States was going from strength to strength. It had just completed the annexation of vast territories stretching from ocean to ocean, and was exploiting its enormous riches. It was growing in economic power and influence, and was clearly destined to become a world power. As the Pilgrim fathers and numerous settlers in the Unites States were of British origin, it was clear that the growing fortunes of that nation were part of the divine design. The Unites States was declared the tribe of Menasseh, to whom it was promised (Genesis 48:19) that it would become an independent nation, coequal with Ephraim (Britain). This partnership under divine promise had a great appeal to many in the young American nation, and British Israelism attracted many adherents there. American fervent advocates of British Israelism such as H. W. Poole spread the message in the New World. To this day the notion that they descended from the tribes of Israel is strong among many white, Protestant Americans, although they do not connect themselves with the British Israelite movement, about which they may not even have heard.

Connection by success was at one time extended even beyond the Anglo–American white world. When, soon after the announcement of the Anglo–Japanese Alliance of 1905, it became evident that Japan was growing into a major power, that country was for a short while considered the true Menasseh rather than the United States. Proof by success was the strongest ruling principle in nominating candidates for special connections with the divine.

During the First and Second World Wars the British Israelites took upon themselves to boost British morale, and distributed thousands of pamphlets aimed at strengthening Britain's self-confidence under divine protection. An excerpt from one such publication, *Britain's Triumphant Role*, published in 1942, reads:

> During the height of the Battle of Britain—at a time when in the eyes of the world the destiny of Britain seemed at stake—a Belgian doctor who had taken refuge in this country exclaimed: "Why are you British people so certain that Britain will not be defeated when all the evidence is to the contrary? Do not tell me that you have faith in victory. Give me a reason." It was at this moment that one realized as never before that the strength of British–Israel Truth is the fact that those who are endowed with the British–Israel vision can give a reason ... Our faith is made rational and reinforced by means of prophecy and its fulfillment which demonstrates that just as the prophecies of God regarding

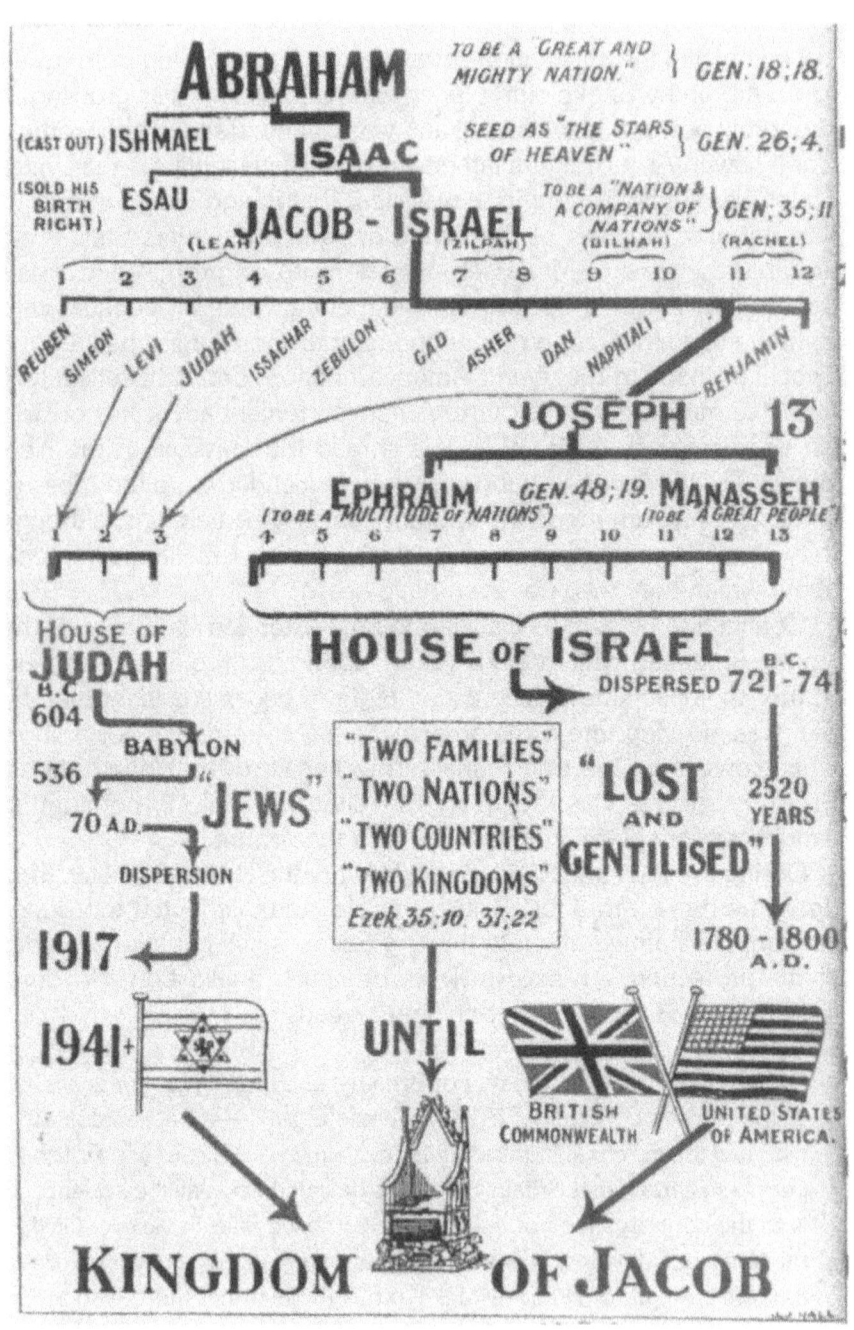

Figure 32: Geneology of the House of Israel, Great Britain, and the United States.

the past have been literally fulfilled so with complete assurance we may look to the fulfillment of the promises of God regarding the future.

Even the decline in the fate of Britain after World War II and the dismantling of the empire did not weaken the belief in its special destiny as the descendant of Israel. It is only a matter of time and a return to the Bible, claim present-day British Israelites, that Britain will see a renewal of its glory under the covenant, because "Britain is Israel."

8

The Red and the White— Israel in America

The discovery of America in 1492 brought about one of the most fascinating encounters between Europe, as represented by Spain, and a new, totally alien world. The meeting with completely unknown and unexpected "creatures" who inhabited the newly discovered lands caused a problem of identification to the conquerors: what were these locals—known first as Indians and now as Native Americans? Were they subhuman or human? How should they be treated? It seems that at first the Spaniards did not attribute human qualities to the Indians, and conducted against them campaigns of degradation, enslavement, and destruction, up to an almost complete annihilation of local populations in the newly conquered territories. Only toward the end of the sixteenth century Bartholome de las Casas, a much respected Catholic priest, bishop of the Mexican province of Chiapas, came out publicly against the attempt to mistreat the local population and destroy them and their cultures. In doing so las Casas strongly disputed the official policy of the Catholic Church and the Spanish Crown, and caused a reevaluation of the official policy toward the Indians.

Las Casas's appeal for a humane treatment of the Indians meant that they had to be officially included within the human race. This inclusion raised the question of their human origins, as, in the intel-

Engraving by Tomás López Enguidanos

Figure 33: Bishop Bartolome de las Casas.

The Red and the White—Israel in America

Figure 34: Persecuting idolaters.

lectual framework of the time, heavily dominated by clerical ideology, it could not be conceived that a people were without documented biblical origins. The need to discover an origin for the Indians, who were not mentioned explicitly anywhere in the Bible, became a serious theological problem, as it threatened the unshakable belief in the sacredness and all-inclusiveness of the Bible. The world at that time, and certainly the strong and belligerent Catholic establishment of sixteenth-century Spain, firmly believed that the Bible was the only reliable source of knowledge of ancient human history. The numerous people who inhabited the world as it was known prior to the discovery of America were all believed to have had Biblical origins. Humanity was neatly divided between the three sons of Noah—Shem, Ham and Japheth—survivors of the flood that annihilated all former humans. The descendants of Shem inhabited Asia; those of Ham, Africa; while the Europeans were the sons of Japheth. The American Indians were thus without human ancestry, without roots in the Bible. As it could not even be imagined that the Bible was guilty of oversight, and its sanctity could in no way be disputed, an early, biblical ancestry had to be quickly found for the newly discovered peoples. This problem was, in the words of Hubert H. Bancroft, so great

> . . . as if another world, upheaved, as it were, from the depth of the Sea of Darkness, was suddenly placed before the philosophers and especially the learned ecclesiastics.

Various theories regarding the possible origin of the American Indians were discussed in the course of the sixteenth and seventeenth centuries. There was no question that they must have originated in the Old World, the location of all known and sanctified world history. It was thus suggested that they were of Phoenician origin, the ancient Phoenicians having been renowned as great sailors; or perhaps they were Carthagenians—those Phoenicians who settled in North Africa and practiced human sacrifices as well as worshipped fire and water, as did the Indians. Others suggested they were descendants of the ancient Greeks, as a stone found in Peru had letters that "looked like Greek" engraved on it; and also, had not the Athenians of old fought the inhabitants of Atlantis, which could not have been situated far from America? The American Indians were also thought to have been offspring of Ophir son of Joktan (Genesis 10:26–29) because of the similarity of the names Ophir to Peru and Joktan to Jucatan. Other opinions attributed to them a Chinese origin, or an ancient Egyptian—builders of pyramids as were the Indians—or an Ethiopian, Trojan, or Scythian origin, or even, rather surprisingly, a descent from more modern peoples like the French, the English, or the Frisians of Denmark. But no theory gained greater popularity, and was discussed down to the minutest details, than that the American Indians were the descendants of the Ten Lost Tribes of Israel.

Israelites behind the Mountains Cordillerae

Perhaps the most touching and one of the best known accounts of the existence of descendants of ancient Israelites in America was written in 1652 by Menasseh Ben Israel, a noted scholar and religious personality of the Portuguese Jewish community in Amsterdam. Interestingly, in Ben Israel's account these Israelies were not identified with the American Indians but with a separate, different, and unidentified group of people. In the introduction to the pamphlet *Menasseh Ben Israel's Mission to Oliver Cromwell*, the author introduces his readers, in the vocabulary and spelling of his time, to a surprising story related to him by one Antonius Montezinus, who claimed to have encountered the Ten Lost Tribes of Israel in America. Ben Israel, being a learned person, had some doubts about the theories that circulated in his time of a possible connection between the Indians and the ancient Israelites:

> There are as many minds as men, about the original of the people of America and of the first Inhabitants of the new World, and of the West Indyes, for how many men soever they were or are, they came of those two, Adam and Eve; and consequently of Noah, after the flood, but that new World doth seem wholly separated from the old, therefore it must be that some did pass thither out of one (at least) of the three parts of the world sc. Europe, Asia and Africa; but the doubt is, what people were those, and out of what place they went. Truly, the truth of that must be gathered, partly out of the ancient Hy stories, and partly from conjectures; as their Habit, their Language, their Manners, which yet doe vary according to mens' dispositions; so that it is hard to find out the certainty.

Nevertheless, after enumerating the various opinions circulating in his days, Ben Israel concludes that:

> I having curiously examined what ever hath hitherto been writ upon this subject doe find no opinion more probable, nor agreeable to rea-

Figure 35: Menasseh Ben Israel.

son, then that of our Montezinus, who saith, that the first inhabitants of America, were the ten Tribes of the Israelites, whom the Tartarians conquered, and drove away; who after that hid themselves behind the Mountains Cordillerae.

The amazing story of Antonio Montezinus's firsthand encounter in America with the descendants of the Ten Lost Tribes was related to Menasseh Ben Israel and other leaders of the Jewish community of Amsterdam by Montezinus himself in the summer of 1644, two and a half years after the traumatic event. Montezinus was a converso, a Portuguese Jew formerly called Aaron Levi, who converted to Christianity under threats of the church and state of Portugal, but continued to practice Judaism in hiding. When in America, he was conducting a mule caravan from Port Honda in the West Indies (as all of what was known of America was called in those days) to the Province of Qu (perhaps Quito, Ecuador). He was accompanied by a group of Indians, one of whom was named Francis but called by all Cazicus. When they crossed the Mountains Cordillerae a great tempest occurred, which inflicted losses upon the caravan, losses that were interpreted by the Indians as punishment for their sins. Francis calmed them and told them that this was nothing compared to the punishment the Spaniards deserved for ill treating God's holy people. Montezinus, who was later imprisoned, suspected of being a secret Jew, was much intrigued with this remark, and in prison had a revelation that the Hebrews were in fact the Indians of his day. After being released he sought Francis, hoping to find more about his comment relating to the persecution of God's people. Eventually Montezinus located Francis and offered to go together on a trip to a remote place, where he confessed that he was a Hebrew of the Tribe of Levi. Francis asked many questions, and, being satisfied with Montezinus's answers, took him on a long and dangerous journey over the mountains. After many days they reached a big river, beyond which, Francis said, Montezinus would see his brothers. Francis waved a linen scarf, and on the other side rose a big smoke. Presently a small boat carrying three men and a woman came near. The woman came ashore while the men remained in the boat. After conversing at length with Francis in a language Montezinus did not understand, the three men came ashore and embraced Montezinus. Two of the men stood on each side of Montezinus, and quoted the Shema invocation in Hebrew. With the help of Francis as interpreter they conveyed to Montezinus the following, rather enigmatic messages:

> Their fathers were Abraham, Isaac, Jacob, and Israel, indicating this by lifting up three fingers. Then they added Reuben, adding another finger to the former three.

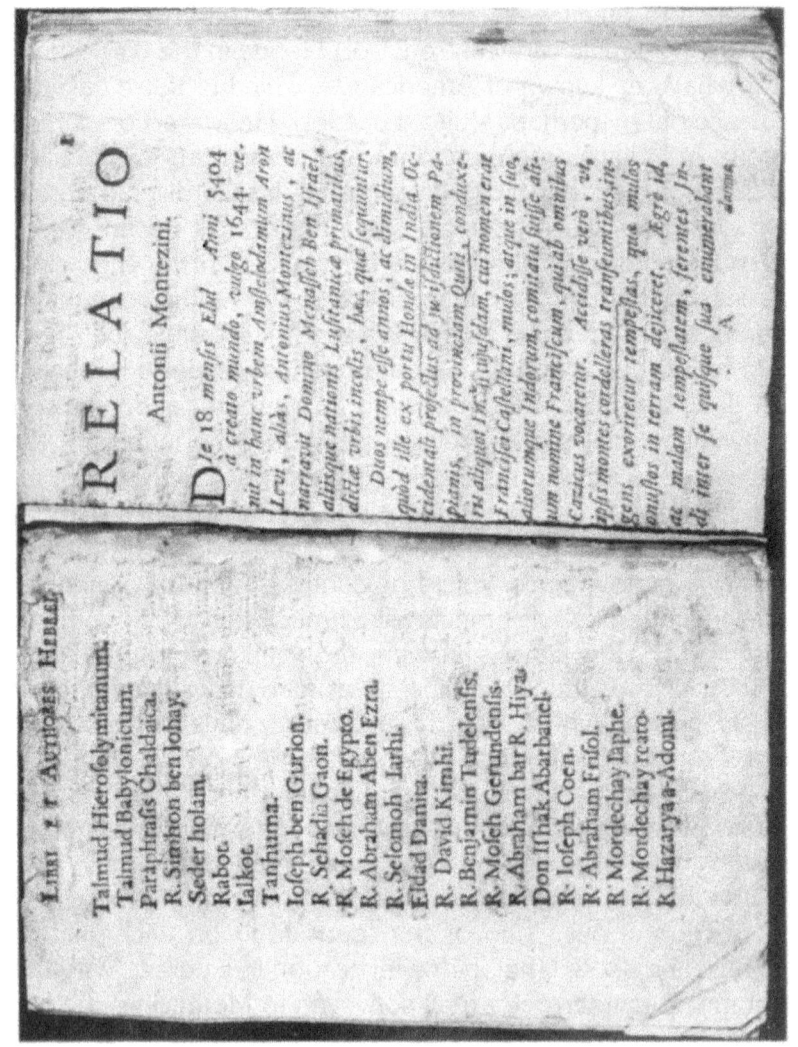

Figure 36: First page of the report of Antonio de Monte Zinos.

Figure 37: Domestic rituals of the Indians.

If someone wanted to come and live with them, they would give him a place.

Joseph lived in the middle of the sea. This they indicated by lifting two fingers together and then parting them.

With excitement they related that shortly they would go to see (someone) and tread (him) under foot. While saying this they winked and stamped their feet.

One day they would all talk together and come forth as if issuing out of mother earth.

A messenger would proceed them.

Francis would tell him more secrets.

They had to prepare themselves, and pray to God that they would not stay long.

They asked Montezinus to send twelve bearded men—indicating this with their fingers—skillful in writing.

The same delegation returned two more times, and repeated the same message, without adding a word and without answering Montezinus's questions. He tried to force himself into the boat but was cast out. The angry messengers warned him against passing the river or inquiring more about them. Other boats, each carrying four people, came and went, repeating the exact same words uttered by the original four messengers. After three hundred of them thus presented themselves to Montezinus, he received food and clothes, and left.

During the journey back Montezinus asked Francis to tell him more about his brothers. Francis related that he had received from his forefathers that these were the Sons of Israel, brought to this place by God. The Indians fought them, and treated them worse than the Spaniards now treated the Indians. With the idea of destroying these Israelite newcomers, the Indians raised three large armies, but none of the soldiers ever came back and no young man was left among them. Considering their terrible defeats, the Indians realized that the God of the Children of Israel was the true God, and that in the end of the days the Israelites would subdue the whole world as they had in the past. Realizing that it was best to make a treaty with the Israelites, five Indian chiefs (known as Cazici) undertook the mission, and negotiated through the above-mentioned woman. It was agreed, by penalty of death, that each side would keep to his own territory and not cross over to the other's, except that the five Cazici could visit the Israelite land every

Figure 38: Musicians and dancers.

seventy months. It was also agreed that secrets could be told only to one who was over three hundred months old; that these secrets could be told only in a desert, in the presence of the Cazici. This agreement was strictly kept. The Indians could approach the Israelites only if something outstanding occurred, and this happened three times in the lifetime of Francis: when the Spaniards came, when ships came from the South Sea, and when Montezinus came—who was long expected. Shortly afteward, the Indian Cazici began to believe that they themselves were also Israelites.

Montezinus also told Menasseh Ben Israel that three other Cazici came to see him in Port Honda and identified themselves as his brothers and promised that they would return and deliver him of his bondage.

It is not known who Montezinus was, and what his stories were based on. In a strange way one is reminded of the sudden appearance of Eldad the Danite, with his fabulous stories of the Ten Lost Tribes. As far as is known, nobody undertook to explore the issue, and search for the mysterious people who lived beyond a great river behind the mountains. Menasseh Ben Israel himself was skeptical, saying:

> If you aske, what is my opinion upon the relation of Montezinus, I must say, it is scarce possible to know it by any Art, since there is no demonstration, which can manifest the truth of it; much lesse can you gather it from Divine, or humane Writings; for the Scriptures doe not tell what people first inhabited those Countries. . . .

However, Ben Israel was convinced that Montezinus was an honest man, who kept his Jewish religion secretly despite the terror of the Inquisition, did not look for profit, and swore many times in the presence of venerable men, including on his deathbed, that his stories were true. Menasseh Ben Israel used the stories of Montezinus in his appeal to Oliver Cromwell, ruler of England at that time, to allow the Jews to return to England, from which they had been expelled some four hundred years before (chapter 7).

The Indians as Israelites

According to Montezinus, the Indians were not descendants of the Ten Tribes of Israel in America. As related in his report, the two peoples were apart, and at one time hostile relations even prevailed between them. However, when the parties signed a treaty, the Indian chiefs began to believe that they themselves were Israelites.

The testimony of Montezinus is the only "firsthand" account of the existence of descendants of the Ten Tribes of Israel in America, but they were not the Indians. The more conventional theory, discussed from the late sixteenth century onward, was that the Indians themselves descended from these Lost Tribes. It is possible that Bishop Bartolome de las Casas himself was the first to speculate on this matter, thus suggesting a solution to the vexing theological problem of the origins of an unaccounted-for people. Other possible originators were, not surprisingly, also Catholic clergymen, perhaps Father Duran, a native of Tezcucu in Mexico, who was active at the end of the sixteenth century, or Father Garcia, active at the beginning of the seventeenth century. Father Garcia frankly stated that his suggestion of the relation between the Indians and the Lost Tribes of Israel was not based on his own original research, but rather summarized the observations of others. He thus indicated that the search for connection between the two had been going on for quite a while. The Indian–Israelite theory was first written in English by the Reverend Thomas Throwgood in the middle of the seventeenth century, and won support among Protestant clergy working with the Indians of North America. Numerous others, especially explorers and clergymen, supported the Indian–Israelite theory, and added their own observations and publications to an ever growing library dealing with the subject. One of the most famous of these was Lord Kingsborough (Edward King), who, as late as the nineteenth century, devoted all his resources to propagate the theory in a nine-volume monumental work.

The great enthusiasm the Indian–Israelite theory aroused was caused first and foremost by the fact that it gave a respectable biblical ancestry to unaccounted-for people. It also catered to the hope that the conversion of the Indians to Christianity as Israelites, not as pagans, would hasten the Second Coming of Christ. Indeed Throwgood's theories inspired missionaries to the Indians in New England in their attempts to convert the Indians. It is therefore interesting that already shortly after the theory relating the Indians to the Israelites was published, it was disputed, some of its opponents being themselves members of the clergy. Friar Juan de Torquemada disputed the notion of an Israelite–Indian connection as early as 1615, while Throwgood's ideas were answered in 1651 by Sir Hamon L'Estrange.

The originators of the Indian–Israelite theory based themselves on a variety of clues, drawn from various sources. First they quoted biblical verses that mention that the exiled Israelites would be scattered in islands in the middle of the sea (Isaiah 60:9, Jeremiah 31:10, Psalms 97:1). Indeed America, or the West Indies as the newly discovered territories were called then, lay beyond the sea and also had many islands. Second, they based themselves on the fourth book of Esdras, the source of so many other theories regarding the whereabouts of the Ten Lost Tribes. Esdras described the escape of the Ten Tribes from their places of exile in Assyria, and gave the length of their journey—a year and a half—until they reached the uninhabited land Arzaret, where they settled. This journey, according to the Indian–Israelite theory, must have taken the tribes through Tartaria (as the whole of Central Asia was called at that time) to the eastern shores of Asia, from where they crossed the Straits of Anias (Bering Straits) to America.

Other clues in support of the Indian–Israel theory were based on observations and vivid imagination. Among them were clues from demography, namely that the large number of Indians corresponds to the prophecies of Hoshea that Israel will be as numerous as the sand on the seashore. The clues from linguistics were based on the observation that the language of the Indians is corrupted Hebrew, just as ancient Spanish is corrupted Latin. It was said that Cuba was the name of the chief of the first Israelite tribe who came to the island. The names of provinces, rivers, men and women, rituals, and other things were believed to be corrupted Hebrew words. In a similar vein were clues from social customs and anthropology: The Indians preserved all the customs of the Ten Tribes, some to a greater, some to a lesser degree. Some practiced circumcision; others washed themselves in the sea and rivers; some celebrated a jubilee every fifty years; still others did not touch the dead, or rent their garments on occasions of misfortune or death. Other tribes had rules of purification for women, or dismissed their wives and married others (divorce is forbidden to the Catholics). The chiefs of some tribes took many wives as in the Old Testament; others married their sisters-in-law if they were childless widows; others took interest on loans of money; and others, according to Micha 3:3, ate each other. Of course it was known that the Indians practiced also heretic customs, but these, so it was speculated, were adopted when they forsook their original biblical law.

Clues from religious practices were similarly interesting. Father Georgia Garcia maintained that both Israelites and Indians were reluctant to accept the miracles performed by Christ, and were therefore punished. The Jews were scattered over the entire face of the earth, while the Indians were persecuted and were rapidly being exterminated. In a similar vein, both people showed ingratitude for favors bestowed on them—the Israelites for favors from God, the Indians for favors granted them by the Spaniards. Kingsborough, to refer to only a few of his very long and detailed list of similarities, was convinced that the religions of the Israelites and the Mexican Indians were practically alike in their very foundations: Both believed in a supreme being, which was very similar in nature in both religions. At the same time both acknowledged a multitude of angels and other celestial beings, and both had an archdevil, with other devils by his side. Both sacrificed to gods and demons in temples and also on hilltops and under trees. Clues from behavioral patterns were also important. One Philippus de Utre, when visiting a province near Garracas, Venezuela, reported that he encountered two farmers who, instead of running away at the sight of his company of armed men, turned around and wounded de Utre with their spears. As the Indians were not known for their brave behavior, de Utre concluded that these farmers were Israelites whom God preserved in that place until the day of redemption. This is surprising, as others claimed that one of the traits similar to both the Indians and the Israelites was their cowardly nature. Father Garcia noted other behavioral traits that were common, in his opinion, to both the Indians and the Israelites. Bringing to the fore all his prejudices against the two people, he claimed that both did not show kindness to the poor, the sick, and the unfortunate, that both were despicable liars, idle, dirty, and boastful, and that both were sorcerers, swindlers, and vicious.

Archaeology supplied important clues. The vast sites and ruins encountered by the Spaniards, especially in Mexico and the Andean Mountains of South America, aroused their sense of wonder and opened new avenues of speculative thought. One such site, explored by one de la Vega, was located in Tiahuanaco in the Province of Collai in Bolivia. The huge site included large buildings and a very wide paved court with a huge chamber on one side, all surrounded by a thick wall. All these structures looked as if they were built of one stone; apparently the building-stones were laid tightly without mortar. The local Indians told de la Vega that that edifice was dedicated to the Maker of the World. That did not make sense, thought de la Vega, and boldly suggested that the whole complex was nothing but a synagogue built by the Israelites. He had sound reasons for this suggestion, as the Indians did not know the use of iron and therefore could not have cut such perfect stones. Moreover, they were idol worshipers, and could not have built a house to one supreme God. Similarly Petrus Cieza, who explored Peru, reported that in the city of Guamanga there were very large buildings, ruined when he visited the site and therefore very ancient. The local Indians told him that white, bearded people, who ruled this area long before the Indians, were the builders of these structures. To the mind of the explorers, these, and other magnificent ruins of America, must have been built by ancient Israelites of the Ten Lost Tribes.

Mythology also supplied clues: Many writers found similarities between stories of creation and ancient history of the Indians and the Israelites. Kingsborough, for example, maintained that stories of the creation of the world told by the Indians of Mexico were similar to those of the Israelites. He reported that the Indians, like the Israelites, believed that the origin of death was in a sin committed by the first man at the suggestion of a woman. Similarly both had versions of the stories of the tower of Babel and of a universal flood that destroyed the world. Even the events of the Exodus were supposed to have had their equivalent in America. Father Duran reported that he heard from some Old Indians, who heard it from their ancestors, that at some time in the past they were suffering hardships and persecutions, as were the Israelites in Egypt. A great man came to their rescue, became their leader, and persuaded them to flee into another land, as did Moses. In their flight they witnessed miracles like those that occurred to the Israelites during the Exodus: When they came to the seashore, the leader struck the water with a rod. The sea opened and they all marched through, and the enemies who pursued them were all drowned. Furthermore, another tradition, recorded in pictures, relates that while on the journey to the Promised Land they rested near a high mountain. A terrible earthquake occurred, and some wicked people were swallowed up into the earth, much like what happened to several Israelites who rebelled against their leader Moses during the wanderings in the desert.

Perhaps most surprising of all clues were rumors and reports circulating among the Indians of the existence in America in the distant past, prior to the arrival of the Spaniards, of tall, white, bearded men, as against the Indians who were of brown color and beardless. They perhaps echo early encounters with Vikings or other white people who landed on the shores of America. The Spaniards picked these stories from the native Indians, and turned them into yet another cornerstone in the Indian–Israelite theory. It is amazing that several Spaniards reported that they actually saw such white people in their own days, or at least heard that they existed. One reported that he encountered white, bearded people on the shore of the river Huariaga, a tributary of the Maragnon (the Amazonas). He related that they were well bred and clothed, lived in a large city, and were rich with gold and silver. Another explorer claimed that he heard of such people living on the banks of another river in the same general vicinity. Yet another report told of encountering white people in a plain on top of a high mountain range.

Interestingly, several ecclesiastics, including Father Garcia, speculated that the Indians were not a separate race from the tall, white people, but were in fact their descendants. Such a change of race could not have occurred naturally, and was, no doubt, a special act of God.

Israel and the Indians of North America

The exploration of North America was conducted later than that of Central and South America. Some of the explorers, being versed with the speculative Indian–Israelite theory, devoted themselves to look for similarities between the Indians they came to know and the ancient Israelites, using the same speculative methods used by the Spaniards. The North American Indians were mainly nomads, with a lower degree of civilization than those of Central and South America. Therefore the clues to their being of Israelite origin were of a somewhat different nature than those found for their more civilized brothers farther to the south.

Among the first to investigate the North American Indians and endorse the Indian–Israel theory was the eighteenth-century James Adair, a trader with the Indians, and resident in their country for forty years. Adair lived mainly in the southeastern regions of the United States, where he encountered wild tribes whom he considered to be "real red men." Some of Adair's arguments in favor of the connection between these people and the ancient Israelites were rather surprising. He suggested that the red color of the Indians was the result of climatic conditions. The hotter or colder the climate, he claimed, the greater proportion of the population had either red or white skin. Adair reported that he observed the Shawano tribe to be much fairer than the Chikkasa tribe that lived farther to the south. Many incidents and observations led him to believe that the Indian color is not natural, but that the external differences between them and the whites proceeded entirely from their customs and method of living, and not from their inherent nature. Their own tradition records them to have come to their present lands by the way of the west, from a far distant country, where there was no variegation of color in human beings. They were entirely ignorant of which was the first or primitive color. Adair believed that the fine red web under their outer skin, as against the fine web in whites, resulted from parching winds and hot sunbeams. In addition the Indians constantly smeared themselves with bear's oil mixed with a red substance, which alone could turn white skin into red even in adults. Adair believed that the general physiognomy was also a clue to the connection between the Indians and the Israelites. Much like Father Garcia, Adair had a low opinion of both, saying that whoever attentively views the features of the Indian, and his eyes, and reflects on his fickly, obstinate, and cruel disposition will naturally think of the Jews.

The social organization of both people seemed similar to Adair. As the Israelites were divided into tribes, so were the Indians. Each tribe in both cases had a chief, each formed a particular section of the nation, and each had its own badge or insignia. In both cases every individual was known by his family name. In every Indian encampment there was a central meeting place, where almost every night the chiefs met to discuss public matters, much as the Israelites did in their Sanhedrin (council of elders during the Second Temple period). Indian marriages, divorces, and punishments of adultery were very much like the Jewish laws and customs. So were their codes of punishments in general.

A similarity was observed also in the religious beliefs. Both people believed in one supreme living God, although the American Indians also believed in numerous gods, and the Israelites had a whole range of angels. The religious ceremonies of both were similar, as both did not worship images or idols. Adair found interesting similarities in the approach of both to death. The American Indians affirmed that there was a certain fixed time and place, when and where everyone must die, without the possibility of averting it; such was the belief also of the ancient Greeks and Romans, who were much addicted to copying the rites and customs of the Jews. Another important point of similarity was that both people believed that they were God's chosen and beloved people. This belief caused both to hate the rest of the world, and in turn to be hated and despised by all. The Indian religious practices, as well as their festivals and ceremonies, followed those of the Hebrews. Like the Israelites, the Indians had prophets, high priests, and lower priests. In the temples of their gods there was a Holy of Holies, as in the temple in Jerusalem. Similarly, some Indian tribes, as the Cherokee and others living on the banks of the Mississippi, had a portable temple that they carried around during their wanderings, as did the Israelites in the desert. The dress of the Indian high priest was similar to that of his Israelite equivalent. The Indians washed and dipped themselves frequently in rivers, had laws of uncleanness and purification, and abstained from unclean things, just as the Hebrews did. Their customs of purifying themselves and fasting before going to war also resembled those of the ancient Hebrews.

Linguistics was another avenue explored by Adair. According to his observations the Indian language and dialects appeared to have the "very idiom and genius of the Hebrew." The Indian words and sentences were expressive, concise, emphatical, sonorous, and bold, and often both in letters and signification synonymous with the Hebrew language. As for general customs, the Indians counted the time and had lunar months in the manner of the Israelites. Like the Israelites they believed that diseases occurred because of divine anger, and cured their sick in the same way. Both Indians and Israelites took great care to carefully bury the dead. The Indians gave their children names appropriate to their circumstances, as did the Israelites. The Indians, much like the ancient Israelites, were fond of decorating themselves with beads and other ornaments. They believed that these decorations were a preventive measure against every evil.

Adair was not alone in his belief in the Indian–Israelite theories. He was joined by others, some of whom claimed that all the North American Indians deserved this honor, while others pointed to specific tribes. It has been claimed that the Navajos in particular showed strong Hebraic traits. They led a peaceful, pastoral life; they had a strong aversion to hog's flesh; they believed that they came out of the water and would return to the water, instead of going to hunting grounds like other tribes. They had prophets and received revelations on particular days; they were keen traders; and they treated their women comparatively well. It is possible that these attributions seeped into the lore of the tribes of the southwestern United States, and surfaced in the declaration of my Zuni friend in Albuquerque that he and his tribe were descendants of the Ten Lost Tribes of Israel.

The missionary Charles Beaty, who was active among the Indians of the frontier lands of Pennsylvania, and west of the Allegheny Mountains in the 1760s, adds some interesting observations in support of the Indian–Israelite theory. He reports that he had taken pains to search into the usage and custom of the Indians, in order to see what ground there was for supposing them to be part of the Ten Tribes. He came to the conclusion that, to his not small surprise, a number of their customs appeared so much to resemble those of the Jews, that he wondered whether the Indians were not indeed descendants of the Ten Tribes.

Beaty observed that among the Indians he came to know, the women conducted themselves according to the Law of Moses. They totally separated themselves for seven days during their monthly period, or after they delivered a child, after which they bathed themselves, and washed all their clothes and utensils. The Indians also observed feasts similar to those of the Israelites. They had a Feast of the First Fruit, during which twelve elders divided a hunted deer and a cake made of new corn into twelve parts, held it up, and prayed for bounty. They had a public feast with elements similar to Passover. Much meat was distributed to the participants and guests, but what was left was burned. Some tribes, however, did not eat the hollow thigh of a deer but cut it off and threw it away, just as the Jews extract the thigh sinew of ritually slaughtered animals. The Indians also consulted prophets upon any extraordinary occasion. Old people related that circumcision was once practiced among the Indians, but this custom fell into disrepute. No people in the world, perhaps, had a higher sense of liberty than the Indians and the ancient Israelites. Both were fearless warriors. The Indians had a tradition that they once possessed a book, and as long as they kept it and acted according to it, their God was kind to them. In their old country they sold the book to white people, and began to decline. God took pity on them and directed them to America.

The evidence of relics:

As in Central and South America, ancient relics discovered in various places in North America supposedly carried Hebrew inscriptions, adding credence to the belief in the Indian–Israelite theory. One Joseph Merrick, Esq., reported that in 1815, when he was leveling some ground on a place named Indian Hill in Pittsfield, Pennsylvania, he discovered a black strap about six inches long and one and a half inches wide. It was folded over, and had a loop at each end. Although the piece was very hard he managed to unfold it and discovered that it was formed of two strips of thick rawhide sewed together with sinews. It contained four folded pieces of written parchment. One was torn to pieces by his curious neighbors, the other three were sent to Cambridge (Massachusetts? England?), where it was declared that the inscriptions were biblical verses written in Hebrew with pen and ink. It seems almost certain that this relic was an old phylactery lost by some local Jew.

A second discovery was made in Ohio around the middle of the nineteenth century. About eight miles southeast of Newark there was a large pile of loose stones, from which the settlers took construction materials. Eventually the mound was excavated, and found to contain a burial in a wooden coffin. At some depth under the burial a stone casket was found, in which was a small slab of hard stone of fine quality. On the face of the slab was scratched a figure of a man with a long beard, dressed in a long robe. Over his head and on the back side and edges of the slab were characters. The stone was shown to a clergyman in Newark, who pronounced the writing to be the Ten Commandments in Hebrew. The whereabouts of both objects is not known, and the decipherment of the inscriptions cannot be verified. If indeed they ever existed, they most probably did not belong to pre-Columbian times.

The Mormons

The story of the Mormons (or the Church of Jesus Christ of the Latter-Day Saints by its official name) is another angle of the belief in the existence in America of early Israelites, brought there by the grace of God. The story strongly reflects the reverent, not to say utopian, attitude of many waves of migrants to the Promised Land, to America, "a land which is choice above all other lands" (II Nephi 1:5). It also presents a most ingenious explanation to the origin of the American Indians.

According to the Book of Mormon, the events relating to the earliest population of America began with the Tower of Babel. When mankind was scattered to all corners of the world as a punishment for building the tower, God aided the Jaredites, sons of Jared, five generations removed from Adam, to cross the ocean and land in America. They were the first settlers of the continent. With time they forgot God's favor and did evil, and so, six hundred years before the birth of Christ, were destroyed. The next wave of migrants were Hebrews who left Jerusalem in the first year of the reign of Zedekiah king of Judah, and traveled eastward until they reached the big ocean. They crossed the ocean by boat, and landed on the western coast of South America. Several years later they were joined by other Jerusalemites who came after the destruction of their city by the Babylonians.

Once in America, the Hebrew arrivals divided themselves into two nations: the good Nephites, named after the prophet Nephi, who led them to America, and the wicked Lamanites, named after Laman, their corrupt leader. The Nephites were persecuted and fled northward, the Lamanites remained farther to the south. The Nephites had in their possession plates of brass engraved with the Five Books of Moses and the books of all the prophets down to Jeremiah, who was active at the time they left Jerusalem. They made a copy of this literature on a new set of brass plates, which they transmitted from generation to generation. They were rewarded by God, who gave then the whole continent of America as their Promised Land. They grew in number, prospered, and spread in all directions, built large cities with temples, cultivated the land, domesticated animals, and discovered gold, silver, lead, and iron. They had many prophets, and engraved their prophecies on plates of gold.

The Lamanites, on the other hand, went from bad to worse, and failed in all their efforts to wage war against the Nephites. The many tumuli scattered all over America cover the remains of their slain warriors. When they arrived in America they were white, but God cursed them for their wickedness. Their physical features were changed and their skin became dark. They were thus the ancestors of the American Indians. One of the primary missions of the Mormon Church was to reconvert the Indians, so that they might be restored to their original state and become white people. The attitude of the Mormons to the Indians, their fallen brothers, has, as a result, always been rather favorable.

The cycle of backsliding of the good and dominance of the bad did not end here. Despite the numerous blessings received by the Nephites, they eventually fell out of grace. Terrible earthquakes destroyed many towns and killed numerous people—Nephites and Lamanites alike. Christ visited those who survived and preached a new law, engraved on plates of gold. The survivors of the catastrophe were converted to Christianity and lived peacefully for three centuries. Toward the end of the fourth century an all-out war broke between the Nephites and the Lamanites, at the end of which the Nephites were driven northward, and were finally destroyed near the Hill of Cumorah (in the State of New York). The Lamanites, who by now had completed their transformation into being red Indians, had the upper hand, and became sole inhabitants of America. Only very few Nephites survived the catastrophe, among them Mormon and his son Moroni.

Mormon wrote on tablets a summary of the history of his ancestors, and buried them in the Hill of Cumorah along with all the original records he possessed. Moroni continued his father's endeavors and recorded all the events that occurred to the Nephites down to the year A.D. 420. He buried his book in the same place. Joseph Smith, founder of the Mormon Church, discovered all these records on September 22, 1827. Smith deciphered the records with the aid of a special miraculous instrument called "Urim Tummim," and included them in the Book of Mormon. To this day the Mormons view themselves as descendants of Israel, although outwardly not of the Ten Lost Tribes. However, during their "Patriarchal Blessing," the participants are identified by their tribal lineage. The majority of Mormons are declared sons of Joseph through his son Ephraim, others attribute themselves to other tribes, and thus do hint at the Ten Tribe lineage. They also designate their non-Mormon neighbors "gentiles," as the Jews designate all non-Jews.

And so, a powerful white Christian denomination, as well as members of Indian tribes, see themselves today as descendants of Israelites who migrated to America. Both hold on to divine promises. To the Mormons these promises have been fulfilled in America, the Promised Land, where they keep growing in numbers and prosperity, in accordance with the words of the biblical prophets. To the Indians, on the other hand, the fulfillment of the promises is yet to come. They live with the hope that sometime in the future, with the help of God, their conditions will change and their situation greatly improve.

9
Israel in the Far Reaches of the World

Enthusiastic travelers, explorers, and missionaries, whose calling, or sense of adventure, took them in past centuries to the remotest corners of the world, were confronted with strange people and outlandish customs. Armed with the Bible as the only relevant guide to the world, they compared their observations of the new and exotic tribes and nations they encountered to familiar biblical descriptions. They were confronted with strange customs that seemed to them in one way or the other reminiscent to those of the ancient Israelites. They observed physical features in which, they believed, they saw a resemblance to those of the imaginary biblical Hebrews. They listened to the way native people spoke, and strove to pick out words that seemingly sounded like Hebrew. By employing these methods these explorers endeavored to relate their discoveries to the Bible, and give the newly found people a biblical ancestry so that they could be treated with some familiarity. The newly discovered tribes could be accounted for only if they were connected to some biblical set of events, and no better candidate presented itself than the drama of the Ten Lost Tribes of Israel, who were lost but carried a divine promise to be found again. Descendants of these Lost Tribes were thus said to be discovered in the remotest corners of the world. A constant stream of publications notified the world that descendants of these tribes were found in all areas reached by Europeans—in Africa, in Asia, in America, and even in far away New Zealand.

While the travelers were exploring, observing, and speculating, the peoples of the newly discovered regions were soon reduced to a status of inferiority, both because of their non-Christian, pagan beliefs, and because their technology was considered primitive and their culture low and even savage. With time, these people, oppressed by their new white overlords, began to identify with some of the Christian doctrines, which they interpreted as reflecting their own situation. Many indigenous populations, while being persecuted by their European oppressors, became familiar with the Bible, and found in the plight of the persecuted Jews a counterpart of their own plight, and therefore felt entitled to claim direct descent from the Lost Tribes of Israel. This process, which sometimes took interesting twists and turns, has occurred among widely separated peoples, some of whom will be described in this chapter.

Israel in India

Beliefs that descendants of the Lost Tribes of Israel lived in India have been circulated since the twelfth century, by one Prester John, a legendary king and priest who allegedly ruled a Christian kingdom in India. Prester John, whose letters describing his imaginary kingdom won great popularity in Medieval Europe, reported that next to his own realm was a very mighty kingdom inhabited by nine tribes of Israel. King Daniel, who had under him three hundred Jewish kings and numerous dukes and counts, ruled this Israelite kingdom. His kingdom was so rich that its houses were built of precious stones. Two rivers that issued from the Garden of Eden flowed there. On the basis of these fabulous legends, it comes as little surprise that several peoples of India consider themselves to this day, or have been proclaimed so by others, descendants of Israel. The supposed existence of ancient Israelites in India is manifested in a wide variety of forms.

The Shinlung tribes

"Our million brothers in India"; "Millions in India claim: we are descendants of a lost Jewish Tribe" announced several Israeli newspapers in the early 1990s. Indeed, members of the Shinlung group of tribes living in Misoram, a remote province in northeast India near the border with Miramar (formerly Burma), insist that they and their many brothers in Burma, as well as the small Tiddim tribe of Burma, are of the ancient Israelite tribe of Menasseh. News of this unusual claim have been circulating for a while, but only in the late 1980s messengers from Israel succeeded in entering Misoram province, closed to visitors by the Indian authorities. Some of these visitors reported with great conviction that members of the Shinlung tribe prayed in Hebrew to the God of Abraham, Isaac, and Jacob, put on phylacteries, and covered their heads, all unshakable signs of their Jewishness. The enthusiasm that this news kindled in some circles in Israel prompted several tribe members to migrate to Israel and begin a process of strict orthodox conversion. A few families made Israel their home, and in 1998 several more families came to Israel and joined the growing Shinlung community in the country.

Very little is known of the history of the Shinlung tribes. It is assumed that they, like many other tribes in the remote hills of the region, originally came from China. They themselves claim that, having been exiled by Shalmanesser of Assyria, they settled in the Province of Yunan in China. They kept moving, arriving in central China where they came in contact with the Jewish community that existed in Kaifeng. From there they moved to the town of Sinlung in the province of Szechwan, and finally arrived in their present place of residence on both sides of the India–Miramar border. During the nineteenth century Christian missionaries arrived, and succeeded in converting almost all the tribes to Christianity. Although the Shinlung claim that they have always kept their Judaism, it is most likely that the missionaries, in the common vein of the time, observed tribal customs vaguely suggestive of ancient Israelite ones, and declared the tribes descendants of the Ten Tribes of Israel. It seems that they were thought to belong to the tribe of Manasseh because the word Manase frequently appears in their tribal prayers. These people, who lived in desolate conditions of poverty, adopted and internalized the attractive notion that they were of Ten Lost Tribes of Israel lineage, as this assured them of divine protection and promises for a better future. When news of the creation of the State of Israel reached these remote regions, these notions were awakened, and the tribesmen began to openly declare their affiliation with the Chosen People.

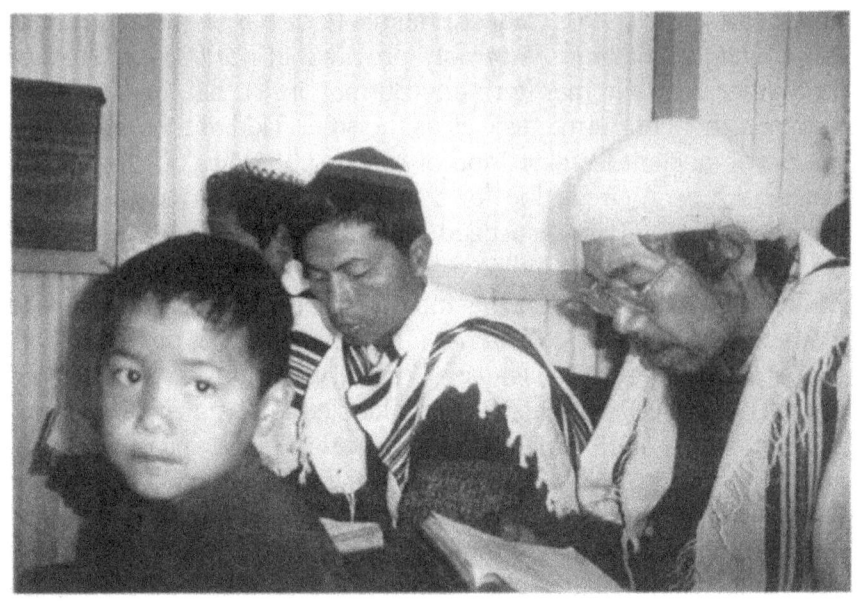

Figure 39: Prayer at the "Tribe of Menasshe" synagogue, Mizoram, 1995.

Figure 40: Members of the "Tribe of Menasseh," Mizoram, 1995.

The Karens

The Shinlung are not the only tribal group of people of the vast Indian subcontinent who claim to be descendents of ancient Israel, or who have been designated as such. George Moore, a nineteenth-century English physician and author, made an ingenious claim that Buddhism was connected to the Israelite religion. Also, on the basis of a report by the American missionary Mr. Mason, Moore suggested that the Karens, yet another tribe that occupied a region on the Burma–India border, were a Hebrew tribe. This tribe, he reported, was also of Chinese origin. It was once very large, and occupied vast areas extending from Siam (Thailand), to Bengal in today's India, and including all of Burma. The Karens practiced many Israelite customs such as domestic habits, according to which they held their women in high regard and forbade polygamy. They had high morals, and were industrious and hospitable to strangers. Their personal appearance and dress were also suggestive: Their dress was dissimilar to that of the Burmese. Moore quoted Mason as saying that the Jewish look of the Karens could not fail to strike anyone. They greatly respected the beard and had a saying: "A man with a beard belongs to the race of ancient kings."

The word for the Karen deity is Yoowah, supposedly connected with Jehova. The Karens claimed that their God gave them in ancient times his word written on leather. The scroll was placed on a shelf, but a fowl scratched it and a swine destroyed it. Therefore they offered a fowl as atonement to God, as did the Jews, and the swine was detested by one sect in the tribe. They also had wizards or prophets to curse their neighbors. Their creation stories are similar to those of the Jews: God first created heaven and earth; then he created man and from his rib created a woman, and then breathed life into them. God also created a tree of death and a tree of life and forbade man to eat from the tree of death. Man disobeyed, being tempted by Satan and a woman. They alone of all neighboring tribes painted two of the posts of their house one white, the other red, in reference to their deliverance from danger, as the Jews smeared their doorposts with blood in commemoration of the exodus (Exodus 12:22). The Karens believed that these and other traditions came to them in a book that God himself wrote.

Moore, perhaps somewhat suspicious that these traditions were transmitted by Christian missionaries, stated that the Karens had no

Christian symbol or tradition. And yet, a Christian origin is the only logical explanation for the existence of these traditions. Unlike the Shinlung, the Karens did not seem to internalize the Lost Ten Tribe origin suggested to them, and did not claim to be of that descent. Enthusiasts from Israel have not yet reached them to convince them that indeed they were.

The Kanaanites

The Kanaanites of Travandrom in southern India are yet another group that prides itself of Jewish origins, though not related to the Ten Lost Tribes. First encountered in 1980, they claim that their name is the clue to their origin. According to their story, they originated in the village of Kana in the Galilee, the site of the famous wedding where Jesus turned water into wine. According to their tradition they became the first Christians, and were therefore persecuted and had to escape to Syria from where they proceeded to India. Nevertheless, they claim that they never forsook the Jewish religion. Several Kanaanites have since come to Israel, converted to Judaism, and hope to influence all members of the community to do the same.

The Jews of Cochin

Also in southern India, in and around Cochin on the Malabar Coast, lives to this day the Jewish community of Cochin. Although they are full-fledged Jews, and themselves have no specific tradition as to their origin, they have drawn the attention of tribe seekers, in the hope of bestowing on them ancient, Ten Lost Tribe roots. Such an attribution was made already by Rabbi Benjamin of Tudela, the Spanish Jewish traveler of the twelfth century, who reported that he heard that a few thousand Jews of black complexion lived in "Cush," usually identified with southern India (although sometimes with Ethiopia). Benjamin relates that they were good Jews, versed with the law of the Torah but not with the Talmud. Because they seemed to Benjamin to lead a life of independence, he identified them with the Lost Tribes he was so eager to find.

Rumors of the existence of a Jewish community in India is mentioned also by Abraham Ferissol (Farizol), a noted Jewish geographer of the sixteenth century. Ferissol reported, in the name of the Italian

Figure 41: Madai family in festive attire, Cochin, ca. 1900.

Christian writer Vespucio, the existence of numerous Jews "above Calicut" (ancient Culcutta), related to those living in islands of the Indian Ocean, and to others living "above Mekka." Ferissol mentioned also the river Ganges, which, so he reported, issued above Calicut and separated the Jews from the inhabitants of India, and identified it with the biblical river Gozan but also with the fabulous Sambatyon. Ferissol also related that the Jews of India were rich, their wealth deriving from trade in spices and pepper. This last remark points to the Jewish community of Cochin that definitely existed and was well established at the time, Cochin having been, and still is, a major center of commerce in spices. The names Calicut and the river Ganges, in the context of a report on a Jewish community living in southern India, indicate the confusion that existed in the sixteenth century regarding the geographic configuration of far-lying and mysterious India.

When first encountered by European missionaries in the nineteenth century, this small Jewish community was divided into two, the so-called black Jews and the so-called white Jews, a situation that aroused much speculation. It was suggested, on the basis of an erroneous interpretation of a set of inscribed copper tablets in the local language Malayalam, that the white Jews were the people of Jerusalem who arrived in India after the destruction of their city by Nebuchadnezzar king of Babylon. As for the black Jews, the Reverend Claudius Buchanan suggested that they were descendants of the Ten Tribes, exiled by Shalmanessar of Assyria and arrived in India from Chaldea. The Reverend Charles Forester suggested, on the other hand, that they descended from Bani Israel tribes in Afghanistan, some of whom had a black complexion. Research has shown that the copper plates dated to the tenth century, and had nothing to do with the white Jews who arrived in Cochin much later. The plates recorded certain rights conferred by the ruler upon the local Jewish community. It is not known when Jews first arrived in Cochin. They were probably traders from Yemen, Iraq, or other Near Eastern countries, who settled in Cochin in connection with the spice trade routes that passed through Cochin. The white Jews were latecomers, exiles from Spain and Jews from Mediterranean and Middle Eastern countries, who arrived in Cochin since the sixteenth century.

The Ten Tribes in China

Unlike India, in which several tribes are said to have descended from the Ten Lost Tribes of Israel, vast and varied China has not attracted tribe seekers until quite recently. However, two separate groups of people did capture the imagination of some, although neither became directly identified as of Lost Tribe descent.

A small Jewish community that existed in the central Chinese town of Kaifeng was discovered in the early seventeenth century by the Italian Jesuit missionary Matteo Ricci. The community attributes its origin to Jews from Central Asia or India, who, because of persecution, or in connection with their business interests along the Silk Route, settled in China around the eleventh century. Their first synagogue, constructed in 1163, was destroyed by natural disasters and restored several times, but already in the eighteenth century it fell into disuse. At the same time, mainly because the community was cut off from the Jewish world, a slow process of assimilation occurred. Members of the community adopted Chinese customs and names, intermarried with their Chinese neighbors, and gradually lost their Jewish identity. Christian missionaries who visited the community in the nineteenth century obtained many prayer books and other documentary material. Several of the missionaries suggested a Ten Tribe descent to these people, although the community itself never mentioned such descent in any of its traditions, and did not adopt it.

When the Reverend Thomas F. Torrence began his missionary work among the Chiang Min people of Szechwan in western China in 1916, he was greatly impressed by their fortlike villages perched on the steep slopes of high mountains. He was much surprised, when studying their religion and observing their rituals, to find that they believed in one single supreme God called "Abba Chee," or Father Spirit. Torrence therefore interpreted their religion as being monotheistic, and came to the conclusion that the Chiang Min religion was related to that of the Israelite patriarchs. The Chiang Min must thus have migrated to China from the Middle East in the dim past. Torrence did not, however, connect them specifically to the Ten Tribes of Israel, though later searchers did suggest such an origin.

Israel in Africa

Africa is rich with tribes who claim an Israelite origin, believing that they arrived from Egypt, Yemen, Morocco, or by sea along the trade routes. The best known of the African Israelites are the Beta Israel, the Jews of Ethiopia, whose story, and the dramatic declaration that they were of the lost tribe of Dan, has already been related. Other people with such claims are not Jewish, having picked this notion from Christian missionaries who were active all over the continent. Several tribes have internalized this attribution to the point of believing in it themselves.

The Zulu

In the nineteenth century the Reverend Joshia Tyler spent forty years in South Africa among the Zulu tribes. He, like so many other missionaries and explorers, strove to understand the strange behavioral traits he encountered, and found parallels to them in the biblical world

Figure 42: Chiang Min village in Szechwan province, China, 1996.

familiar to him. Tyler reported that the Zulu circumcised themselves, and that they rejected swine flesh, two unfailing signs of an Israelite connection. The Zulu also refrained from stepping on a fresh grave lest they contract a disease of the feet, to Tyler another sign of a connection between them and the Israelites, although such a custom is not mentioned in Jewish law or lore. As with the Israelites, a widow married the brother of her deceased husband. Other related customs were the naming of children after some circumstance connected with their birth, the purchase of wives, and the bestowing on a rooster the disease of the people and sending it into the wilderness—similar to the Jewish scapegoat. Like the Israelites, the Zulu cursed their enemy before going to war, had their servants pour water on their hands after a meal, and sprinkled the doorway of their huts with medicinal water to keep away disease. Interestingly, Tyler reported that the Christian Zulu declared: "We understand the Old Testament better than the New; it describes so perfectly our home life!" It seems that the attribution of an Israelite origin came entirely from Tyler, as it is not reported that the Zulu themselves ever made any such claim.

The Lemba

By contrast, numerous members of the Lemba tribe of South Africa, Zimbabwe, and Mozambique recently declared themselves descendants of the Ten Lost Tribes of Israel, who arrived in Africa some fourteen hundred years ago from a place called Sena. Since then, they say, they were cut off from mainstream Judaism. Their history was never recorded in writing, but was transmitted orally. When they were first encountered in 1957 it was observed that their facial features were not typical Negroid, that they refrained from eating swine, separated milk from meat, and did not marry outside their community. It was also reported that they valued education, a very clear Jewish trait, and were well acquainted with the New Testament. Again one senses the fingerprints of Christian missionaries. The Lemba observed customs that they claimed were reminiscent of Jewish ones. Men were being circumcised, although at the age of fifteen. Women who wanted to marry a Lemba had to take a very strict course of Lemba traditions, similar to the requirement for a Jewish conversion. The course ended, as with the Jews, with a purification ceremony—in this case jumping through a burning circle. The Lemba also washed their hands ritually before partaking of food.

Recently the British anthropologist Tudor Parfit picked up the Lemba tradition that they originated in a place called Sena. He traveled back along the supposed route of the Lemba migration from Africa to Yemen, where he discovered a settlement by this name in the region of Hadermout. Indeed Jews are known to have lived there in the ancient past. This strengthened his belief in the Jewish descent of the Lemba. A rather surprising study of the DNA of several Lamba men carried out by David B. Goldstein of Oxford University, and reported by Associated Press on May 10, 1999, revealed a genetic similarity between them and Jews of the priestly group (cohanim). This similarity further seems to support the Lemba tradition of their Jewish ancestry. But does this necessarily connect the Lemba with the Lost Tribes of Israel?

A tribe in Cameroon

Claimants for an Israelite origin are to be found also in Cameroon, as related by Nagimbus Bodol, son of a chief of one of the tribes of that country. Bodol told that his tribe considered itself Israelite and refused to be registered as Christian, Moslem, or pagan. Therefore its members were not granted birth certificates. Bodol moved to Israel, converted, and changed his name to Uriel Ben Abraham. His father the chief, tells Ben Abraham, was very educated and very religious, and knew the Psalms by heart. He was very active in the struggle against the colonial regime in his country. Not much more is known about the beliefs and claims of the tribe.

The black Jews of Ondo Forest

A tribe that lived in Dahomei, formerly known as Western (French) Sudan, south of Timbuktu at a distance of three days' travel on foot, attributed to itself an ancestry in the Israelite tribe of Ephraim. Bata Kindai Amgoza Ibn LoBagola, a member of the tribe, gave a fascinating description of this tribe, to which he referred as the black Jews of Ondo Forest. In the 1930s, he claimed, the tribe numbered about two thousand people, scattered in some twenty villages. They believed that they were of Jewish origin, and came to this place via Morocco, where their ancestors had lived for many generations. Being persecuted in Morocco, they traveled across the Sahara Desert for many years, until finally reaching an uninhabited place in the heart of Africa, where they found water, cleared the forest, and built a village. Other tribes of wild pagans, who called them Emo-yo-Guaim (strange people), came to live nearby. The black Jews were independent of all outer rule, completely self-sufficient, and lived very much like their neighbors.

LoBagola reported that his tribe had very distinct Jewish elements. Their most prized possession was a Torah scroll written in Aramaic, its letters believed to have been engraved into the parchment with a hot iron, not written with ink. No letter could therefore be changed. They believed their ancestors brought the scroll more than one thousand and eight hundred years before the time they settled in Africa. They did not have the other parts of the Bible, nor did they know anything about the Talmud. They observed Passover, Shavuot, New Year, the Day of Atonement, and Succot. They circumcised their boys at eight days, but, unlike other Jewish communities, performed this act using their teeth and nails. Seven rabbis, all born into rabbinical families, headed the community. These rabbis supervised the education and religious behavior of the community, which was very strict in observing the law.

The tribe had a temple where the scroll was kept, which the people entered only once a year, on the Day of Atonement. The rabbis entered the temple every Sabbath, read the Torah, and explained the laws to the community, which was seated on the ground around the temple.

The interesting thing about the story of these black Jews is that it contains no Christian element. There were Jewish communities in Morocco, who lived on the verge of the Sahara desert, who claimed an ancestry from the tribe of Ephraim. Perhaps the black tribe from the Ondo Forest picked up this notion through trade relations with Morocco?

Israel in New Zealand

The story of the Maori, the autochthonous population of New Zealand, and their identification with the Israelites has some particular, political elements. Indeed the first British who arrived on the islands looked for, and claimed they found, elements of resemblance between the two. But things were not left at that. Here the confrontation between the Maori and the British (paheka as the Maori called them) led to the creation of a new cult, known as Hau-hau. This cult, a combination of local and Christian beliefs and practices, led the fight against the British with the hope of expelling them from the islands. The supreme deity of the cult was called Jehova, a deity that possessed many elements of Tane, the local pagan deity, despite its Jewish name. Members of the cult believed that they and the Jews were the children of the same father, and that they descended from the tribes of Israel, in particular from Judah. Their plight under the British led them to a strong identification with the sufferings of the ancient Israelites, especially under the Egyptians. The history of the Israelites, as taught by the Christian missionaries, became a model for political action of the Maori against the British oppressors. For example, they preached against any contact with the British, just as the Israelites refrained from communicating with the gentiles. The self-ordained prophet of the cult also promised his adherents that the day would come when the British would be banished from the land, the dead Maori warriors would rise, and the Jews would come and join them to become a single nation. Together they would build a new life for the whole world.

Conclusion: Why the Search?

The search for the Ten Lost Tribes of Israel, an endeavor that has been going on for over two millennia, has satisfied various needs, and has been kept alive by diverse interests. It is a historical fact that the Ten Tribes were exiled, and after a short period of time were never heard of again. Why then would the Ten Tribes of Israel, exiled some 2,800 years ago, be considered only temporarily lost? Why should they, of all the numerous peoples and tribes that have been lost over the centuries, be expected to reappear? In other words—why are they not left alone to rest in oblivion? The answer to these questions lies in the realm of religious belief. According to the Bible, God has issued to the tribes of Israel specific promises that they will eventually return from their land of exile to their homeland, and then enjoy a glorious future. Such divine promises, repeated many times by several biblical prophets, cannot but be fulfilled. Religious beliefs and sentiments lie therefore at the heart of the search for the Ten Lost Tribes of Israel.

For those who evaluate historical processes in a coolheaded, scientific way, the hope for the return of the tribes does not seem realistic. History is full of tribes and peoples who appeared on the stage of history for a period, acted their part, and then, owing to a variety of circumstances, the curtain fell on them and they disappeared. Such realists even rely on biblical sources, according to which some of the exiled Israelites joined their Judean brothers in Babylon, and together they returned to Judea to rebuild the Temple in Jerusalem. The promise for the return of the tribes of Israel was thus partially, if not wholly, fulfilled. However, despite the dramatic permission to return to Judea given by Cyrus king of Persia, many Israelites remained in their places of exile, where they underwent the natural process of assimilation into the society in which they lived, and lost all contact with the Israelite nation. On the other hand, the Judeans who were exiled by Nebuchadnezzar about 130 years after the Israelite exile, and remained in Babylon, maintained their religious faith and with time grew in number to become a large and prominent Jewish diaspora.

For those for whom the word of God, as pronounced by his prophets, is infallible, this realist explanation does not hold. If indeed some of the exiled have already returned, the great majority of the Lost Tribes have not. They are still considered lost, and the promises are yet to be fulfilled. Accordingly the search has to go on. If an active search cannot be pursed, then at least a hope has to be sustained that the lost tribes will eventually be found and return to unite with their brothers, the descendants of the un-lost tribes of Judah and Benjamin.

The Jewish search

Among those who have always expected the Ten Tribes to be found, one has to differentiate between the Jews and the Christians, each sustaining the search for different purposes. For the Jews, a persecuted minority in all countries of their exile, the idea that a segment of the Jewish people exists somewhere and eventually will be found has been a source of consolation and a hope for the future. The need for such hope has been so great that the idea of the continuous existence of the Ten Tribes has grown and developed over the centuries, and has acquired attributes that stand in sharp contrast to the situation of the Jews in their countries of exile. The Ten Tribes have come to be viewed as living an independent life in their own kingdom, ruled by their own kings and princes. They have been believed to be numerous and strong, sometimes even of gigantic physical proportions, and to have a powerful army with which they subdue their neighbors. They have also been supposed to be very rich. What a wondrous soul-lifting picture and a source of pride for the Jews who have lived under the yoke of unsympathetic and hostile neighbors, under the threat of being exiled, robbed, and killed, and whose living conditions have been mostly sordid.

However, the Jewish belief in the glorious existence of the Ten Lost Tribes has created a problem: If indeed they have been so powerful and rich, why did they not come to the rescue of their downtrodden brethren? Why have they gone on living in peace and quiet while atrocities against the Jews keep occurring? The explanation has been found in the wondrous Sambatyon River, a powerful and insurmountable physical—and no doubt also psychological—barrier between the Ten Tribes and the rest of the world. The Sambatyon River has served the role of distancing the Ten Tribes from the realm of reality. Thus they are there but unreachable, real but untouchable. No communication could have been with them, except in legends. They have served an important purpose and catered to real needs, but remained remote and assumed a dreamlike quality. The hope for their appearance has been postponed to the time when the Messiah will come, an event that could occur any minute, but could also take place in the distant future.

Will the Jews continue the search for the Ten Lost Tribes? Indeed some do. The return of many Jews to their old homeland, and the creation of the State of Israel, has aroused in some the strong desire to increase the numbers of the Jewish population and add to it people on whom a Ten Tribe descent could perhaps be bestowed. The Jerusalem-based Amishav organization has been the most enthusiastic and active in this endeavor. However, the belief in the existence of great multitudes of Ten Tribe descendants and their ultimate immigration to Israel is perhaps a matter of wishful hopes. It is to be fulfilled in a mystically shrouded future, much in line with the attitude of the Jews to the issue of the Ten Tribes throughout history.

The Christian search

While the Jewish belief in the continuous existence of the Ten Lost Tribes has been based on one single motif—hope of rescue from the reality of exile—the relation of Christianity to the saga of the Ten Lost Tribes of Israel was motivated by at least two different and separate needs. On the one hand the belief in the Ten Tribes has presented a ready explanation to the customs and beliefs of tribes and people encountered in many lands during the age of geographic and imperialistic expansion. Many Christians, especially missionaries, have bestowed a Ten Tribe–descent status on many newly discovered peoples, and have then converted them to Christianity. On the other hand there have been those who found in the legacy of the Ten Tribes answers to their concern about their own situations, and developed the belief that they themselves were of such illustrious ancestry.

Rumors that peoples who threatened Europe, such as the Tatars and Mongols, were of Ten Tribe of Israel ancestry already circulated in the Middle Ages. However, the Christian world did not begin to concern itself in earnest with the Ten Tribe issue until the discovery of America and the opening up of the world to the white man. Since the sixteenth century Europeans have been continuously confronted with a whole array of people of a variety of complexions and physical appearances, adhering to strange customs and ways of life, and having a set of religious beliefs and practices that have had nothing to do with the Judeo–Christian heritage. This confrontation has been perplexing to the Europeans, and often deadly to the native peoples. Armed with the Bible, the Europeans, through the agencies of enthusiastic missionaries, have striven to convert the natives to what for them was the one and only true faith—Christianity—and to rescue them from ignorance and barbarism. While doing so, some missionaries, along with various adventurers and soldiers, have studied the native tribes with which they have come in contact, described their customs and lifestyle, and striven to understand them through comparisons with the world known to them. Several have found what they believed to be a resemblance between the customs they observed and those of the ancient Israelites, and developed it into an intriguing theory. Based on a wide array of such supposed similarities, they have bestowed on some of the native peoples a Ten Lost Tribe ancestry. This attribution has inflamed the minds of some missionaries, who have doubled their effort to convert these peoples to Christianity, believing that such a conversion would have a double benefit. Not only would it add members to the church, but these new members would be of Israelite—or Jewish—origin, as no specific distinction has been made between the two. Moreover, not only would such a conversion be a great achievement to the Christian Church, which has tried for centuries to convert the Jews; but these converts would be innocent of the heavy sin of the Jews—the crucifixion of Jesus—since they had already been lost at the time of that event. If these sinless Israelites recognized Jesus, it would be a crowning accomplishment for the church, and open the way to the Second Coming of Christ. The zeal with which Christian missionaries have pursued the idea that the tribes and peoples they have encountered in various parts of the world originated from the Ten Tribes of Israel is thus understandable.

With the advent of natural and human sciences, and a better understanding of the origins of mankind and its development in time and space, the Christian quest for the Ten Lost Tribes has dwindled. It is not likely that missionaries nowadays will declare a tribe of Israelite origin, and compare its beliefs and customs to those of ancient Israel.

The other aspect of the relationship between Christian people and the Ten Lost Tribes of Israel has arisen from within Christianity itself, and several ideologies of a connection to these people have been born. The British Israelites who started out in Britain and spread to its former colonies, and the Mormons, a Christian sect born in the Unites States, believe, each from its own point of view, that they have descended from ancient Israel. Both attribute their success in the world to divine blessings, thus making them the true carriers of promises made long ago to Israel. These two movements exist to this day, but while the British Israelites are dwindling in numbers, the Mormons keep growing. Both cater to their own members rather than try to bestow Israelite origin upon others, as Christian missionaries and others did in the past.

Native tribes and their search for a new identity

Christianity has been so successful among various tribes and peoples around the world that some have even come to internalize the supposed resemblance between themselves and ancient Israel, and have wholeheartedly adopted the idea that they are of Ten Tribe origin. It seems that this process has happened mainly among the more vulnerable of native people, those who were stripped of their beliefs, their livelihood, and their honor by the advent of the white man. Having lost the belief in their own tradition, and looking for an alternative to the set of new doctrines imposed on them by their overlords, they found in the Jewish Bible stories of suffering Israelites with whom they could identify. The fate of Israel, enslaved in Egypt under

Figure 43: Newspaper clippings on the search for the Ten Lost Tribes, 1970s–1980s.

a tyrant who would not release them from slavery, and their defeat by the equally cruel Assyrians who exiled them to distant lands, has had a great appeal to peoples who have felt themselves oppressed. We are the lost Israelites, carriers of divine blessings for a glorious future to come, claim several of these peoples. Thus among the Japanese and the Maori of New Zealand, among tribes in India, Africa, and America, there are those who have adopted the notion of an Israelite descent, which has given them strength and hope.

Will other groups adopt this idea? Under the influence of the Amishav organization there seems to be a modest awakening of such notions among several remote tribes, although the heyday of this ideology seems to be over.

Will the search continue? Have the divine promises been fulfilled?

Judging by literature that is constantly being published, lately especially on the Internet, it seems that although the active search for the Ten Lost Tribes of Israel has been on the decline throughout the twentieth century, interest in the subject is on the rise. There seems to be a growing curiosity about various Ten Tribes of Israel contenders, and about the ideology behind their claims. The British Israelite group seems to be particularly active in presenting its case on the Internet, perhaps hoping to make new adherents to their decreasing numbers. News of various tribes who claim Ten Tribes of Israel descent pop up from time to time. On November 28, 1999, the Israeli newspaper *Haaretz* carried the story that the Maori tribes of New Zealand claim to be of the tribe of Ephraim, having reached the islands where they presently live some 3,000 years ago. It was reported that in the year 2000 a Maori delegation planned to come to Israel to resume contact with the Jewish people.

As for the question of whether the divine promises for the return of Israel to its ancient homeland have been fulfilled—the answer lies with each individual. Many see in the creation of the State of Israel and the ingathering to it of so many Jews a fulfillment of the promises. Others perhaps still wait for the Sambatyon river to dry and expect multitudes of powerful Israelite tribesmen to march forth.

Bibliography

Adair, James. *History of the American Indians*. London: E. & C. Dilly, 1775.

Bancroft, Hubert H. *The Native Races of the Pacific States of North America*. (I) London: Longmans, Green, 1875; (II) New York: Appleton, 1875.

Beaty, Charles. *Journal of a Two Months Tour with a View of Promoting Religion among the Frontier Inhabitants of Pennsylvania, and of Introducing Christianity among the Indians to the Westward of the Allegheny Mountains*. London: W. Davehill and G. Pearch, 1768.

Bellew, Henry Walter. *Journal of a Political Mission to Afghanistan in 1875 under Major (now Colonel) Lumsden*. London: Smith, Eldar and Co., 1862.

———. *A New Afghan Question*. Self-Published Lectures Delivered in Simla in 1880.

———. *The Races of Afghanistan: Being a Brief Account of the Principal Nations Inhabiting that Country*. Calcutta: Thacker, Spink, 1880.

———. *An Inquiry into the Ethnography of Afghanistan*. Graz: Academische Druck, 1973.

Ben Israel, Manasseh. *Sobre el origen de los Americanos*. Madrid: S.P. Junquera, 1881.
Benjamin, Israel Joseph. *Eight Years in Asia and Africa*. Hanover: Published by the Author, 1865.
Benjamin of Tudela. *The Itinerary of Benjamin of Tudela*. London: A. Asher, 1840.
Ben-Zvi, Itzhak. *The Exiled and the Redeemed*. Philadelphia: Jewish Publication Society, 1961.
Blome, Richard. *Geographical Description of the Four Parts of the World*. London: Printed by T.N. for R. Blome, 1670.
Brothers, Richard. *A Revealed Knowledge of the Prophecies and Times wrote under the Direction of God by the Man that will be Revealed to the Hebrews as their Prince*. (I) London: [s.n.], 1794; (II) Philadelphia: Robert Campbell, 1795.
———. *A Description of Jerusalem: Its Houses and Streets, Squares, Colleges, Markets and Cathedrals, the Royal and Private Palaces, with the Garden of Eden in the Center*. London: George Riebau, 1796.
Buchanan, The Reverend Claudius. *Christian Researches in Asia*. London: Cadell and Davies, 1840.
Dunlop, D. M. *The History of the Jewish Khazars*. Princeton: Princeton University Press, 1954.
Duran, Father Diego. *The Aztecs: the History of the Indies of New Spain*. New York: Orion Press, 1964.
Edrei, Moshe. *An Historical Account of the Ten Tribes, Settled Beyond the River Sambatyon in the East*. London: Printed for the Author, 1836.
Eidelberg, Joseph. *The Japanese and the Ten Lost Tribes*. Givatayim: Sycamore Press, 1985.
Elphinstone, Mountstuart. *An Account of the Kingdom of Caubul*. London: Longman, Hurst, Rees, Orme, Brown (et al.), 1815.
L'Estrange, Sir Hamon. *Americans no Jews, or Improbabilities that the Americans are of that Race*. London: Henry Seile, 1651.
Ferissol, Abraham. *Igeret Orhot 'Olam*. Offenbach, 1720.
Flavius, Josephus. *The Jewish War*. Grand Rapids, Michigan: Zondervan Publishing House, 1982.
Fletcher, Giles. *Israel Redux or the Restauration of Israel*. London: John Hancock, 1677.

Forester, The Reverend Charles. *The One Primeval Language*. London: Richard Bentley, 1851.
Frazer, Sir James. *The Golden Bough*. London: Macmillan, 1922–1925.
Fujisawa, Chikao. "The Spiritual and Cultural Affinity of the Japanese and the Jewish People," *Japan and Israel*. Tokyo; 1925.
Garcia, Father Gregorio. *Origen de Los Indios de la Nuevo Mundo*. Madrid: F. Martiniz Abad, 1729.
Gawler, John Cox. *Our Scythian ancestors identified with Israel*. London: W. H. Guest, 1883.
———. *Dan, the Pioneer of Israel. His Early Enterprise, his Settlements, and connections with the Scythians*. London: W.H. Guest, 1880.
Godbey, Allen N. *The Lost Tribes, a Myth: Suggestions towards rewriting Hebrew History*. Durham, N.C.: Duke University Press, 1930.
Ha-Levi, Yehuda Ben Shmuel. *The Khuzarsi*. New Jersey: J. Aronson, 1998.
Halhead, Nathaniel B. *Testimony of the Authenticity of the Prophecies of Richard Brothers*. London: [s.n.], 1795.
Hyamson, Albert M. "The Lost Tribes, and the Influence of the Search for them on the Return of the Jews to England," *The Jewish Quarterly Review* 15 (1902–1903), 640–676.
Ibn LoBagola, Bata Kindai Amgoza. *An African Savage's own Story*. Leipzig: B. Tauchnitz, 1930.
Kaempfer, Engelbrecht. *History of Japan*. Glasgow: J. MacLehose, 1906.
King, Edward (Lord Kingsborough). *Antiquities of Mexico*. London: A. Aglio, 1831–1848.
Lanternari, Vittorio. *The Religion of the Oppressed*. New York: Knopf, 1963.
McLeod, N. *Epitome of the Ancient History of Japan*. Nagasaki: Rising Sun, 1879.
Mechoulan, Henry & Nahon, Gerard (eds.) *Manasseh Ben Israel— The Hope of Israel*. Oxford: Littman Library of Jewish Civilization, Oxford University Press, 1987.
Mongait, A. L. *Archaeology in the U.S.S.R.* Great Britain: Pelican Books, 1961.

Moorcraft, William. *Travels in the Himalayan Provinces of Hindustan and the Punjab, in Ladak and Kashmir, in Peshawar, Kabul, Kunduz and Bukhara from 1819 to 1829*. Pataila: Language Department Punjab, 1970 (reproduction of the 2nd edition first published in 1837).

Moore, George. *The Lost Tribes and the Saxons of the East and of the West, with New Views of Buddhism, and Translations of Rock-Records in India*. London: [s.n.], 1861.

Nakada, Bishop Juji. *Japan in the Bible*. Tokyo: Oriental Missionary Society, Japan Holiness Church, 1933.

Nennius. *History of the Britons*. London: Society for Promoting Christian Knowledge, 1938.

Neubauer, A. "Where are the Ten Tribes?" I–IV, *Jewish Quarterly Review* I (1888–1889): 14–28; 95–112; 185–201; 408–423.

Osborn, The Reverend A. M. "Were the Ten Tribes of Israel Ever Lost?" *The Methodist Quarterly Review* 37 (July, 1855): 419–440.

Zen'ichiro, Oyabe. *The Origin of Japan and the Japanese People*. Tokyo: [s.n.], 1929.

Parfit, Tudor. *The Thirteenth Gate: Travels among the Lost Tribes of Israel*. London: Weidenfeld and Nicolson, 1987.

Paris, Matthew. *The Illustrated Chronicles of Matthew Paris: Observations of 13th Century Life*. Cambridge: Corpus Christi College, 1993.

Plinius, Secundus Gaius the Elder. *The Natural History of Plini*. London: G. H. Bohn, 1855–1857.

Poole, H. W. *Anglo–Israel, or the British Nation and the Lost Tribes of Israel*. Toronto: William Briggs, 1879.

Ro, A. S. "Sambatyon," *Encyclopedia Judaica* 14 (1971): 762–764.

Rose, Sir George Henry. *The Afghans, the Ten Tribes or the Kings of the East*. London: J. Hatchard, 1852.

Rosenau, William. "What Happened to the Ten Tribes?" *Hebrew Union College Jubilee Volume 1875–1925* (1925): 79–88.

Sadler, John. *Rights of the Kingdom*. London: J. Kidgell, 1682.

Samuel, The Reverend Jacob. *The Remnant Found or the Place of Israel's hiding discovered, being a summary of proofs showing that the Jews of Daghistan on the Caspian Sea are the remnants of the Ten Tribes*. London: J. Hatachard, 1841.

Saphir, Jacob. *Even Saphir*. Lyck: M'kitze Nirdamim, 1874.

Six Outline Missionary Lessons for Bible Classes in Japan. London: Missionary Society of London (not dated, but in the 1910s).

Teshima, Ikuro. *The Ancient Jewish Diaspora in Japan, the Tribe of Hada, their religion and Cultural Influence*. Tokyo: Makuya Tokyo Bible Seminary, 1976.

Torquemada, Frair Juan. *Monarquia Indiana*. Mexico City: Universidad Nacional Autonoma de Mexico, 1964.

Torrence, The Reverend Thomas F. *China's First Missionaries*. Chicago: Daniel Shaw Co., 1988.

Tuchman, Barbara. *Bible and the Sword*. New York: New York University Press, 1956.

Tyler, The Reverend Joshia. *Forty Years among the Zulus*. Cape Town: C. Sturik, 1971 (photocopy of the Boston 1891 edition).

Vasittart, Henry. *On the Descent of the Afghans from the Jews*. London: The Asiatic Research Series, 1790.

White, W. C. *Chinese Jews*. Toronto: University of Toronto Press, 1966.

Wilson, John. *The Title-deeds of the Holy Land, and Identification of the Heir*. London: J. Nisbet, 1871.

Wilson, John. *Our Israelitish Origin*. Philadelphia: Daniels & Smith, 1851.

Wolff, The Reverend Joseph. *Narrative of a Mission to Bokhara in the Years 1843–1845*. London: J.W. Parker, 1846.

Index

Abd el-Rahman III, 71
Abraham Ben-Daud, 72
Abraham, son of Benjamin Herat, 93, 95
Absalom, 12
Adair, James, 161–162, 163
Afghana, 84
Afghanistan
   the Afghan-Israelite connection today, 101
   the Afghans and the House of Saul, 84–86
   Afghans and Scythians, 90–92
   the Afghans as Ten Tribes, 86–89
   Islamic traditions connecting the Afghans with ancient Israel, 82
   matching Israelite and Afghani tribes, 92–95
   matching place-names, 95–96
   modern Afghanistan and its people, 81–82
   on the physiognomy of the Afghans and the Jews, 96–99
   similarity of habits and customs, 99–101
   the two exiles, 89–90
Africa, Israel in, 177
   the black Jews of Ondo Forest, 180–181
   the Lemba, 179–180
   a tribe in Cameroon, 180
   the Zulu, 177, 179
Ahab, 14, 15
Akiva, Rabbi, 34, 36
Alexander the Great, 32, 57, 98, 138
America, Israel in, 145–149
   British Israelism and the U.S., 140–141

America, Israel in (*continued*)
  the evidence of relics, 164–165
  the Indians as Israelites, 156–161
  Israel and the Indians of North America, 161–164
  Israelites behind the Mountains Cordillerae, 149–156
  the Mormons, 165–167
American Indians, 145, 147–149
Amishav (organization), 49, 101
Amos, 26
Anglo-Ephraim Association, 140
Anglo-Japanese Alliance, 118, 141
Animal sacrifices, 99–100
Antioch, city of, 32
Antiquities of the Jewish People (Josephus Flavius), 28
Aphgan, 95
Apocrypha, 29, 32
Arzareth, 30, 96
Asaaf, 84
Asher, tribe of, 1, 2, 6, 7, 10, 92
Ashkenazi Jews, 51, 115
Asiatic Research Series (Jones), 87
Asiatic Society, 87
Asrarul Afghinah, 87
Assyria, 14–16, 17
  dispersal in the lands of the Assyrian Empire, 20–23
Avdan, 7
Avihail, Rabbi, 49

Babylon, 23–24, 28
Bakri, 70
Bancroft, Hubert H., 148
Bani Israel, 82, 84, 86, 92
Bar Kochba Revolt, 34
Baruch, Rabbi, 50
Baruch, son of Samuel of Pinsk, 51–52
Beaty, Charles, 164
Bellew, Henry Walter, Afghan-Israelite connection, 82, 88–91, 92–93, 95–96, 98, 99, 100
Bene Israel, 40–41, 49
Ben Israel, Manasseh, 128–129, 149–150, 151, 156
Benjamin, tribe of, 14, 28, 84, 95, 114, 115, 184
Benjamin of Tudela and the Ten Tribes, 37–39, 41, 49, 174
Ben-Zvi, Izhak, 93
Berechiah, Rabbi, 32
Berekia, 84
Bereshit Raba, 34
Beta Israel, 177
Bible
  absence of American Indians in the, 147–148
  biblical verses of the location of the tribes, 20
  King James Bible, 128
  the search for the lost tribes, 183
Bible History and Britain, The (pamphlet), 125
Blome, Richard, 58
Bodol, Nagimbus, 180
Book of the Khozars (Yehuda Ha-Levi), 71

Index

Book of Mormon, 165–166
Bradwardin, Thomas, 57
Britain's Triumphant Role, 141,143
British-Israelite connection, 63, 118–119, 125, 189
  early notions of, 127–129
  the ideology of British Israelism, 134–136
  Manasseh Ben Israel and the return of the Jews to England, 129–134
  motto of British Israelism, 126–127
  nationalism and biblical ancestry, 140–143
  Richard Brothers, 131–134
  Saxon-Israel and Celtic-Israel connections, 129–131
  Scythian ancestors, 137–140
Brothers, Richard, 131–134
Buchanan, Rev. Claudius, 176
Buddhism, 118
Bulan, 72
Byzantine Empire, 79

Caedmon, 130
Catholic Church, 127, 145, 148
Caucasian Mountains, 4, 53–54, 57
  Jews in the, 73–74, 75
Celts, 129–131, 137–138
China, the Ten Tribes in, 176–177
Christianity
  the Christian search for the lost tribes, 185–187
  conversion of American Indians to, 157

  conversion of the Japanese to, 118
  Jews converted to, 46, 62, 151
  the search for the Tribes and Christian doctrines, 62
Chronica Majora (Paris), 57, 58
Chronicles, Books of, 20
Church of Jesus Christ of the Latter-Day Saints, 165–167
Cieza, Petrus, 159–160
Cimmerians, 137, 139
Clement VII, 46
Constantine V, 79
Conversos, 46, 151
Cromwell, Oliver, 128, 129, 149, 156
Cumans, 57
Customs and habits
  comparisons of ancient Jewish, 77–78
  similarity of, 99–101
Cyrus, 24, 184

Daghastan, Mountain Jews of, 74–80
Daniel, Book of, 135
Daniel, king, 34, 170
Dan, tribe of, 6,7, 10, 41, 95, 138, 139, 177
  Eldad from, 2, 37
  Lesghians and, 76–77
  Tamarlin and the, 61
Dapne, 32
Darius I, 65
David, 12, 14, 84
David the Reubenite, 44, 45–46, 51

Dead Sea Scrolls, 28
De la Vega (explorer), 159
Deportation of the Ten Tribes, 16–17, 19–20, 26
Derbent Passage, 68
Derbent Pass, Battle of the, 68
Deuteronomy, Book of, 100, 114–115
De Utre, Philippus, 159
Diary
  of Benjamin of Tudela, 37, 39
  of Eldad, 4, 39, 57
Dimashqi, 70
Diodorus, 64
Du Nuas, Joseph, 39
Duran, Father, 157, 160
Durranis, 82, 93

Eastern group, tribes of the, 4, 7
East India Company, 96
Edrei, Moses, 50
Egypt, 15
Eidelberg, Joseph, 123
Elah, 15
Eldad the Danite
  could Eldad have been an imposter?, 9–10
  diary of, 4, 39, 57
  geographical background of the Tribes, 53–54
  as a Khazar, 73
  stories of, 1–4, 6, 7, 32, 34, 37, 44, 51, 72, 156
Eleazar, king, 50
Eleventh tribe, 8–9
Elijah of Ferrara, 39–40
Elphinstone, Mountstuart, 88, 96
Ephraim, 135, 140, 141, 167
Ephraim, tribe of, 4, 12, 14

Eretz Aheret, 30
Esdras the Fourth, mystical visions of, 29–30, 87, 90, 110, 157–158
Essene sect, 28
Esther, 86
Esther, Book of, 86
Ethiopia, Jews in, 39–44
Ezekiel, 25
Ezekiel, Book of, 114
Ezra the Scribe, 28

Falasha (Ethiopia), 41, 44
False messiahs, 46–47
Ferissol, Abraham, 174–175
Finleyson, John, 134–135
Five Books of Moses, 166
Fletcher, Giles, 59–61, 62
Forster, Rev. Charles, 73, 88, 93, 176
Francis (Indian), 151, 154, 155
Francoise I, 46
Fraser, Sir James, 100
French Revolution, 133
Fujisawa, Chikao, 119–120
Fuller, Thomas, 128
Furuhata, Tanemoto, 120

Gad, tribe of, 6, 7, 10, 15, 38, 41, 46, 119
Garcia, Father Georgia, 157, 158, 159, 161
Gawler, Colonel, 63, 64, 137, 138–139
Genesis, Book of, 138
Genghis Khan, 38, 61
Getae, 138
Ghilzays, 82
Gion Festival, 103, 105

Golden Bough, The (Fraser), 100
Goldstein, David B., 180
Gol, Michael, 95
Goths, 138
Gozan River, 20, 21

Haaretz, 189
Habib Ala Khan, 95
Habor, city of, 20, 21, 89
Hadad, 15
Haidar, Ghulam, 93
Halah, city of, 20, 89
Halhed, Nathaniel, 133, 134
Ham, 109, 148
Hananel, 44
Hanina, Rabbi, 32
Hara, city of, 20, 21, 23, 89
Harun al-Rashid, 70
Helbo, Rabbi, 32
Henry VIII, 127
Herod the Great, 27
Herodotus, 137
Hill, Aaron, 61
Hisdai Ibn-Shaprut, 71–72
Hoditch, Sir Thomas Hungerford, 93
Holiness Church Movement, 119
Hoshea, king, 15–16, 89, 90
Hoshea, prophet, 24, 140, 158
Husain, 87

Ibn-al-Athir, 70
India, Israel in, 39–44, 170
  the Jews of Cochin, 174–176
  the Kanaanites, 174
  the Karens, 173–174
  the Shinlung tribes, 170–171
Irmia, 84
Isaacites, 63, 67
Isaiah, 24, 26, 114
Islam, Jews converted to, 86
Islamic traditions and ancient Israel, 82
Israel in the far reaches of the world, 169–170
  Israel in Africa, 177–181
  Israel in India, 170–176
  Israel in New Zealand, 181–182
  the Ten Tribes in China, 176–177
Israel, Joseph, 47, 49
Issachar, tribe of, 4, 6, 44, 72
Istakhri, 69

Jacob, 12, 130
Japan, Israel in, 103–106
  brief history of Japan relevant to the Tribe issue, 106–108
  the Japanese and the Japan-Israel theory, 118–123
  McLeod and the Japan-Israel theory, 108–109
  McLeod's observations and interpretations, 109–114
  ways of identifying the tribes, 114–117
Japan-Russia War of 1903, 118
Japheth, 109, 113, 148
Jeremiah, 26, 65, 130, 166
Jeroboam, 7, 14
Jewish messengers to the Ten Tribes, 47–49

Jews in search of their lost
    brethren, 31
  Benjamin of Tudela and the
    Ten tribes, 37–39
  David the Reubenite, 45–46
  the fate of the Lost Tribes,
    34–37
  Jewish messengers to the
    Ten Tribes, 47–49
  messiahs and the Lost Tribes,
    44–45
  news of Jews in India,
    Yemen, and Ethiopia,
    39–44
  the river Sambatyon, 32–34
  the sages of the Mishnah
    and Talmud and the
    Lost Tribes, 31–32
  Shabbtai Zvi, 46–47
  the Ten Tribes in popular
    legends, 50–52
Jimmu Tenno, 110, 119,
    123
Jonathan, son of Saul, 95
Jones, Sir William, 88, 96
Joseph of Arimathea, 130
Joseph, king of the Khazars,
    71, 72
Joseph, tribe of, 12
Josephus Flavius and the Ten
    Tribes, 28–29, 33
Joshua, son of Nun, 44
Judah, tribe of, 4, 12, 14, 28,
    114, 115, 184
Judaism
  conversion of the Khazars to,
    69–71
  Shintoism and, 119–120
Justinian, 79

Kabbalah, 41
Kaempfer, Engelbrecht, 106,
    107–108
Kalkhu, city of, 21
Karl V, 46
Khan, Gulam Nebu, 95
Khazars, the, 67
  the conversion of the Khazars
    to Judaism, 69–71
  correspondence between
    Spain and Khazaria, 71–
    72
  the Jewish kingdom and the
    Jewish world, 72–73
  who were, 67–69
Kingdom of Israel
  end of, 15–16
  formation of, 7, 14, 15
Kingdom of Judah, 19
  fate of the, 23–24
  formation of, 7, 14, 15
  Scythian invasion of, 65
King, Edward (Lord
    Kingsborough), 157, 158–
    159
Kobayashi, Mr., 105
Kofar al Torak, 38
Konoe, Ayamoro, 120

Laman, 166
Lamanites, 166, 167
Las Casas, Bartholome de,
    145, 156–157
Law of Moses, 28, 84, 99,
    100, 128, 164
Lee, Samuel, 62
Leo IV (the Khazar), 79
Lesghians, 76–77, 79
L'Estrange, Sir Hamon, 157

Leviticus, Book of, 100
Levi, tribe of, 8–9, 12, 41, 84, 151
LoBagola, Bata Kindai Amgoza Ibn, 180, 181
Luminous Religion, 120
Lumsden, Henry, 88

McLeod, N., Japan-Israel theory, 108–115, 118
Maimonides, 41
Malkiel, 50
Martel, Charles, 68
Mason, Mr. (missionary), 173
Mas'udi, 69–70
Medes, city of, 20, 23, 89, 90
Meiji Restoration, 108, 113, 118
Menasseh, tribe of, 4, 7, 12, 15, 38, 46, 72, 119, 141, 171
Merrick, Joseph, 164–165
Messiahs and the Lost Tribes, 44–47
Messiah, the, 129
Mishnah, 34, 36, 37, 40, 41
Missionary Society of London, 118
Mongols, the, 57
Montezinus, Antonius, 149–151, 154, 155, 156
Moorcraft, William, 96
Moore, George, 173
Mordecai, 86
Mormons, the, 165–167
Moroni, 167
Moses, 12, 66, 67
Moses (Levi), tribe of, 8–9
Mountains Cordillerae, 151

Mountain tribes and plain tribes, 53–56
  Jews and the Caucasian Mountains, 73–74
  the Khazars, 67–73
  Mountain Jews of Daghastan, 74–80
  the Scythians, 62–67
  the Tatars, 56–62
Mural al-Dhahab (Mas'udi), 69–70

Nadir Shah, 76
Nakada, Juji, 119
Naphtali, tribe of, 6, 7, 10, 50, 92
Nathan of Gaza, 46, 47
Native Americans, 145, 147–149
  the Indians as Israelites, 156–161
  Israel and the Indians of North America, 161–164
Nebat, 7, 14
Nebuchadnezzar, 23–24, 84, 184
Nennius, 138
Nephi, 166
Nephites, 166–167
Nestorian Church, 120
New Zealand, Israel in, 181–182, 189
Nicolay, 7
Noah, three sons of, 109, 113, 148
Northern group, tribes of the, 4
Numbers, Book of, 100, 140

Obadiah of Bertinoro, 40–41
Obadiah, king, 72
Omri, 137
Ophir, 148
Otto I, 72
Ottoman Turks, 46
Oyabe, Zen'ichiro, 119

Pakistan. *See* Afghanistan
Pardes, 34
Parfit, Tudor, 180
Paris, Matthew, 57, 58
Patan, 95
Pathans, 82
Pekah, 15, 62, 89, 90, 92
Perry, Matthew C., 108
Persia, 38, 65, 86, 89
Philistines, 12
Phoenicians, 138–139, 148
Physiognomy
  of the Afghans and the Jews, 96–99
  of the Japanese, 115
  of the Lesghians and the tribe of Dan, 76
Pliny the Elder, 33, 138
Poitiers, Battle of, 68
Poole, H. W., 141
Prester John, 34, 38, 40, 41, 44, 46, 50, 170
Protestantism, 127–128, 141
Pukhtunwal, laws of the, 99, 101
Puritanism, 128
Pushtuns, 82

Qairawan, Tunisia, Jewish community of, 1, 2–3, 9–10

Rehoboam, 14
Reuben, tribe of, 4, 6, 15, 38, 44, 72, 95
Revelation, Book of, 60, 135
Rezin, 62
Riblathah, city of, 32
Ricci, Matteo, 176
Riebau, George, 134
Ritual laws, 10, 99–100
Rose, Sir George, 98

Sacrifices, animal, 99–100
Sadler, John, 128
Salmon, prince, 39
Samaria, 17, 21
Sambatyon, river, 9, 32–34, 40, 41, 44, 45, 49, 50, 51, 52, 185, 189
Samuel Ben Nahman, 32
Samuel, Rev. Jacob, 75–78, 80
Sanson, Monsieur, 58
Sappir, Jacob, 47
Saul, 12, 82, 84, 86, 95
Scythians, the, 62–63
  Afghans and, 90–92
  British Israelism and, 137–140
  excavating Scythian remains, 66
  in history, 64–65
  how did the Scythians become Israelites?, 63–64
  reconstructed Scythian history, 67
  Scythian "prehistory", 65–66

Search, the, 183–184
  the Christian search, 185–187
  the Jewish search, 184–185
  native tribes and their search for a new identity, 187–189
  will the search continue?/have the divine promises been fulfilled?, 189
Second Monarchy of Judah, 24
Second Temple, 24, 27, 31
Sennacherib, 23
Shabbtai Zvi, 46–47
Shalmanesser II, 14–15
Sharp, William, 133
Shem, 109, 113, 148
Shintoism, 118, 119–120
Shishak, 15
Shlomo Molcho, 46
Simeon, tribe of, 4, 7, 44, 72
Simon bar Kosba, 34
Simon Bar Yohai, 36
Skutis, 63, 65, 66, 67
Smith, Joseph, 167
Solomon, 12, 14, 84, 96, 119
Sons of El Shaddai, 41
Sons of Isaac, 63, 65, 137
Sons of Israel, 82, 154
Sons of Moses, 41, 51
Sons of Rechab, 38, 41
Southern groups, tribes of the, 4, 6, 7
Stone of Scone, 130
Strabo, 64, 66, 138
Sulleiman Mountains, 96
Syria, 14, 15

Talmud, 32, 37
Tamarlin, 61
Tatars, the, 56–57, 91
  early attempts to connect the Tatars with Israel, 57–58
  early geographic knowledge and, 58–59
  Giles Fletcher and the Tatar-Israel theory, 59–61
  the search for the Tribes and Christian doctrines, 62
  Tamarlin and the tribe of Dan, 61
Tchornei, Jehuda, 80
Ten Lost Tribes
  could Eldad have been an imposter?, 9–10
  an eleventh tribe, 8–9
  location of, 4, 6
  stories of Eldad the Danite, 1–4
  the way of life of the tribes, 6–8
Teshima, Ikuro, 120
Throwgood, Rev. Thomas, 157
Tiglath Pileser, 15, 17, 23, 62, 92
Tineius Rufus, 34
Titus, 33
Tokugawa, Ieyasu, 106
Torquemada, Juan de, 157
Torrence, Rev. Thomas F., 177
Tower of Babel, 109, 165–166
Twelve tribes, splitting of, 14
Tyler, Rev. Joshia, 177, 179
Tyndale, William, 128

United States, British Israelism and the, 140–141
Usbeck Tartars, 62
Uziel, 7

Vasittart, Henry, 86–87
Vespucio, 175
Virgil, 138
Visions of Esdras, 29
Vulgate, 128

Wedgwood, Ralph, 135
Where are the Ten Lost Tribes?, 11
  ancient Israel: the beginnings, 12
  dispersal in the lands of the Assyrian Empire, 20–23
  division of the kingdom, 12–15
  end of the Kingdom of Israel, 15–16
  the exiled and the remnants, 16–20
  the fate of the kingdom of Judah, 23–24
  from Assyria to the ends of the world, 26–28
  Josephus Flavius and the Ten tribes, 28–29
  the mystical visions of Esdras the Fourth, 29–30
  where are the Ten Tribes hiding?, 26
  why are the Ten Tribes of Israel kept alive?, 24–25
White Huns, 92
Wild, Dr., 140
Wilson, John, 135, 139–140
Wolff, Rev. Joseph, 96, 98
World War I and II, Britain during and after, 141, 143
Wycliff, John, 128

Yamaguchi, Mr., 105
Yavneeli, Shmuel, 49
Yehuda Ha-Levi, 71
Yehuda ha-Nassi, 36
Yemen, Jews in, 39–44

Zaddok, 50–51
Zamolxis, 66, 67
Zaurov, Hiya, 95
Zebulun, tribe of, 4, 6, 72, 93
Zemah Gaon, 9–10
Zohar, 36

www.ingramcontent.com/pod-product-compliance
Lightning Source LLC
Chambersburg PA
CBHW062218300426
44115CB00012BA/2123